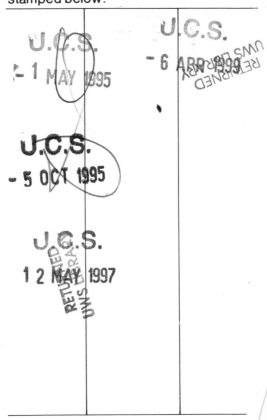

This book must be returned immediately it is asked for by the Librarian,
and in any case by the last date
stamped below.

The Dynamics of Technology, Trade and Growth

Edited by

Jan Fagerberg,
NUPI, Oslo, Norway

Bart Verspagen
MERIT, Maastricht, The Netherlands

and Nick von Tunzelmann
SPRU, Brighton, UK

Edward Elgar

Published by
Edward Elgar Publishing Limited
Gower House
Croft Road
Aldershot
Hants GU11 3HR
England

Edward Elgar Publishing Company
Old Post Road
Brookfield
Vermont 05036
USA

British Library Cataloguing in Publication Data

Dynamics of Technology, Trade and Growth
  I. Fagerberg, Jan
  338.9

Library of Congress Cataloguing in Publication Data

The Dynamics of technology, trade and growth / edited by Jan
  Fagerberg, Bart Verspagen and Nick von Tunzelmann.
    240p. 23cm.
    Proceedings of a conference.
    1. Technological innovations—Economic aspects—Congresses.
  2. Industrial productivity—Congresses. 3. Comparative economics–
  –Congresses. I. Fagerberg, Jan. II. Verspagen, Bart. III. Von
  Tunzelmann, Nick.
  HC79.T4D96 1995
  338'.064—dc20   94–22218
                                       CIP

Printed and bound in Great Britain by
Hartnolls Limited, Bodmin, Cornwall

ISBN 1 85278 922 0

Contents

Foreword

This book is the result of a conference jointly organized by the STEP-group for Studies in Technology, Innovation and Economic Policy at the Norwegian Computing Center (Oslo), the EUNETIC network, and the Norwegian Institute of International Affairs (NUPI, Oslo). The EUNETIC network is sponsored by the SPES-program of the European Union. The conference was sponsored by the Programme for Future-Oriented Technology Policy of the Research Council of Norway (programme coordinator Keith Smith), EUNETIC, the STEP-group and NUPI. Bart Verspagen's work was made possible by a fellowship of the Royal Netherlands Academy of Arts and Sciences. We thank all these institutions for their generous financial support. We are also indebted to the people who made the conference such a big organizational success: Wilma Coenegrachts (MERIT), Liv Høyvik (NUPI) and Erik Reinert, Keith Smith and Heidi Wiig (all from the STEP-group). Of the many papers of high quality that were presented at the conference, we were able to include only a few in this volume. The papers which do appear, however, have benefited from discussions among all conference participants. The production of the book was greatly assisted by the work by Mieke Donders (MERIT) who skilfully typeset the manuscript.

Jan Fagerberg
Bart Verspagen
Nick von Tunzelmann

List of Contributors

Moses Abramovitz
Department of Economics
Stanford University
Stanford, CA 94305–6072
United States

Erik Beelen
MERIT, University of Limburg
P.O. Box 616
6200 MD Maastricht
The Netherlands

Mario Cimoli
Department of Economics
University of Venice
Ca'Foscari, Dorsoduro 3246
I–30123 Venice
Italy

Steve Dowrick
Economics RSSS
Australian National University
P.O. Box 4
Canberra, A.C.T. 2601
Australia

Jan Fagerberg
NUPI
Grønlandsleiret 25
N–0190 Oslo
Norway

Christopher Freeman
MERIT, University of Limburg
P.O. Box 616
6200 MD Maastricht
The Netherlands

Erik S. Reinert
STEP-group, Norsk Regnesentral
P.O. Box 114, Blindern
N–0314 Oslo
Norway

Nick von Tunzelmann
SPRU, University of Sussex
Mantell Building
Falmer, Brighton BN1 9RF
United Kingdom

Fernando Vega-Redondo
Universidad de Alicante
Fac. CC. Economicas y
   Empresariales
Ap. Correos 99
E–03071 Alicante
Spain

Bart Verspagen
MERIT, University of Limburg
P.O. Box 616
6200 MD Maastricht
The Netherlands

Edward N. Wolff
Department of Economics
New York University
269 Mercer Street, 7th Floor
New York, NY 10003
United States

1. The Economics of Convergence and Divergence: An Overview

Jan Fagerberg, Bart Verspagen and Nick von Tunzelmann

Why do some countries grow faster, and reach higher levels of productivity, while other countries fall behind? This – and similar – question(s) have been central to the literature on economic growth from the very beginning. There are good reasons for this. If clear answers can be provided, these may have wide implications for economic policies and welfare.

With the neoclassical revolution in economic thinking around the turn of the century, however, the focus shifted away from questions related to growth and development. It was brought to the forefront again by some of Keynes' followers who wanted to generalize his ideas to the long run. The resulting models (Harrod 1939, Domar 1946) supported the Keynesian view that market forces left alone should not be expected to lead to full employment in the long run. Not unexpectedly, this result was not greeted with enthusiasm by the neoclassicals. They pointed out that this result rested on very restrictive assumptions, above all that of a fixed relation between the factors of production. While defendable, perhaps, in the very short run, this assumption was not regarded as appropriate for the long run. Following this, Solow (1956) and Swan (1956) suggested models that allowed for substitution between factors of production on the basis of economic criteria.

These models, based on standard neoclassical assumptions on the behaviour of agents and markets, 'eliminated' the Keynesian problems of long-run unemployment and economic instability. At the time this was regarded as a remarkable achievement, although in retrospect it may be argued that the neoclassical models in some sense proved 'too much'.

Another problem with these models was that they predicted that in the absence of exogenous technological progress, there would be no productivity growth in the long run. An alternative perspective, more in the Keynesian tradition, was offered by Kaldor and others (see Kaldor 1957, Kaldor 1961 and Kaldor and Mirrlees 1962). They suggested models where long-run productivity growth was made possible through endogen-

1

ous technological progress and shifts in the distribution of income. However, this alternative approach quickly fell out of fashion, although Kaldorian ideas kept inspiring some (European) economists. From the point of view of technological change, the marginal role assigned to Kaldor's approach was certainly a misfortune, for his model was the only one that already incorporated an endogenous technology factor in the 1950s.

Although the neoclassical contributions seemed to triumph in the theoretical arena, empirical research reported findings that questioned the explanatory power of these models. Abramovitz (1956) showed that the overwhelming share of observed growth in the US could not be explained in a straightforward manner by the factors taken into account by the neoclassical model, unless one was willing to see exogenous technological change as a satisfactory explanation. This result was soon corroborated by Solow (1957) and others.[1] The stage was set for a continuing search for mostly empirical explanations of the 'measure of our ignorance', as Abramovitz labelled the unexplained part of productivity growth (some of which might be technical progress proper).

In the first two decades following the publication of the papers by Abramovitz and Solow, attempts to explain growth and growth differences were aided by theoretical perspectives laid down in the neoclassical theory of growth. The contributions consisted mainly of so-called 'growth-accounting' studies and estimated production functions. However, as will become apparent below, this search did not succeed in eliminating the questions raised already in the 1950s.

By the mid-1970s, just as the world economy went from a period of high and stable growth to one characterized by low and sluggish growth performance, neoclassical growth theory, and applied work intimately related with it, had fallen out of fashion. The terrain was taken over by others, mostly economic historians and economists with a more heterodox background. These authors – some of them inspired by Schumpeter, Kaldor and other economists outside the mainstream – pointed to the existence of gaps in technology between countries. One strand of research focused on the potential for catch-up by countries behind the technology frontier and the prerequisites for exploiting this potential (see for example Gomulka 1971, Cornwall 1977, Maddison 1979 and Abramovitz 1979). These studies were mostly descriptive in nature, but sometimes included estimated models as well. Others pointed out that the existence of technology gaps between countries does not necessarily imply convergence, but may equally well be consistent with a diverging pattern. Models and applied work in this spirit – to a large extent inspired by Kaldor – were presented by Dixon and Thirlwall (1975), Thirlwall (1979) and others.

In the middle of the 1980s, the mainstream re-entered the terrain, through the advent of the so-called 'new growth theories'. This resurgence of mainstream interest was to some extent related to the increasing anxieties about US technological and economic leadership of the world economy. (Europeans had a much longer history of such anxieties.) Suddenly, explanation of convergence – or lack of such – in the world economy became one of the most fashionable issues in mainstream economics. Impressive mathematical models were developed, and econometric work flourished, the latter also a consequence of the publication at the same time of new and large data sets (consisting of more than one hundred countries). However, the neoclassicals who took part in this did in general not acknowledge – or take into account – that the issues they suddenly had become so strongly interested in, had been addressed by others for several decades already. This has led to the strange result that although many neoclassicals increasingly adopt views that until recently were associated with more heterodox economists, there is still not much communication and interaction between economists with different theoretical backgrounds in this area. This book – and the conference that preceded it – is intended as a contribution to challenge this situation.

1. NEOCLASSICAL GROWTH: THE PERSISTENT RESIDUAL

The neoclassical growth model as formulated by Solow and others was an impressive theoretical achievement, but one that arguably led theoretical and empirical research on growth and growth differences astray (see Dowrick in this volume). It was successful in showing that in a world where perfect competition prevails, there is no conflict between growth and full employment, in contrast to the predictions of earlier models. It did so at a high cost, however. Disregarding exogenous technological progress, higher productivity could be achieved only by increasing capital per worker, and this caused the marginal productivity of capital to decline. Ultimately the marginal productivity of capital would approach a level where productivity growth ceased. Thus, in the absence of exogenous technologial progress, this model predicted a stagnant level of productivity in the long run. Another prediction was that countries with similar rates of population growth and propensities to save would converge towards the same level of productivity (ouptut per unit of labour). The introduction of exogenous technological progress allowed for productivity growth in the long run. Convergence would still take place provided that all countries benefited equally from the exogenous growth in technology (which was generally taken for granted in applied work based on this perspective).

As noted, the empirical work that accompanied these theoretical developments showed that the explanatory power of this model was indeed very limited. In the analysis of Abramovitz, around 90% of US productivity growth had to be accounted for by the residual, which following Solow (and Tinbergen, see note 1) should be expected to reflect exogenous technological progress. Obviously this was not very satisfactory and various attempts were made to 'squeeze down the residual' (Nelson 1981). One strategy was to embody as much as possible of the unexplained productivity growth into the factors themselves by adjusting for changes in quality (Jorgenson and Griliches 1967). Although the latter authors succeeded in largely eliminating the residual in the examples they quoted, their procedure effectively wrote such phenomena as technical change into their 'quality adjustments', which still warranted an explanation. The residual has also been 'eliminated' by Scott (1989), who is at pains to stress that his approach differs from Jorgenson and Griliches, and indeed more closely resembles the 'new growth theories'. Scott considers that R&D should be treated like any other form of investment as expended to change the situation, and therefore he conflates all forms of investment before computing the residual. The net result, however, is – as with Jorgenson–Griliches – to leave the variable itself in need of further clarification.

Another strategy, suggested by Denison (1962, 1967), was to add other explanatory factors, such as changes in the employment mix (from low productivity to high productivity activities) and better exploitation of economies of scale. In the case of the USA, what was not accounted for in this way was assumed to reflect technological progress. For other countries, what was left when the estimated contribution from all factors plus the US residual (technological progress) was deducted, was ascribed to technological catch-up and other unknown sources. Obviously, assumptions such as economies of scale and productivity differences across sectors contradict the strong equilibrium assumptions on which the neoclassical growth theory was based. Thus, the growth-accounting exercises increasingly lost sight of theory. However, the growth accountants are not the only ones to be blamed for this. The major problem, of course, was that the theory that was intended to form the basis of this work had very little to tell about growth.

An alternative empirical approach to explain differences in growth across countries was to estimate neoclassical production functions on cross-country samples. Attempts to do that (Chenery *et al.* 1970, Feder 1986) showed that the explanatory power of the model was also poor in this case. In general (for samples including developing countries) a positive correlation between growth and investment rates could be found, but the impact of population growth was generally non-significant (and sometimes took on unbelievably high values). These authors and others therefore followed the route of the 'growth accountants' and added other (disequilibrium) factors. To improve the 'explanatory power' of their models, many authors replace growth of the labour force with growth of employment, thereby effectively neglecting the unemployment problem. This is, of course, very difficult to justify within a model framework that assumes full utilization of all resources (including labour) from the very start.

2. TECHNOLOGY GAPS AND CATCH-UP

During the 1970s, these and other weaknesses of the neoclassical approach to growth became more and more apparent. It was pointed out by several authors (Abramovitz and David 1973, Nelson 1973, 1981) that some of the basic weaknesses referred to how technology was conceived in these models. Technological progress, it was argued, could not be assessed independently of capital accumulation, economies of scale and – for the more recent period – educational investment (human capital). Above all, technology was not a truly public good, not only because a large part of it was appropriable by legal and other means, but also because technology and technological progress to a large extent was embedded in organizations and firms. Thus, following this approach, imitation was more difficult than originally conceived by the neoclassicals.

Maddison (1979, 1982, 1991), Abramovitz (1979) and others presented analyses of growth post-World War Two, which showed that the productivity differences within the OECD area were markedly reduced during this period, at least until the end of the 1970s. The narrowing of the gap was to a large extent ascribed to the higher rates of capital accumulation in the follower countries (a vintage effect operating through the presumed greater productivity of newer capital stock, see Wolff in this volume). These writers also pointed to more favourable general economic conditions in this period as an important contributing factor to the 'catch-up boom'.

In later work, Abramovitz (1986, 1992, and this volume) elaborated this framework further to take other conditioning factors more explicitly into account. This relates, for instance, to factors such as education, an appropriate financial system, labour market relations etc. which he – following Ohkawa and Rosovsky (1973) – labelled 'social capability'. Another important set of factors are those which are classified under the heading of 'technological congruence', referring to the assumption that technological progress depends on leader-country characteristics, and that backward countries – to implement leader-country technologies – need to emulate some of these characteristics. For instance, the rise of the US to technological leadership is conceived as based on capital and scale-intensive technologies that were not equally appropriate in countries with less capital and smaller markets.

It is fair to say that this elaborate framework, although very attractive, remains untested, at least when it comes to econometric tests. One obvious problem, admitted by Abramovitz, is the difficulty of conducting tests on the impacts of social capability or technical congruence on the kinds of data typically available for a range of countries. One result of the empirical work in this general area, however, is that the unconditional convergence hypothesis, which can be derived from Solow's growth model, is falsified. However, subsequent contributions (Fagerberg 1987, 1988a, 1991, Baumol *et al.* 1989, Dowrick and Nguyen 1989, Verspagen 1991, to mention a few) have established that the scope for catch-up, as proxied by GDP per capita or the like, stands up well when other factors explaining differences in growth performance across countries are added (so-called 'weak' convergence). Variables that have been shown to be successful in this respect are investment rates, education and national technological activity. Admittedly, these results are open to different interpretation, but they do suggest that catch-up, to be successful, requires other supporting factors.

3. THE HERITAGE FROM KALDOR AND MYRDAL

There is more to technology gaps than the prospects for their elimination through catching-up. Gaps are also created, through a process of divergence. Arguing along Kaldorian lines, several authors have presented models and analyses where structural differences across countries may lead to long-run differences in growth rates. The traditional approach to growth did not attempt to explain this possibility. On the contrary, early models in this tradition – based as they were on the assumption of perfectly competitive markets – led to convergence predictions. No wonder, perhaps, that the first attempts to account for diverging growth patterns across countries were firmly rooted in the Keynesian (or post-Keynesian) tradition. Some of this work can be traced back to Harrod's and Hicks' early attempts to develop a Keynesian understanding of open-economy macroeconomics. In this approach the growth of a country was seen as constrained by the demand for its exports. However, the main contributor and source of inspiration in this area has been Kaldor.

In the 1950s Kaldor developed models of economic growth in which technological progress was assumed to be endogenous (the technological progress function, see Kaldor 1957, 1961, Kaldor and Mirrlees 1962). The basic idea was that investment and learning were interrelated, so that technological progress could best be represented as a function of capital accumulation per worker. These models contained only one production sector and structural aspects were therefore not taken into consideration. In his applied work, however, he was at pains to stress that the prospects for technological progress were not equal across sectors or industries. Generally these prospects were assumed to be more favourable in manufacturing than elsewhere (Kaldor 1966, 1967), giving manufacturing the role as an 'engine of growth' in the economy. Following Verdoorn (1949), Kaldor saw productivity growth in manufacturing as related to growth of manufacturing output, e.g. the higher the rate of growth of manufacturing output, the higher the rate of learning, and hence the rate of productivity growth. He also noted the interaction between the growth of manufacturing and demand: since income elasticities of demand vary across production sectors, rising national income will (in a closed economy) go hand in hand with structural changes in the composition of output, a theme later elaborated by Pasinetti (1981). However, export markets may allow a country to change – and grow – at a faster rate than the domestic markets would have allowed. Thus, for Kaldor growth of manufacturing exports was one of the chief ways to increase manufacturing output and, hence, learning, technological progress and the competitiveness of a country (Kaldor, 1978, 1981).

Kaldor often stressed the interactive character of the factors taking part in the growth process, leading to 'cumulative causation' or 'virtuous' and 'vicious' patterns of development. These arguments go back to Myrdal (1957). Myrdal argued that the growth of advanced countries could have both 'spread' (i.e., spillover) and 'backwash' effects for the less developed countries. For example, the growth of capital in the advanced countries, instead of leading to declining capital prices or outflows of capital to the rest of the world, might encourage technical progress in those advanced countries, which could then augment their capital formation. In this way 'causation' became 'circular and cumulative'. The less developed countries became caught in the 'backwash', as capital and technology (and other developmental resources) flowed increasingly to the already advanced countries.

In a paper from 1970, devoted to the issue of why growth rates of countries – and regions – differ, Kaldor sketched an approach which combined the Keynesian assumption of growth as constrained by export demand with his own emphasis on endogenous technological progress. This approach was soon formalized by Dixon and Thirlwall (1975). In this model the impact of growth in export demand on economic growth through the multiplier is magnified by the Kaldor–Verdoorn relationship: the increase in demand induced by export growth affects productivity positively, this leads to improvements in the price competitiveness for exports (assuming wages constant), and, hence, further increases in the rates of growth in exports and GDP. The most likely outcome (according to Dixon and Thirlwall) would be one of countries growing at different rates – reflecting differences in structural characteristics – implying neither convergence nor divergence in productivity levels. Thirlwall (1979, 1980) introduced a constraint on the external account into this framework (balanced trade), arguing that export-led growth models otherwise may overestimate growth. On the additional assumption that relative prices are relatively sticky, so that their impact can be ignored (eliminating the feedback from endogenous technological progress), Thirlwall showed that the growth rate of a country's GDP relative to the rest of the world depends on the relation between the demand elasticities for its exports and imports, e.g. on structural aspects of the economy. This means that a country that produces goods which are in high demand both at home and abroad will grow faster. Thirlwall (1979) showed that with the exception of Japan this simple model 'explained' postwar growth remarkably well. His empirical results, although highly suggestive, have been subject to some controversy (for an overview see McCombie 1986). Furthermore, the precise meaning of the concept of an income elasticity of demand – highly relevant on a disaggregated level – is intuitively difficult to grasp when applied to the total exports or imports of a country. Kaldor (1981, p. 603) suggested that these elasticities should be seen as shorthand for 'the innovative ability and adaptive capacity' of the producers in the different countries. Following this suggestion Fagerberg (1988b) presented a balance-of-payments constrained growth model where exports and imports were determined by the differences across countries in the potential for catch-up, indigenous technological efforts, investments and other factors. This model presented a reasonable explanation of the finding of Kaldor (1978) that the market shares for exports for countries seem to move in line with relative costs (and not the other way around).

The balance-of-payments restriction to economic growth, and its underlying Kaldorian and Myrdalian ideas, also provided ample inspiration for authors in the recent neo-Schumpeterian tradition (for example Cimoli 1988, Dosi *et al.* 1990, Cimoli and Soete 1992, Verspagen 1993 and Cimoli's chapter in this volume). The models presented in this tradition combine the Thirlwall argument on the influence of elasticities of demand with explicit dynamics for national and sectoral technological capabilities, and/or the way in which technological competitiveness affects market-shares dynamics. Thus, these models allow for both differences in techno-logical progress and differences in income elasticities of demand across sectors and countries. As a result, growth paths in these models are in most cases highly dependent on structural (i.e., related to sector composition) features (as in Pasinetti 1981). In an international context, the possibilities for sectoral specialization, combined with different learning possibilities and demand patterns, will then induce differences in growth rates among countries. There is also a distinct possibility for path dependency and lock-in effects in these models.

4. NEOCLASSICAL GROWTH: THE REVIVAL

The problems with the old Solowian theory – at least as conceived by many of the adherents of the new theories – were first, that long-run growth in productivity could not be explained without reverting to some exogenous factor, and second that it predicted a global convergence in productivity levels that was not seen to be taking place. The answer of theorists in the neoclassical area was to follow in the footsteps of Arrow (1962), Uzawa (1965) and others in attempting to endogenize the contribution from technological progress to economic growth.

Romer's (1986) paper postulated a production function in which both traditional factors (labour and capital) and a factor related to 'technology' were accumulated. He simply assumed the latter factor had some external effects, i.e., the individual entrepreneur would find both her own and the economy-wide technology stock in her production function. Lucas (1988) provided a similar model in which human capital was accumulated.

While these models still seemed to start from the 'classical' idea that accumulation is the source of growth, a subsequent class of models was more explicitly based on the Schumpeterian idea that innovation by private firms drives the growth process. In these models, technology is seen as a separate, endogenous factor explaining productivity growth in the economy (see for example Romer 1990, Grossman and Helpman 1991, Aghion and Howitt 1992). Users of new technologies have to pay a price to cover the cost of the new technology. In return they receive an exclusive monopoly right to its use. Thus, technological progress is at least partly appropriable, and this introduces an element of imperfect competition into these models. At the same time, new technologies also add to the existing pool of knowledge, and in this way facilitate new technological developments. Thus, new technologies also contain a non-appropriable – or public – element. The combination of these two elements, the incentive to innovate due to the appropriability of technological progress, and the positive externality from this process, allows growth to go on. In these models growth therefore depends positively on the amount of resources available for development of new technologies (human capital, R&D), the extent to which new technologies are appropriable and how 'patient' investors are. Thus, variables related to human capital and R&D stand out as the prime candidates for distinguishing empirically between countries that do catch up and countries that do not. Another prediction, which is intuitively much more difficult to accept, is that large countries will experience faster technological progress and hence faster growth than small countries. There is, as pointed out by Verspagen (1992), little if any empirical evidence to support this.

The theoretical development in this area has spurred empirical work, also greatly facilitated by the publication of large data sets containing more than one hundred countries and several decades (Summers and Heston 1991). The tested models are all very alike, indeed they are in many cases indistinguishable from those used by the adherents of the traditional growth theory or the technology-gap theories. Generally, they are single-equation models, where growth is assumed to be a function of the technology gap, proxied by GDP per capita, and other factors assumed to affect growth positively. A useful summary has recently been published by Levine and Renelt (1992). For large samples, the scope for imitation combined with investment or education or both works well to explain differences in growth across countries. In contrast, most other variables that have been suggested in the literature, are shown not to be robustly correlated with growth (measures of national technological activity were not included though).

However, when both investment and education are included, the impact of each – or at least one – of these variables is reduced. This is consistent with the view of many new growth theorists that investment should be considered as an endogenous variable (Romer 1989, Barro 1991). An exception is De Long and Summers (1991), who argue that equipment investment (as contrasted to investment in structures and transport) has a much higher explanatory power than education variables. They estimate the pay-off to equipment investment to be around 30%, and interpret this result in support of the hypothesis of positive external effects of capital accumulation. However, they are not able to rule out that this result is caused by interaction between investments and other factors. Wolff (in this volume) provides some evidence supporting this interpretation. In contrast, a recent study by Lichtenberg (1992) indicates that the returns to R&D are much higher than the returns to physical capital.

5. TECHNOLOGY GAPS: SOME POLICY ISSUES[2]

Baumol's seminal paper of 1986 which initiated the 'convergence-controversy' argued that the phenomenon was best explained by technological spillovers. Baumol, however, shrank from recommending that the United States should implement controls or restrictions on the export of technology, as some politicians were supporting at that time. Similar policy issues arose via the 'new growth theory', which were sharpened as its practitioners came to contrast generic technological information ('blueprints'), assumed to have high spillover potential, with learning-by-doing that would depend on specific production activity by the follower. Abramovitz's contemporaneous paper of 1986, as we have pointed out, although giving some weight to spillovers, placed greater emphasis on 'social capabilities' in trying to account for why only some countries seemed able to catch up. This placed greater policy stress on indigenous efforts to develop the context for socioeconomic development within the catching-up country. Those within the 'new growth' school who developed increasing returns out of returns to human capital formation and their spillovers could be regarded as offering similar policy advice. Finally, the evolutionary school, although it had originally drawn a rather sharp contrast between innovation and imitation (e.g., in Nelson and Winter 1982), was by this time coming to emphasize the tacitness, cumulativeness and idiosyncrasy of technological accumulation; from which it could be inferred that the later comers could benefit to only a limited degree from technological spillovers – even in technology they would have to undertake serious innovative efforts of their own. This implied the need for technology policies in the follower countries that would go well beyond technology imports.

We can here briefly survey the types of policies that have been implemented by some of the larger industrializing nations. Further details of these strategies are provided in von Tunzelmann (1994).

1. Controlling technology spillovers. Once it had begun to establish itself as 'workshop of the world', Britain attempted for a time to restrict the outflow of skilled personnel and advanced equipment. These laws, on the export of 'artizans and machinery', first introduced at the end of the seventeenth century, were supported by the 'Manchester School' of businessmen who by the 1830s were becoming the most vociferous supporters of free trade in agricultural products. However, as Reinert briefly remarks in his chapter below, the laws were quite ineffective, and were abolished by 1843, several years before the 'Manchester School' got its own way through the repeal of the Corn Laws, to usher in Britain's

classic era of free trade. Such ambivalent attitudes to trade policies, which the cynic might label as hypocrisy, also characterized the converse policies adopted by the countries aiming to catch up, as we shall see below.

Here we can consider the attempts by the follower countries to import technologies. It has often been observed that British industries were carried to Continental Europe and to the USA in the early nineteenth century embodied in just those 'artizans and machinery' which the laws were trying to prohibit (e.g., Jeremy 1981). This may have been a necessary condition for international technology transfer, but it was not a sufficient condition, as Bruland's detailed study (1989) of the attempts to build an English-style textile industry in Norway indicates. In similar vein, the Japanese government, in the aftermath of the Meiji restoration of 1868, sought to induce highly skilled or educated Westerners to remain long enough in Japan for their knowledge to become transplanted. The reverse policy, of getting one's trainees to spend time in more advanced facilities abroad, was used at about the same time by the Scandinavians (Bruland 1991), rather later by the Japanese, and in particular by the Newly Industrializing East Asian countries of the late twentieth century.

Aside from migrations of skilled labour, there was also the possibility of exports/imports of the plant and equipment. Foreign Direct Investment (FDI) was widely canvassed as a vehicle for technological catch-up. In the nineteenth century, FDI was used almost entirely for infrastructural development (railroads, ports, etc.) – little of the massive capital outflows from Britain and later the USA went into, say, foreign manufacturing at this stage. Recipient countries were also guarded about the loss of control implied in FDI. Japan typically allowed the first plant incorporating a particular technology to be built by foreigners (usually Germans), and then made every effort to construct and operate subsequent plants itself. Similar policies have been followed more recently in South Korea and Taiwan, although the city-state 'tigers' (Singapore and Hong Kong) have permitted a greater degree of foreign ownership. Even so, there appears to be a much stronger role for local control in the NICs (newly industrializing countries) of East Asia than their counterparts in Latin America, and this appears to have been a major factor in the relatively greater success of the former region (Freeman 1993 and his contribution to this volume).

2. Domestic credit and technology policies. In a well-known study, Gerschenkron (1962) argued that banks and the financial system would have to take on a more pro-active role in catching-up countries, the more so the further the country needed to catch up. Later studies have certainly confirmed the existence of differences in the structure of organized finance. The current belief appears to be that the differing structures of financial systems may have been less a pro-active decision to leap ahead

than a reaction to changes in the demands for long-term industrial finance. Most catching-up countries did also take some steps to provide a credit system to support industrial growth. However, they did not all use the financial sector in the same pro-active way. The prime examples of such a pro-active policy are Japan and Korea, while many other countries to a large extent relied more on other policy instruments.

As part of the industrialization effort, some governments or ministries sought to avoid merely repeating the growth patterns of their predecessors, and tried to leapfrog into modern capital-intensive industry. Very different examples are provided by Soviet Russia under Stalin in the 1930s (following the 'industrialization debate' of the 1920s), and by Japan under the Ministry of International Trade and Industry (MITI) in the 1950s. Though there was some opposition within the country and overseas, MITI considered that unbalanced growth based on heavy industry could lead to faster expansion, and for exports sought to replace comparative advantage (in labour-intensive industries) with 'competitive advantage' (in capital and scale-intensive industries producing goods with a high income elasticity of demand). The growth performance of the Japanese economy over those years suggests a very effective strategy, but it ran into increasing domestic problems, and in 1971 MITI moved towards encouraging instead information technologies and the 'knowledge industry' (von Tunzelmann 1994 and references therein). The policy literature relating to present-day NICs and developing countries has tilted towards the crucial role of indigenous technological capabilities in the catching-up countries (Fransman 1985, Bell and Pavitt 1993), if need be through developing along different technological paths (for an elegant theoretical analysis of technological paths, see Vega-Redondo's chapter in this volume).

The above suggests that inflows of technology embodied in labour and/or capital may help to trigger catch-up but are unlikely to sustain it. The same implication of the necessity for developing domestic capabilities comes out of many of the papers presented at our conference – for example by nearly all of the papers published in this volume. The required scope of such domestic policies is hinted at in Abramovitz's chapter.

3. Commercial policies. The MITI strategy implied creating rather than simply adjusting to comparative advantage. For trade policies, the main concern has been the so-called 'infant industry' argument for protectionism towards fledgling industries in the catching-up countries. Reinert shows at length in his chapter below how Britain began as a catching-up country in late medieval times, and adopted some infant-industry protectionism (it also 'imported' skilled workers from the Continent). As Britain moved into world leadership, the torch for industrial protectionism was taken up

by its later rivals – by Alexander Hamilton in the USA, by J.-B. Say (otherwise a free-trader) and Saint-Simon in France, and by Friedrich List in Germany. Most such writers argued that free trade was the optimum when the industrial imbalances were overcome, so such protectionism ought to be temporary. The modern counterpart is 'strategic trade policy' (e.g., Krugman 1986, Helpman and Krugman 1989, Krugman 1990), which has links with the 'new growth theory' described earlier. Empirical studies of the American experience with protective tariffs, for example by David (1970) on cotton and by Fogel and Engerman (1971) on iron, do not give great encouragement for the view that indigenous capabilities can be nurtured successfully behind protective tariffs. Much appears to depend on retaining appropriate elements of competition – not just internally as Reinert stresses, but also externally, through properly designing the policies to sustain domestic efforts at catching-up. Nor did all countries use tariffs for this purpose – Japan was barred by the 'Unequal Treaties' imposed on it in 1858 (repealed only in 1911) from extensive tariff-making, and had to pursue protectionism mainly through other means, such as the limitation on FDI noted above. The United States has from 1824 to the present day tried to justify the use of tariffs in industries where it considers it suffers from a disadvantage and free trade where it is dominant. One can conclude from this that infant-industry protectionism is certainly not sufficient for growth.

4. Social capabilities. Abramovitz's (1986) paper discussed the role of development of corporate and managerial capabilities, a theme which he expands upon in his contribution to this book. Here, however, the scope for imitation seems very weak indeed. The United States overtook Britain at the end of the nineteenth century by basing itself on a quite different corporate tradition, as the justly celebrated works of Chandler (1977, 1990) have demonstrated. In the same way, the Japanese rivalry with the USA in the late twentieth century has been based on a quite different set of beliefs and practices in the corporate sphere. MITI was however much less successful in changing the industrial structure in Japan (e.g., forcing mergers) than in changing technologies. Attempts to graft leadingedge practice into a different sociocultural setting, as for example by Latin American countries adopting North American managerial practices, have been much less successful (von Tunzelmann 1994).

Abramovitz also placed much attention on the role of education, partly because of its theoretical contribution via spillovers as advocated by some of the new growth theorists (e.g., Lucas 1988, Barro 1991), and partly because it is relatively straightforward to measure. Cross-country correlations between educational attainments and growth rates have generally been high, but these have been disputed on grounds (a) that when education and investment are both included in the equations, one or other usually drops out of significance; (b) that this may reflect 'reverse causation', running instead from growth to education. The precise links between education and industrialization – for instance, what type of education it is best to offer – also remain in doubt. In the 'first industrial revolution' in Britain, educational attainments were low, but it can be argued that the nature of technology was such that better educational standards might not have made much difference to the rate of industrialization at this stage (Mitch 1993) – although the deficiency probably weakened Britain's attempts to keep up with later industrializers like Germany and the USA. Much has been made of the argument that the rapid industrialization of East Asia's 'four tigers' has been led by education (e.g., World Bank 1993). This has been disputed by Amsden (1989) for the case of South Korea, who contends that the education offered was too abstract to help industry very much. However, it does seem that widespread and preferably universal primary education, even if the curriculum is rather non-vocational, is associated with 'learning to learn' – provided that this is backed up with extensive efforts in training on-the-job.

Gerschenkron's study in 1962 argued that the extent of government interventionism would have to rise, the larger was the technology gap between the leader country and the country in question. This was based on his assessment of growth patterns across Europe in the nineteenth century (for a recent reappraisal, see Sylla and Toniolo 1991). Others pointed out that, if the gaps were larger still, as when moving to different regions of the globe (Asia, Latin America, etc.), there was less evidence for any simple expansion of government involvement. Different strategies might be required in the 'late late comers' (Hirschman 1958). This pattern seems consistent with the asymmetric growth responses demonstrated in some chapters here, e.g., by Dowrick and especially by Beelen and Verspagen. The progress of indigenization of industrial technologies is studied in several modern analyses of technology transfer (e.g., Rosenberg and Frischtak 1985, Katz 1987), and the nature of the government policies established in the recent literature on 'new growth theory' (Krugman 1986, Shaw 1992), on evolutionary theory (Smith 1991), and on 'National Systems of Innovation' (OECD 1992, Nelson 1993, etc.). Catching-up emerges as very far from the passive process that might seem to be implied by technological spillovers.

NOTES

1. In an early contribution, Tinbergen (1943) had already pointed out that a large part of economic growth around the turn of the century had to be explained by 'exogenous' growth in the efficiency of capital and labour inputs. His article sets out, in a Cobb–Douglas framework, the exact method for calculating what later became known as the 'Solow-residual'. Tinbergen found that growth in total factor productivity was highest in Germany (1.5% annual average over the period 1870–1914), followed by the United States and France (both 1.1%). The United Kingdom, at that time losing its leadership of the world economy, only realized a 0.3% increase in total factor productivity.
2. The editors are grateful to Keith Smith for assistance with this section, based on the paper he gave at the Oslo meeting.

REFERENCES

Abramovitz, M. (1956), 'Resources and Output Trends in the United States since 1870', *American Economic Review*, 46: 5–23.

Abramovitz, M. (1979), 'Rapid Growth Potential and its Realization: The Experience of Capitalist Economies in the Postwar Period', in E. Malinvaud (ed.), *Economic Growth and Resources*, London: Macmillan.

Abramovitz, M. (1986), 'Catching Up, Forging Ahead, and Falling Behind', *Journal of Economic History*, 66: 385–406.

Abramovitz, M. (1992), 'Catch-Up and Convergence in the Postwar Growth Boom and After', Paper presented at the Workshop on Historical Perspectives on the International Convergence on Productivity, New York, April 23–24.

Abramovitz, M. and P. David (1973), 'Reinterpreting Economic Growth: Parables and Realities', *American Economic Review*, LXIII: 428–39.

Aghion, P. and P. Howitt (1992), 'A Model of Growth Through Creative Destruction', *Econometrica*, 60: 323–51.

Amsden, A.H. (1989), *Asia's Next Giant: South Korea and Late Industrialization*, New York and Oxford: Oxford University Press.

Arrow, K. (1962), 'The Economic Implications of Learning by Doing', *Review of Economic Studies*, 29: 155–73.

Barro, R. (1991), 'Economic Growth in a Cross Section of Countries', *The Quarterly Journal of Economics*, 106: 407–43.

Baumol, W.J. (1986), 'Productivity Growth, Convergence and Welfare: What the Long Run Data Show', *American Economic Review*, 76: 1072–85.

Baumol, W.J., S.A. Batey Blackman and E.N. Wolff (1989), *Productivity and American Leadership: The Long View*, Cambridge, Mass.: MIT Press.

Bell, M. and K. Pavitt (1993): 'Technology Accumulation and Industrial Growth: Contrasts between Developed and Developing Countries', *Industrial and Corporate Change*, 2: 157–210.

Bruland, K. (1989), *British Technology and European Industrialization: the Norwegian Textile Industry in the Mid Nineteenth Century*, Cambridge: Cambridge University Press.

Bruland, K. (ed.) (1991), *Technology Transfer and Scandinavian Industrialization*, New

York and Oxford: Berg.

Chandler, A.D. jr (1977), *The Visible Hand: the Managerial Revolution in American Business*, Cambridge, Mass. and London: Belknap Press.

Chandler, A.D. jr (1990), *Scale and Scope: the Dynamics of Industrial Capitalism*, Cambridge, Mass. and London: Belknap Press.

Chatterji, M. (1992), 'Convergence Clubs and Endogenous Growth', *Oxford Review of Economic Policy*, 8: 57–69.

Chenery, H., H. Elkington and C. Sims (1970), *A Uniform Analysis of Development Patterns*, Harvard University Center for International Affairs, Economic Development Report 148 (July), Cambridge, Mass.

Cimoli, M. (1988), 'Technological Gaps and Institutional Asymmetries in a NorthSouth Model with a Continuum of Goods', *Metroeconomica*, 39: 245–74.

Cimoli, M. and L. Soete (1992), 'A Generalized Technological Gap Trade Model', *Economie Appliquée*, 45: 33–54.

Cornwall, J. (1977), *Modern Capitalism. Its Growth and Transformation*, London: Martin Robertson.

David, P.A. (1970), 'Learning by Doing and Tariff Protection: a Reconsideration of the Case of the Ante-Bellum United States Cotton Textile Industry', *Journal of Economic History*, 30: 521–601.

De Long, J.B. and L.H. Summers (1991), 'Equipment Investment and Economic Growth', *The Quarterly Journal of Economics*, CVI: 445–502.

Denison, E.F. (1962), *The Sources of Economic Growth in the United States and the Alternatives Before Us*, New York: Committee for Economic Development.

Denison, E.F. (1967), *Why Growth Rates Differ: Post-War Experience in Nine Western Countries*, Washington, D.C.: Brookings Institution.

Dixon, R. and A.P. Thirlwall (1975), 'A Model of Regional Growth-Rate Differences on Kaldorian Lines', *Oxford Economic Papers*, 27: 201–14.

Domar, E.D. (1946) 'Capital Expansion, Rate of Growth and Employment', *Econometrica*, 14: 137–47.

Dosi, G., K. Pavitt and L. Soete (1990), *The Economics of Technological Change and International Trade*, Brighton: Wheatsheaf.

Dowrick, S. and D.T. Nguyen (1989), 'OECD Comparative Economic Growth 1950–85: Catch-Up and Convergence', *American Economic Review*, 79: 1010–30.

Fagerberg, J. (1987), 'A Technology Gap Approach to Why Growth Rates Differ', *Research Policy*, 16: 87–99.

Fagerberg, J. (1988a), 'Why Growth Rates Differ', in G. Dosi *et al.* (eds), *Technical Change and Economic Theory*, London: Pinter, 432–57.

Fagerberg, J. (1988b), 'International Competitiveness', *Economic Journal*, 98: 355–74.

Fagerberg, J. (1991), 'Innovation, Catching Up and Growth', in *Technology and Productivity: The Challenge for Economic Policy*, Paris: OECD, 37–46.

Feder, G. (1986), 'Growth in semi-industrialized countries: a statistical analysis', in H. Chenery *et al.* (ed.), *Industrialization and Growth*, Oxford: Oxford University Press.

Fogel, R.W. and S.L. Engerman (1971), 'A Model for the Explanation of Industrial Expansion during the Nineteenth Century: with an Application to the American Iron Industry', in R.W. Fogel and S.L. Engerman (eds), *The Reinterpretation of American Economic History*, New York etc.: Harper & Row, 148–62.

Fransman, M. (1985), 'Conceptualising Technical Change in the Third World in the 1980s: an Interpretative Survey', *Journal of Development Studies*, 21: 572–652.

Freeman, C. (1993), 'Interdependence of Technological Change with Growth of Trade and GNP', in M. Nissanke and A. Hewitt (eds), *Economic Crisis in Developing Countries*, London and New York: Pinter, 157–77.

Gerschenkron, A. (1962), *Economic Backwardness in Historical Perspective*, Cambridge Mass.: Belknap Press.

Gomulka, S. (1971), *Inventive Activity, Diffusion and the Stages of Economic Growth*, Aarhus: Skrifter fra Aarhus Universitets Økonomiske Institut, Nr. 24.

Grossman, G.M. and E. Helpman (1991), *Innovation and Growth in the Global Economy*, Cambridge, Mass.: MIT Press.

Harrod, R. (1939), 'An Essay in Dynamic Theory', *Economic Journal*, 49: 14–33.

Helpman, E. and P.R. Krugman (1989): *Trade Policy and Market Structure*, Cambridge, Mass.: MIT Press.

Hirschman, A.O. (1958), *The Strategy of Economic Development*, New Haven and London: Yale University Press.

Jeremy, D.J. (1981), *Transatlantic Industrial Revolution: the Diffusion of Textile Technologies between Britain and America*, 1790–1830s, Oxford: Blackwell.

Jorgenson, D. and Z. Griliches (1967), 'The Explanation of Productivity Change', *Review of Economic Studies*, 34: 249–84.

Kaldor, N. (1957) 'A Model of Economic Growth', *Economic Journal*, 67: 591–624.

Kaldor, N. (1961), 'Capital Accumulation and Economic Growth', in F.A. Lutz and D.C. Hague (eds), *The Theory of Capital*, London: Macmillan.

Kaldor, N. (1966), *Causes of the Slow Rate of Economic Growth of the United Kingdom*, Cambridge: Cambridge University Press.

Kaldor, N. (1967), *Strategic Factors in Economic Development*, Itacha, New York: New York State School of Industrial and Labor Relations, Cornell University.

Kaldor, N. (1970), 'The Case for Regional Policies', *Scottish Journal of Political Economy*, 17: pp.

Kaldor, N. (1978), 'The Effects of Devaluation on Trade in Manufacture', in *Further Essays on Applied Economics* (Collected Papers Vol. VI), London: Duckworth, 99–118.

Kaldor, N. (1981), 'The Role of Increasing Returns, Technical Progress and Cumulative Causation in the Theory of International Trade and Economic Growth', *Economie Appliquée*, 34: 593–617.

Kaldor, N. and J.A. Mirrlees (1962), 'A New Model of Economic Growth', *Review of Economic Studies*, 29: 174–92.

Katz, J.M. (ed.) (1987), *Technology Generation in Latin American Manufacturing Industries*, Basingstoke and London: Macmillan.

Krugman, P. (1986), *Strategic Trade Policy and the New International Economics*, Cambridge, Mass.: MIT Press.

Krugman, P. (1990), *Rethinking International Trade*, Cambridge, Mass.: MIT Press.

Levine, R. and D. Renelt (1992), 'A Sensitivity Analysis of Cross-Country Growth Regressions', *American Economic Review*, 82: 942–63.

Lichtenberg, F.R. (1992), 'R&D Investment and International Productivity Differences', *NBER Working Paper*, No. 4161, Cambridge, Mass.: National Bureau of Economic Research.

Lucas, R.E. (1988), 'On the Mechanisms of Economic Development', *Journal of Monetary Economics*, 22: 3–42.

Maddison, A. (1979), 'Long Run Dynamics of Productivity Growth', *Banca Nazionale del Lavoro Quarterly Review*, 128: 1–37.

Maddison, A. (1982), *Phases of Capitalist Development*, New York: Oxford University

Press.

Maddison, A. (1987), 'Growth and Slowdown in Advanced Capitalist Economies: Techniques of Quantitative Assessment', *Journal of Economic Literature*, 25: 649–98.

Maddison, A. (1991), *Dynamic Forces in Capitalist Development*, New York: Oxford University Press.

McCombie, J.S.L. (1986), 'On Some Interpretations of the Relationship between Productivity and Output Growth', *Applied Economics*, 18: 1215–55.

McCombie, J.S.L. and A.P. Thirlwall, (1994), *Economic Growth and the Balance-of-Payments Constraint*, Basingstoke and London: Macmillan.

Mitch, D. (1993), 'The Role of Human Capital in the First Industrial Revolution', in J. Mokyr (ed.), *The British Industrial Revolution, an Economic Perspective*, Boulder Colo.: Westview Press, 267–307.

Myrdal, G. (1957), *Economic Theory and Underdeveloped Regions*, London: Duckworth.

Nelson, R. (1973), 'Recent Exercises in Growth Accounting: New Understanding or Dead End?', *American Economic Review*, 63: 462–8.

Nelson, R. (1981), 'Research on Productivity Growth and Productivity Differentials: Dead Ends and New Departures', *Journal of Economic Literature*, 19: 1029–64.

Nelson, R. (ed.) (1993), *National Innovation Systems, a Comparative Study*, Oxford: Oxford University Press.

Nelson, R. and S.G. Winter (1982), *An Evolutionary Theory of Economic Change*, Cambridge, Mass. and London: Belknap Press.

OECD (Technology/Economy Programme) (1992), *Technology and the Economy, the Key Relationships*, London: OECD/HMSO.

Ohkawa, K. and H. Rosovsky (1973), *Japanese Economic Growth*, Stanford: Stanford University Press.

Pasinetti, L.L. (1981), *Structural Change and Economic Growth. A Theoretical Essay on the Dynamics of the Wealth of Nations*, Cambridge University Press: Cambridge.

Romer, P.M. (1986), 'Increasing Returns and Long-Run Growth', *Journal of Political Economy*, 94: 1002–37.

Romer, P.M. (1989), 'What Determines the Rate of Growth and Technological Change?', *Working Papers*, Macroeconomic Adjustment and Growth, Country Economics Department, The World Bank, March 1991 WPS 279, Washington D.C.: The World Bank.

Romer, P.M. (1990), 'Endogenous Technological Change', *Journal of Political Economy*, 98: 1002–37.

Rosenberg, N. and C. Frischtak (eds) (1985), *International Technology Transfer, Concepts, Measures, and Comparisons*, New York: Praeger.

Scott, M.F.G. (1989), *A New View of Economic Growth*, Oxford: Clarendon Press.

Shaw, G.K. (1992), 'Policy Implications of Endogenous Growth Theory', *Economic Journal*, 102: 611–22.

Smith, K. (1991), 'Innovation Policy in an Evolutionary Context', in P.P. Saviotti and J.S. Metcalfe (eds), *Evolutionary Theories of Economic and Technological Change*, London: Harwood, 256–75.

Solow, R. (1956), 'A Contribution to the Theory of Economic Growth', *The Quarterly Journal of Economics*, 70: 65–94.

Solow, R. (1957), 'Technical Change and the Aggregate Production Function', *Review of Economics and Statistics*, 39: 312–20.

Summers, R. and A. Heston (1991), 'The Penn World Table (Mark 5): An Expanded Set of International Comparisons 1950–1988', *The Quarterly Journal of Economics*, CVI: 327–68.

Swan, T.W. (1956), 'Economic Growth and Capital Accumulation', *Economic Record*, 32: 334–61.

Sylla, R. and G. Toniolo (eds) (1991), *Patterns of European Industrialization, the Nineteenth Century*, London: Routledge.

Thirlwall, A.P. (1979), 'The Balance-of-Payments Constraint as an Explanation of International Growth Rate Differences', *Banca Nazionale del Lavoro Quarterly Review*, 32: 45–53.

Thirlwall, A.P. (1980), *Balance-of-Payments Theory and the U.K. Experience*, London: Macmillan.

Thirlwall, A.P. (1986), 'A General Model of Growth and Development along Kaldorian Lines', *Oxford Economic Papers*, 38: 199–219.

Tinbergen, J. (1943), 'Zur Theorie der Langfristigen Wirtschaftsentwicklung', *Weltwirtschaftliches Archiv*, 55: 511–49.

Uzawa, H. (1965), 'Optimum Technical Change in an Aggregative Model of Economic Growth', *International Economic Review*, 6: 18–31.

Verdoorn, P.J. (1949), 'Fattori che Regolano lo Sviluppo della Produttivita' del Lavoro', *L'Industria*, 1: 3–10.

Verspagen, B. (1991), 'A New Empirical Approach to Catching Up or Falling Behind', *Structural Change and Economic Dynamics*, 2: 359–80.

Verspagen, B. (1992), 'Endogenous Innovation in Neo-Classical Models: A Survey', *Journal of Macroeconomics*, 14: 631–62.

Verspagen, B. (1993), *Uneven Growth Between Interdependent Economies. The Evolutionary Dynamics of Growth and Technology*, Aldershot: Avebury.

von Tunzelmann, G.N. (1994), *Technology and Industrial Progress*, Aldershot: Edward Elgar (forthcoming).

World Bank (1993), *The East Asian Miracle, Economic Growth and Public Policy*, Washington: World Bank.

2. The Origins of the Postwar Catch-up and Convergence Boom

Moses Abramovitz[1]

1. CONVERGENCE EXPERIENCE

The growth of the presently advanced market economies in the quarter-century after World War II is the experience that has brought the convergence hypothesis the attention it now enjoys. During this period, roughly 1948–1973, the growth of this group of countries had a character closely consistent with the implications of the convergence hypothesis.[2]

- The cross-country variance of productivity levels declined steadily and swiftly.
- There was a close inverse correlation between countries' initial productivity levels and their subsequent growth rates.
- On the average, and in most individual countries, the gap between their own productivity levels and that of the productivity leader, that is, the USA, was greatly reduced. There was 'catch-up' as well as 'convergence'.
- We know, however, that the postwar quarter-century was historically exceptional. For much of the nineteenth century, until about 1860, divergence, not convergence, was the rule among the smaller number of presently advanced countries for which productivity estimates are available (Baumol, Batey Blackman and Wolff 1989).
- Between 1870 and 1938, there was a more or less steady decline in productivity variance, but the rate of decline was slower than it became in the postwar quarter-century; and the correlations between initial levels and subsequent growth rates were weaker. And while some countries at times enjoyed faster productivity growth than the USA, that was not true for the group of presently advanced countries on the average. The record, therefore, showed relatively slow, though steady, group convergence, but no group catch-up. On the contrary, at least until 1913, the USA, already the leader, was forging further ahead.
- During the wartime decade of the 1940s, there was neither convergence nor catch-up. Variance of productivity levels increased and the

American productivity lead over almost all the members of the group became still greater.

- Then after the strong convergence of the postwar quarter-century, there was another change. The pace of convergence slowed down and almost stopped. Catch-up to the USA continued but at a slower pace. The figures in Table 2.1 amply confirm these observations.[3]
- Finally, we now know that, while some less developed countries have had periods of catch-up towards the levels of the advanced countries, the East Asian countries are the only substantial group of LDC's whose per capita incomes have grown faster than those of the advanced countries for a substantial period and that only since the war. In general, as one enlarges a sample initially confined to the richest countries to include poorer and poorer countries, the strength of the tendency to convergence declines and divergent tendencies become stronger (Baumol, Batey Blackman and Wolff 1989, Ch. 5 and Appendix to Ch. 5, esp. pp. 303–5).

Table 2.1.   Means and variance of the relative labour productivity levels of 15 presently advanced countries compared with the USA (US GDP per hour = 100)

	Means		Variance[a]		Rates of change in variance[a] (% per year)		
	A	B	A	B		A	B
1870	77	62	0.51	—	*1870–1913*	–1.01	—
1890	68	—	0.48	—	1870–1890	–0.30	—
1913	61	54	0.33	0.37	1890–1913	–1.62	—
1929	57	—	0.29	—	*1913–1950*	0.24	0.00
1938	61	—	0.22	—	1913–1929	–0.76	—
1950	46	44	0.36	0.37	1929–1938	–3.02	—
1960	52	—	0.29	—	1938–1950	4.19	—
1973	69	66	0.14	0.14	*1950–1973*	–4.02	–4.14
1989	—	81	—	0.13	*1973–1989*	—	–0.46

Sources: A-columns based on Maddison (1982), Tables 5.2 and C.10; B-columns based on Maddison (1993), Table 13.
[a] Coefficient of variation.

This chapter has two connected aims. Its broader, underlying objective is to help us understand the nature and strength of the forces making for convergence and at the same time to expose the conditions that limit and constrain these convergent tendencies. I try to do this by asking why the pattern of convergence and the pace of catch-up among the group of advanced market economies were so much stronger and clearer during the postwar quarter-century than they had been earlier. Suggesting an answer to this narrower question is my second and more immediate objective.

The answer I give to this historical question is that a special conjuncture of antecedent developments, which enlarged the ability of 'laggard' countries to pursue the American resource-intensive, capital-using but scale-dependent path of technological progress, worked together with new institutions and public policies to produce the strong convergence of the postwar boom period. Many of the elements of this conjuncture, however, were by their nature self-limiting, and were undermined by the convergence and catch-up they had supported. Others which might perhaps have continued, nevertheless weakened or disappeared. The weaker convergence and catch-up of the last 20 years followed. I have set out my views about the post-1973 weakening of catch-up and convergence in Abramovitz (1993b). I confine myself here to the origins of the postwar catch-up and convergence boom itself.

2. THE ELEMENTS OF CATCH-UP POTENTIAL AND ITS REALIZATION

My historical analysis proceeds from a view about a set of conditions that govern, first, the relative *potential* of different countries to raise their productivity and, second, a set that influences their ability to *realize* their potential.

I begin with potential itself. Consider two countries, otherwise similar, but one is a productivity leader, the other a laggard. There are at least four reasons why the laggard will tend to have a stronger potential for labour productivity growth than the leader.

First, as the leader's capital stock turns over, its embodied technological progress is limited by the advance of knowledge over the lifetime of its capital instruments. But a laggard can make a larger leap by substituting modern, state-of-the-art equipment for instruments that were obsolete even when originally installed. The same applies to modernization in disembodied technology.

Secondly, laggards typically suffer from relatively low levels of capital intensity. On this account, as well as because new capital can embody a large technological leap, the inducement to invest tends to be stronger in the laggard country than in an otherwise similar leader. So there is a potential for rapid progress by capital accumulation and by speeding the embodiment of best-practice technology.

Thirdly, in laggards one usually finds relatively large fractions of workers attached to low productivity farming and to similarly low productivity self-employment and family employment in very small-scale fabrication and petty trade. Productivity differentials between labour in these sectors and in larger-scale industry and commerce are, in general, more marked in poorer countries than in richer (Kuznets 1966, Lewis 1954, Kindleberger 1967, Denison 1967). Such differentials are an opportunity for relatively large gains in productivity from the better allocation of labour.

Fourthly, the chance for rapid productivity advance along all these channels means a chance for rapid growth in aggregate output and size of markets, which brings a productivity bonus from the economies of scale.

This is the simple core of the tendency to convergence. And if that were all there was to it, we should expect to see laggards 'always and everywhere' advance faster than a leader. Rates of productivity growth across countries in any period would be an inverse function of their initial levels of productivity, and national levels of productivity would converge towards the leader's. By the same token, as the process of convergence went on, the gaps separating laggards from leaders would become smaller, and laggards' rates of growth would decline. The catch-up effect supporting growth would be self-limiting, weakening steadily as catch-up proceeded.

But things are not so simple. Leading and lagging nations are not 'otherwise similar'. The relatively low productivity of laggard countries is not, in general, just a transient accident. It arises from conditions that have limited their past growth and that may continue to limit their ability to make the technological leaps that the convergence hypothesis envisages. Or they may be hampered in other ways that disturb the expected association between productivity levels and subsequent growth rates. There are two broad classes of constraints.

One consists of what may be called the limitations of 'technological congruence'. Such limitations arise because the frontiers of technology do not advance evenly in all dimensions with equiproportionate impact on the productivities of labour, capital and natural resource endowments and with equal effect on the demands for the several factors of production and on the effectiveness of different scales of output. They advance rather in a biased fashion that reflects, first, the direct influence of past science and technology on the evolution of practical knowledge and, secondly, the complex adaptation of that evolution to the natural resource and factor availabilities and to the scale of markets, consumer demands and technical capabilities of those relatively advanced countries operating at or near the frontiers of technology. This is the message of Paul David's now classic paper (1975, Ch. 1). In these circumstances, the resource availabilities, factor supplies, technological capabilities, market scales and consumer demands in laggard countries may not conform well to those required by the technologies that have emerged in the leading countries. The laggards, therefore, face varying degrees of difficulty in adapting and adopting the current practice of leaders. The degree of difficulty, however, is not a constant. It tends to change over time as the production processes and production structures of the leaders evolve and as the laggards' own development adapts to the factor supply and, it may be added (see below), to the organizational and institutional challenges presented by more advanced countries (Abramovitz 1986).

There is, secondly, a more vaguely defined set of matters that I call 'social capability'. This is a term coined by Ohkawa and Rosovsky (1972). It refers to matters that almost every student has to allow for, whatever terms he uses. As I use it here, it is a rubric that covers countries' levels of general education and technical competence, the commercial, industrial and financial institutions that bear on their abilities to finance and operate modern, large-scale business, and the political and social characteristics that influence the risks, the incentives and the personal rewards of economic activity including those rewards in social esteem that go beyond money and wealth.

Over time, there is a two-way interaction between the social capabilities required by technological best practice and the development of those very capabilities. A country's ability to exploit the opportunities afforded by existing best practice is limited by its current capabilities. Capabilities, however, tend to develop in the directions to which the requirements of a leading technology point or, in the case of a leading country, in the directions defined by those of an emerging technology. Levels of general and technical education are raised and their content altered; legal codes are modified; corporate and financial institutions are established and people learn their modes of action. Moreover, experiences gained in the practice of a technology enhance the technical and managerial capabilities that serve it and thus support further advance along the same path. Such interaction, therefore, may for a time solidify a leader's position or, in the case of laggards, may work to counter the tendency that would otherwise exist for their relative growth rates to decline as catch-up proceeds.

Countries' potentials for rapid productivity growth by catch-up, therefore, are not determined solely by the gaps in levels of technology, capital intensity and efficient allocation that separate them from leading countries. They are restricted also by natural resource endowments and more generally because their market scales, relative factor supplies and income-constrained patterns of demand make their technical capabilities and their product structures incongruent with those that characterize countries that operate at or near the technological frontiers. And they are limited, finally, by those institutional characteristics that restrict their abilities to finance, organize and operate the kinds of enterprises that the technologies of the frontiers require.

These then are the elements of countries' effective *potential* for productivity growth. Beyond that there is a group of factors that govern the ability of countries to *realize* their potentials in particular periods of time. Here one has to consider the facilities that laggard countries have for learning about more advanced methods, for appraising them and for acquiring them. Next, there are the issues that arise because long-term, aggregate productivity growth requires structural change. So the determinants of resource mobility, particularly labour mobility, are important. And finally there are the macroeconomic conditions that govern the intensity of use of resources and the volume of investment activity. These last bear on the pace of realization because they influence the cost of capital, the perceived rates of return to investment and the risks to which they are subject. They influence the rate of capital accumulation and, therefore, the pace at which more advanced technology is incorporated into production. And they affect the choices between present and future that control the research, development and investment horizons of business.

3. BASES OF THE POSTWAR POTENTIAL FOR CATCH-UP AND CONVERGENCE

The dramatic postwar record of Western Europe and Japan creates a presumption that their potential for rapid growth by exploiting America's methods of production and organization then was strong. It was strong partly because the productivity gaps separating the laggard countries from the USA were larger than ever before. Larger leaps by technological borrowing and by other means were then in prospect – but only if Europe and Japan could now do what they had not been able to do before: to take advantage of America's relatively advanced methods to grow faster than the USA itself. The insistent question, therefore, is why Europe, which, in the early nineteenth century, was itself the source of America's technology, had proved unable to keep pace with the USA during the three-quarters of a century following 1870, when America forged ahead and when it maintained and enlarged a lead not challenged until after World

War II.

3.1. The Gaps

America's labour productivity lead had widened in two main phases, the first between 1870 and 1913, the second, another large step, during the wartime decade of the 1940s.[4] As for the variance of levels within the whole group of countries, this had been declining, if slowly, from 1870 to 1938, but again there was a dramatic widening across the 1940s (see Table 2.1).

The enlarged labour productivity gaps separating the USA from the other presently advanced countries in 1950 are one preliminary index of a stronger potential for catch-up. The enlarged variance is a similar index of a stronger potential for convergence.

There are indications that these enlarged labour productivity gaps reflected all the proximate sources of catch-up potential mentioned earlier. Wolff (1991, Tables 1 and 2) reports that in four large countries (Germany, France, Italy and the UK), the enlargement took the form of both capital intensity and total factor productivity (TFP).[5] Maddison (1987) reports that in four European countries (France, Germany, the Netherlands and the UK) and Japan, the fraction of total employment on the farms, where productivity is relatively low, increased substantially compared to the USA between 1913 and 1950. For the European countries the average increased by 9.3 percentage points; for Japan the relative rise was 4.3 percentage points. For self-employment and family workers, the change before the war cannot be traced. But the 1950 shares of these groups in Europe and Japan exceeded that in the USA by large margins. For seven countries in Northwest Europe, the excess over the USA was 5.6 percentage points; for Italy 19 points; and for Japan, 50 (Denison 1967, Table 16 and Denison and Chung 1976, Table F–2).

Reflecting these large and enlarged gaps, there is evidence that the postwar catch-up and convergence took the form of advance along all the related avenues of growth. (For the contributions of capital intensity and TFP, see Englander and Mittelstadt 1988 and Maddison 1987, for the contribution of labour reallocation, see Maddison 1987). It would be a mistake, however, to place much emphasis on the apparent specific contributions of these 'proximate' sources as these emerge in the growth accounts. The several sources interact. The prospect of making large productivity gains by modernizing capital equipment supports capital accumulation, and a rise in the rate of accumulation, such as took place in the 1950s and 1960s compared with preceding decades (cf. Maddison 1987, Tables 19 and 20), speeds the pace of embodied technical progress.

In the growth accounts, this appears in TFP. A speedier pace of moderniz-ation, which reflects both technical progress and accumulation, raises the growth rates of production in manufacturing and other urban activities. It enlarges urban employment and speeds up the ruralurban flow of workers.

The fact that the initial low levels of postwar productivity in Europe and Japan stemmed in part from wartime destruction, depletion of stocks and delayed innovation lent added strength to the potential for rapid productivity growth, at least during the earlier part of the postwar expan-sion. Large increases in effective capacity could be obtained by compara-tively small investments in repair, replacement of missing components and rebuilding of inventories (Dumke 1990).

The antecedent questions, however, remain. As early as 1870, the level of labour productivity in the USA was higher than that of every presently advanced European country except the UK itself where the level was four percent higher than in the USA. Setting the US level at 100, the average for the 11 continental European countries was 56. By 1913, the UK relative had fallen to 78 and that for the continental countries on average to 49. Only one European country (Germany) was able to maintain its relative standing, and that was only 50. Clearly there is no suggestion of catch-up in all these years of general peace and development. What was it then that blocked the catch-up process even before the onset of the financial and political disturbances, the Great Depression and the destruc-tion of war between 1913 and 1945? The answer I propose is that the difficulty lay in failures of what I have called 'technological congruence' and 'social capability', and that it was the gradual elimination or weaken-ing of these barriers that opened the way after the war for the strong catch-up experience of the 1950s and 1960s.

3.2. Technological Congruence: Primary Materials[6]

The American advantage, which other countries were unable to match during the late nineteenth and early twentieth centuries, stemmed first from America's more abundant and cheap supplies of primary materials. Such supplies were far more important in the late nineteenth and early twentieth centuries than they have since become. This is true to begin with because food then constituted larger shares of consumer expenditure and GDP, and resources devoted to agriculture were a larger share of total factor input. Beyond that, however, the industrial technology that emerged during the decades from, say, 1870 to 1913, when America rose to productivity leadership and forged ahead, was a minerals-based technology in which the costs of coal as a source of steam power, of coal and iron for steel and the costs of these and still other metals formed a large part of the total costs of manufactured goods to their final users. Cheap supplies of primary materials were, therefore, one of the reasons for America's growing comparative advantage in the trade in manufactures (David and Wright 1992, esp. Table 6).

The USA enjoyed these cheap supplies only in part because of its rich natural resource endowments but even more because it had been successful in uncovering the existence of its rich reserves, in devising new methods for using their sometimes peculiar characteristics and in building an efficient network of transport by rail and water that reached all parts of its very large territory. Government played a part in all these matters and so did the young engineering faculties of the new universities (David and Wright 1992).

The peculiar American law of mining heightened the incentive for exploration and development. The government claimed no ultimate title to the nation's minerals, not even to those on the public domain. It offered free access to prospectors, and no fees or royalties were assessed against the minerals removed. The government's large subsidies for railroad building, particularly in the West, helped provide the transportation that made Western mining profitable. The incentive for minerals exploration and development, however, stemmed even more largely from the demand that appeared, in fact and in clear prospect, as American manufacturing shifted towards the production of minerals-based capital and consumer goods. There was, therefore, a fruitful interaction between the development of primary materials supply, the advance of American technology and the growth of manufacturing industry, construction and transport (Wright 1990, David and Wright 1992, Rosenberg 1980).

The minerals-based, resource-intensive technology proved to be the path of technical progress in all the presently advanced countries, but America enjoyed a substantial advantage in following that path because of her rich and varied natural endowment and the technological effort and investment that developed them. In 1910, reserves of some minerals, for example iron, were as large in Europe as a whole as in North America (Wright 1990, Chart 5). But Europe, to say nothing of Japan, could not rival America in the variety and richness of its developed mineral resources. In 1913, out of 14 important industrial minerals, America accounted for the largest share of world output in 12; it was second in the other two. Its average share in copper, coal, zinc, iron and lead was 40 percent. Given the still high transportation costs of the time and the relative importance of materials in the total costs of finished goods, this translated into large cost disadvantages for Europe in the production of finished manufactures.[7]

The importance of these intercountry differences, however, declined over time (Schultz 1951, Nelson and Wright 1992). For this there were several reasons:

- Both land and water transportation costs declined sharply.
- Resources were discovered in many parts of the world whose existence was unknown as late as 1870 and 1900.
- Technological progress, by increasing farm yields per acre has been land-saving. It has increased the value of mineral resources previously neglected and added new metals and synthetic materials to the range of metals and agricultural raw materials on which production had earlier relied.
- Crude materials came to be processed more elaborately and, on this account also, primary products became a smaller fraction of the final cost of finished goods.
- Services, including distribution, professional services, finance and government, in which the materials component is small have become more important compared with foods and manufactures in which the materials component is larger.

For all these reasons, differences in developed natural resource endowments have counted for less in recent decades than they had done earlier. One striking recent example of these changes deserves special notice. When the postwar period opened it was widely expected that the well-worked, high-cost coal deposits of Europe and the more general lack of energy sources in Japan would pose serious obstacles to development for both. The rapid exploitation of cheap Middle-Eastern petroleum, however, and the development of low-cost transport by supertanker changed the picture. Energy problems became much less severe in Europe and Japan, and this went far to eliminate what had been an important relative advantage of the USA.

3.3. Technological Congruence: Capital-Using and Scale-Intensive Technology

The technology that emerged in the nineteenth and persisted into the early twentieth century was not only resource-intensive, it was tangible capital-using and scale-dependent. The exploitation of the technical advances of the time demanded heavier use of machinery per worker, especially power-driven machinery, in ever-more specialized forms. But it demanded operation on an ever-larger scale in order to make such use of the structures and equipment economical. And it required steam-powered transport by rail and ship, itself a capital-intensive and scale-intensive activity, to distribute the growing output to wider markets. This was the message of all the early economists beginning with Adam Smith and running in a line through Böhm-Bawerk and Sidgwick to Taussig and Allyn Young. It is also the view from economic history (Rosenberg 1980), and it is a view supported by statistical studies of nineteenth and early twentieth century

American growth. An American growth account for the nineteenth century shows that tangible capital accumulation was then the major source by far of the growth of output per manhour and of its acceleration. But these studies also indicate that the importance of capital accumulation in that era rested on a tangible capital-using bias of technological progress. Although a series of studies report that the elasticity of substitution between tangible capital and labour is less than unity – which by itself would have reduced the factor share of capital, the faster growing factor-capital's share of GDP in fact rose markedly in the USA during the nineteenth century and remained stable into the early years of the present century. There is, therefore, a strong presumption that technological progress was tangible capital-using (Abramovitz and David 1973, David 1977, Abramovitz 1993a).

These again were technological paths along which the American economy was drawn more strongly and which America could follow more easily than Europe in the late nineteenth and early twentieth centuries. Just as a rich natural endowment had supported the development of the minerals-based technology of the time, so American high wages, the early consequence of abundant land, encouraged the development of the era's capital-intensive technology. And the heavy use of power-driven capital equipment was further supported by the relatively large, rich and homogeneous domestic market open to American firms.

By 1870, the USA already had a larger aggregate domestic market as measured by GDP than any of the other presently advanced countries. Its GDP growth rate between 1870 and 1913 was also the highest. By 1913, American GDP per capita was 1½–2 times that of the average of the 15 other countries in the Maddison sample. American GDP per capita even in 1870 exceeded that of all the other countries in the same sample except the UK. By 1913, however, it exceeded that in the UK by 20 percent and that of the average of the others by 72 percent. The American population in 1870 was considerably larger than that of most European countries. It was then rivalled only by the UK, Germany and France, but by 1913, it was 45 percent larger than even the largest of the European countries, Germany.[8]

The American domestic market was not only large, it was well unified by an extensive transportation network. And it was unified in other ways as well that the European and Japanese economic and social conditions could not at first match. The rapid settlement of the country from a common base in the East limited regional differences in tastes. The relatively egalitarian conditions of American society, a reflection of its shorter history, its freedom from feudal and aristocratic traditions and its land abundance, fostered a tolerance for simple, functional goods and so provided a large market for the standardized products of large-scale production.[9]

The American development of mass-production methods was also encouraged by that country's widely diffused and high level of per capita income. This supported a large market for the new metals-based durable consumer goods that proved so well adapted to production by scale-dependent and capital-intensive methods. By contrast, Europe's smaller, less equally distributed incomes restricted the market for such goods to its wealthier classes and delayed the full exploitation of America's mass production methods.

Finally, American land abundance and the level terrain of the Midwest and trans-Mississippi Prairies lent themselves to the extensive cultivation of grain and livestock, a condition well-suited to mechanization on a scale not feasible in Europe at the time (Parker 1972).

These again, however, were American advantages that became less important with the passage of time and the further advance of technology and industrialization. The American advantage in scale became less important over time, not because the laggards advanced more rapidly in aggregate output; that did not happen before the postwar boom. It happened in part simply because their aggregate outputs grew larger absolutely and, for some industries and products, approached the levels demanded by the scale requirements of the time. This process was supported by the decline in transportation costs and the more liberal trading regime that emerged between 1880 and 1913. Foreign markets, therefore, went further than they had done to help meet scale requirements. From 1870 to 1913, the average growth rate of the volume of exports of Maddison's sample of 11 countries in continental Europe was 43 percent greater than their GDP growth (Maddison 1991, Tables 3.2 and 3.15). And, of course, there was a great expansion in trade during the 1950s and 1960s when export growth among these countries exceeded that of GDP by 89 percent. Scale requirements in the newer industries producing consumer and producer durables, the typical mass-production industries of our era, were also more easily satisfied because per capita incomes increased. Larger domestic and foreign markets, therefore, appeared and the laggard countries could begin to exploit the capital-using and scale-dependent methods already explored by the USA. This was a path of catch-up that proved especially important after World War II, but it had begun to be followed in earlier decades.[10]

Still another and, I believe, important reason for the decline in American advantage was a gradual alteration in the bias of technological progress, and, therefore, in the relative demands for the several factors of production. The nineteenth century *tangible* capital-using and scale-dependent bias began to shift in the direction of *intangible* capital. The returns to capital formation by education and R&D began to rise relative to that for structures and equipment. This is a judgement based on American experience, but I believe it applies to Europe and Japan as well. One sees this shift, first, in the trend of the share of tangible capital in the factor distribution of GDP. This rose markedly in the course of the last century but then levelled off and declined just as markedly between the early 1900s and the mid-1950s. One sees this shift, secondly, in the stability of rates of return to education in the face of huge increases in the fractions of workers who have had relatively long years of schooling. And one sees it, thirdly, in the rapid increases in the proportion of GDP devoted to expenditures for organized R&D (Abramovitz and David 1973, David 1977, Abramovitz 1993a).

Table 2.2.   *Average years of formal education of the population aged 15–64 in 1913 and 1989.*

		Total	Primary	Secondary	Higher
France	1913	6.18	4.31	1.77	0.10
	1989	11.61	5.00	5.29	1.32
Germany	1913	6.94	3.50	3.35	0.09
	1989	9.58	4.00	5.20	0.38
Japan	1913	5.10	4.50	0.56	0.04
	1989	11.66	6.00	4.95	0.71
Netherlands	1913	6.05	5.30	0.64	0.11
	1989	10.51	6.00	3.82	0.69
UK	1913	7.28	5.30	1.90	0.08
	1989	11.28	6.00	4.75	0.53
USA	1913	6.93	4.90	1.83	0.20
	1989	13.39	6.00	5.72	1.67

Source: Maddison (1991), Table 3.8.

The shift in relative demand from tangible towards intangible assets stems from several sources that manifest themselves mainly, but not only, in a change in the composition of employment by occupation. Jobs requiring more years of schooling have gained at the expense of jobs requiring fewer. I discuss the causes and extent of this and other sources of shift towards intangible assets elsewhere (Abramovitz 1993a). The shift itself, however, bears on my argument because the rising importance of capital formation by education responded to economic and social incentives that must have been to some considerable degree independent of the scale conditions that limited the early response of many European countries and of Japan to the opportunities for growth held out by tangible capital formation in the nineteenth and early twentieth centuries. The figures in Table 2.2, for example, indicate that by contrast with the stock of tangible capital per worker, the average years of education in the USA and in several other of the presently advanced countries were much the same in 1913.

Levels of schooling, of course, rose in later years, but the approximate equality continued to hold. The USA took a more pronounced lead in higher education after 1950, but the roughness of the estimates and still more the quality differences among countries in schooling at each level make the significance of differences in the figures uncertain.[11] Since the table refers to full-time formal education, the level in Germany, which, as Maddison says, 'has an extensive system of post-formal apprentice training combined with part-time education', is understated (1991, p. 64).

The USA led Europe (except possibly Germany) in the development of organized R&D (Mowery and Rosenberg 1989) and increased its lead from early in the present century until sometime in the 1950s, but its lead over most other presently advanced countries has been declining in more recent decades. Nelson and Wright (1992) attribute the continuing American *technological* leadership through the 1950s and 1960s to its investments in higher education and R&D. There is a distinction, however, between leadership in technology and catch-up in labour productivity. The laggard countries achieved their postwar labour productivity catch-up in those years mainly by exploiting the methods explored earlier by American firms. Their capabilities for assessing, acquiring and adapting existing technology were becoming stronger, however, as their R&D investment cumulated, and the emphasis of their effort gradually shifted towards technological advance as they approached American levels of efficiency.

3.4. Social Capability

This is a class of factors that in some ways lies behind the degrees of technological congruence just discussed. It is a large and still poorly defined subject which I treat briefly, partly for lack of space, but still more because I do not know the full scope of the subject or how to deal empirically with many of its elements.[12]

In earlier work (1986, p. 388), I identified a country's social capability with 'technical competence, for which – at least among Western countries

– years of education may be a rough proxy, and with its political, commercial, industrial and financial institutions, which I characterize in more
qualitative ways'. With respect to institutions, I had in mind mainly the
stability and effectiveness of government and 'experience with the
organization and management of large scale enterprise and with financial
institutions and markets capable of mobilizing capital for individual firms
on a similarly large scale'. In later work I have referred also to matters
connected with social attitudes towards wealth and growth and to problems
of incentives and opportunities (1993b, Ch. 1).

With respect to all this, it is tempting, at least by hindsight, to say that,
in the postwar period and for the sample of countries here in question,
social competence was adequate to absorb and exploit the best-practice
technology of the time. This, however, leaves open some obtrusive
questions, e.g. how far Japan's extraordinary postwar performance or
Britain's poor showing can be attributed to differences in the elements of
social capability. It also leaves open the question whether a general rise
over time in the social capability of the whole group of advanced countries
helps account for the unusual strength of the convergence process in the
first quarter century following the war.

I suspect that considerations that fall under the rubric of social capability are important for both these questions. Pleading incompetence, however, I shall say nothing about the relation between social capability and
international differences in performance. And pleading only a slightly
smaller degree of incompetence, I shall say just a little about some general
changes in social capability over time.

1. Levels of education, as Table 2.2 suggests, rose steadily throughout the
   half-century preceding the postwar period. They did so even during the
   war and interwar years between 1913 and 1950. Insofar as education of
   the general population and of a cadre of competent engineers are
   required to discover, assess, and acquire modern technology and to use
   it effectively, countries in Europe and North America, as well as Japan,
   were better equipped after the war than they had ever been before.
2. Businessmen became more experienced in large-scale production, and
   the corporate organization that was adapted to engage in it became
   more common. This, however, had developed more slowly in Europe
   and Japan than in the USA, which helps account for Europe's delayed
   catch-up.

Building on its early advantage in exploiting a capital-using but scale-
dependent technology, the USA had an earlier involvement with large-
scale, corporate enterprise. Large numbers of businessmen gained experience in the organization, finance and operation of such firms. Its engineers
enjoyed an earlier acquaintance with the techniques of mass production

and the design of products adapted to the requirements of long runs of standardized goods. As a condition of expansion, the managerial and administrative staffs needed to control and guide big business developed and came to understand better its personnel and merchandising problems (Chandler 1990).

These considerations suggest that America, having taken an early lead in the development of a capital-using but scale-dependent technology built upon it cumulatively. Nor could European countries duplicate America's performance cheaply and quickly. Since much engineering knowledge and managerial know-how is 'tacit', embodied in the experience of a national network of engineers and administrators, it cannot be easily transferred or imitated. Rather it had to be built up gradually by the laggards on the basis of their own experience as ventures in large-scale business were established and expanded (Nelson and Wright 1992).

The opportunity to gain such experience was, as said, at first hampered by the fact that European conditions were initially not so closely congruent with the scale requirements of the new technology as were American. Even where and when opportunity offered, however, the experience of Europeans with the organization and conduct of large-scale firms was limited in different countries and in varying degrees, by a traditional attachment to family proprietorship and control. Chandler (1990) gives a detailed account of such matters in his history of 'personal-capitalism' in Britain. When the postwar era opened, American economic historians were still debating the thesis that traditions of family ownership and control were limiting the development of large-scale production and modernization in France (Earle 1951).

This last was an anachronism, as the experience of the 1950s and 1960s soon proved. The older traditions and the outlook it reflected had been changing for many years. This can be seen in the 'rationalization' sought by the merger and cartel movement that became important in Western Europe in the 1920s (Pellicelli 1976, Ch. 4). It is part of the experience that formed the European background for Schumpeter's views about the role of large-scale business in capitalist growth, as he was preparing *Capitalism, Socialism and Democracy* in the 1930s. Walther Rathenau's book of 1918 was a still earlier recognition of changes under way. It drew attention to the gradual separation of ownership from the control of large firms and saw this as a desirable change. It was a movement that was to develop more intensively during the 1930s (Pellicelli 1976, p. 193). All this, of course, had long been an established fact of American industry; even so it was not yet a commonplace in public understanding, as the reception accorded to Berle and Means, *The Modern Corporation and Private Property* (1934), suggests.

The constraints on catch-up arising from the more limited experience of

European businessmen and engineers with large-scale operations were matched by a slower development of European financial markets; and this was another constraint imposed by social capability. The finance of large-scale business, when not provided by government itself, manifestly rests on the ability of capital markets to mobilize finance on an equally large scale. This, in turn, involves a solution to the basic problem of such finance, which is to overcome the disjuncture between the assets that ultimate savers desire to hold and the liabilities that ultimate investors are willing to assume. The ultimate savers, who are households, desire safety and liquidity besides an attractive return. The ultimate investors, in this instance large corporations, need capital to finance durable and illiquid assets to be used in a risky business environment. Their debts, therefore, must have commensurately distant maturities, and a portion of their finance must come from the sale of equities, which, failing the presence of an effective capital market, subject holders to all the risks of the business.

Effective capital markets overcome this disjuncture by a complex process of intermediation carried out by a variety of financial institutions. Limited liability corporations with debts and shares tradable on well-functioning securities exchanges convert long-term bonds and shares into liquid assets. Banks in a variety of forms, insurance companies, pension funds and mutual funds are other institutions through which savers obtain assets that have the characteristics they desire, while the liabilities that corporations can assume are held by institutions whose size and professional management permit diversification and reduce risk.

The USA with its early establishment and expansion of large industrial and transport corporations also led in the development, if not the establishment, of securities exchanges. The success of the exchanges encouraged households to purchase corporate securities directly, and they also supported the growth of savings and trust companies, life-insurance companies, investment trusts and the other capital-market institutions that provide channels of intermediation between savers and corporate investors. The development of the capital market tended to raise the real return to the former and to lower the cost of finance to the latter. It was one of the pillars on which the extension of scale-dependent technological progress rested.

European countries and Japan, where large industrial corporations came later than in America, were also slower to develop their capital markets as a channel of intermediation. Although securities markets existed before the turn of the century, their corporate listings were limited; industrial corporations that went to the market depended on the industrial banks, whose own resources were not large. Household saving went mainly to real estate, to the postal savings systems and to government rents.

Although old-age pension schemes created by governments and trade unions were established earlier in Europe than in the USA, their funds also were unavailable to corporate business. Business had to depend more largely in Europe than in the USA on the funds supplied by a group of insiders and on retained earnings. The persistent importance of family proprietorships and close corporations presumably owes something to the lagging development of European financial markets.

The laggard development of financial markets in Europe, as well as Japan, began to be overcome in the course of the present century – not always in imitation of American patterns, but effectively. As the scale of markets open to these countries became wider, the prospects for successful ventures into large-scale operations and mass production became clearer. The demand for widely mobilized finance increased, new institutions were established to meet the demand and the operation of old ones was modified. The public gradually became familiar with their workings and public participation grew. There was, therefore, an interaction between the change in technological congruence, which was basic, and three supporting economic responses: the growth of large-scale business itself; the cumulation of managerial and engineering experience with such operations; and the development of financial markets.

3.5. A Summary of the Origins of Postwar Potential

The upshot of this section's argument is that the enlarged gaps in labour productivity and, insofar as it can be measured, technology, were only one part of the reason that the potential for catch-up and convergence was very strong after World War II. The other part was that the elements of technological congruence and social capability that had limited catch-up potential in the past had become less restrictive over time.

America's early advantage in cheap access to food and industrial raw materials had become smaller and less important. This was a consequence of discovery, technological progress in refinement, cheaper transport, synthetics and simply the elaboration of processing and distribution. America's advantage in exploiting the dominant tangible capital-using but scale-dependent character of nineteenth century technological advance had also been undercut. The domestic markets of the laggard countries had grown larger. Cheaper transport had opened wider markets, at least until 1913 and again, of course, in the postwar period itself. Per capita incomes had risen and begun to provide larger markets for automobiles and the other consumer durables that were especially suitable for mass production. Businessmen in Europe and Japan had gained in experience with the organization, finance and operation of large public corporations, and financial markets had developed. The bias of technological progress had begun to shift from its older scale-dependent, tangible capital-using bias to a newer intangible capital-using bias less dependent on scale.

These changes had all been underway from at least the beginning of the present century. In some respects they continued into the 1920s and 1930s in spite of the troubles of those years. One may, therefore, entertain the thought that if earlier trends had continued after 1913, the 1920s, 1930s and 1940s might have been decades of strong catch-up and convergence. That possibility, however, was foreclosed by the disastrous events of those times. It, therefore, remained for the 1950s and 1960s to release the potential for catch-up that had been accumulating for half a century.

4. CONDITIONS SUPPORTING THE REALIZATION OF POTENTIAL

The actual realization of a strong potential for catch-up depends on a variety of background conditions that govern the responses of business-men, labour and governments to the opportunities that lie before them. This background may be favourable or unfavourable, and it may persist for an extended span of years. Between 1914 and 1950 – counting the years of initial recovery from World War II – they were such as to doom the possibility of any general realization of what might otherwise have been a strong potential source of rapid growth by catch-up. During the quarter-century following World War II, however, the reverse was true.

The lessons of the sad interwar history had been learned. In a generous impulse, supported by the geopolitics of the developing Cold War, the USA played an important part in rebuilding the European and Japanese economies and in creating new institutions of international trade and money. Far from demanding the repayment of war debts, a new loan was extended to the UK and Marshall Plan aid was provided to Western Europe generally. The Western Allies, after setting aside the Morgenthau Plan for the partition and deindustrialization of Germany, abjured large punitive reparations from Germany and Japan with all the international disputes, resentment and economic disorder they would have caused both in these countries and among their neighbours. Instead, the Allies used the period of occupation to help the defeated powers create viable economies. The postwar inflations in Germany and Japan were brought to a short-lived end by monetary reforms that the occupying powers helped to design and carry out. The interwar years present a picture of rising protectionism. After World War II, by contrast, a series of trade liberalization 'rounds', organized by the General Agreement on Trade and Tariffs (GATT) and responsive to American leadership, helped to establish a far freer trade regime. Meanwhile European economic unification was promoted first by the European Payments Union, then by the Iron and Steel Community, finally by the Common Market and the European Free Trade Association (EFTA). At the same time, the new quasi fixed-rate, dollar-exchange standard established at Bretton Woods, together with American monetary policy, provided the necessary expansion of money supplies and reasonable price, interest-rate and exchange-rate stability – at least until the system succumbed in the early 1970s to its own built-in contradictions (see below).

The full development of this subject would be a long story. It is composed of more elements than are suggested by the preceding paragraphs. I choose to take up, however briefly, three broad classes of factors that supported the realization of catch-up potential during the postwar growth boom. Readers can find some additional discussion and a fuller presentation of supporting evidence in an earlier paper (1979, pp. 18–30).

4.1. Technological Effort and Facilities for Diffusion

It is now a commonplace that the exploitation of best-practice products and methods in use elsewhere is a costly process. It involves, first, awareness, then appraisal, then acquisition by purchase or reverse engineering, and finally, adaptation from the forms in which the techniques may have been cast where first applied to forms better suited to the resources, skills, scale of market and style of products of the firms and markets to which they are to be transferred. Sources of materials supply, organization of production and networks of distribution must often be changed. This involves costly investment. The scale and effectiveness of such effort was supported after the war by a number of developments.

First, as evidenced by investment in organized R&D, investment by the 'followers' looking to the acquisition of existing best-practice technology rose from small beginnings to levels that by 1970 approached the American total expenditure, including that for defence, virtually equalling it in private expenditures alone (Englander and Mittelstadt 1988, Table 14).

Secondly, these stronger efforts were made under conditions more favourable to the diffusion of practical knowledge than had ruled earlier. There was a much larger technical and business press. Air transport made international travel far faster and cheaper. The liberalization of international trade and payments acquainted managers throughout the industrialized countries with the products and techniques of firms in other countries, and competition impelled an early response. The Marshall Plan, with its arrangements for the exchange of American and European productivity missions, was an early opportunity for observation of foreign production methods and focused attention on the superiority of the American methods then in use. Governments of the NATO and OEEC (later OECD) countries encouraged the spread of knowledge about productivity-enhancing methods. When the growth of the European market became apparent, American firms became eager to obtain a share of the business through patent licences, technology transfer contracts, joint ventures and foreign subsidiaries. The Common Market, when it was established, encouraged the same sort of activity among its members. By contrast with the portfolio investment which had dominated capital flows before 1914, these direct investments were carriers of technology and advanced capital goods pressing domestic firms to modernize. The revival of trade, supported by the successive GATT rounds, by the Common Market and by EFTA worked to the same end.

4.2. Conditions Supporting Structural Change

The general rule that change in the structures of production, occupations and locations is a necessary concomitant of economic growth is well established. A special conjuncture of conditions after the war made labour supplies particularly responsive to demands and, therefore, facilitated the necessary transfers of labour.

In some countries, these conditions stemmed initially from high levels of unemployment (Denison 1967, Table 5–1A). Next, there were still large reserves of labour in farming and self-employment (Kindleberger 1967, Abramovitz 1979). Repatriation of nationals added large numbers to labour forces in Japan, Germany and France. And permanent immigration and guest workers added many people more, not only in Germany and France, but also in Switzerland and Scandinavia.

Population movements during the war and more particularly in its aftermath left the farm share of all workers in many countries either higher than it had been earlier or higher than it would have been if the war had not occurred. In addition, unusually high rates of productivity growth on the farms kept the level of redundant workers on the farms high for many years. Maddison (1982, Tables 5.11 and 5.13) reports that the average rate of farm productivity growth between 1950 and 1973 was almost 6 times as rapid as it had been from 1870 to 1950.

I have made rough estimates of the relation between migration of workers off the farms (some of whom may have gone abroad, especially from Italy) to the number of workers added to non-farm employment between 1950 and 1970. The average share in the four large European countries and in Japan was 64 percent (1979, p. 26, fn. 2). The rise in farm productivity after the war was doubtless due in part to a rapid expansion in industry's demand for labour and so to the transfer of partly redundant farm labour. But it also reflected the consolidation of small holdings, mechanization, electrification, better fertilizers, insecticides and improved seeds.

All these developments combined to make the supply of labour to industry and commerce flexibly responsive to demand and so helped restrain the rise in wages that would have limited industrial expansion. Two additional considerations supported the transfer of labour and the growth of industry. One was the restriction of immigration in America. Before World War I, when immigration was essentially unlimited by law, a strong labour market in the USA drew large waves of migrants from European farms. After World War II, however, immigration in America was severely limited. Redundant workers on European farms, therefore, went to home industry. A second consideration was the initial postwar weakness of labour unions in several European countries which were less well able to control entry into trades and industries. This condition, which lasted into the 1960s, may also have played a part in permitting the widespread use of guest workers.

4.3. Supports for Investment

Heavy investment was a central element in the rapid postwar catch-up and convergence process. It was the carrier of the more advanced, capital-using and scale-dependent American methods that laggards were adopting and adapting to their own conditions. In large part the investment came as a response to the enlarged productivity gaps that separated Europe and Japan from America when the war ended and to the new conditions of techno-logical congruence and social capability that had made the enlarged gaps a strong potential source of rapid growth by catch-up. By the same token, their war-damaged and unbalanced initial capital stock, its comparative obsolescence and simply its limited quantity conferred on laggards the potential for rich rewards to investors and for rapid productivity growth – provided finance could be obtained.

In the years immediately following the war, however, there were serious obstacles to investment. These stemmed partly from postwar financial and fiscal disorganization and inflation, partly from shortages of materials and inventories generally, and partly from balance-of-payments problems that restricted imports. These problems were gradually overcome in the course of the late 1940s and early 1950s by monetary and fiscal reforms, by Marshall Plan and other extraordinary aid, and by such transitional devices as the European Payments Union. As these obstacles were overcome, both Europe and Japan found that they enjoyed unusual and valuable supports for the investment needed to realize their strong potentials for growth. The question here is: what were the conditions and developments that facilitated and sustained heavy investment for 20 years?

The propensity to save

A strong savings propensity emerged initially because both households and business firms had a pressing need to rebuild the cash assets and other liquid claims to money that had been depleted or entirely lost in the postwar inflations (Wallich 1976, Carré *et al.* 1975). Of longer lasting importance, however, were the rapid rates of rise of household incomes, business profits and government revenues that were engendered by investment and productivity advance themselves. Because the pace of income growth in many countries was unprecedentedly rapid, it also greatly exceeded expectations. It, therefore, outran the planned expenditures of governments and households and the dividend distributions of corporations and left all three with larger surpluses – or smaller deficits – than expected. This condition persisted into the 1960s. The 'Julius Turm', where the Prussian kings had kept their war chest, became a familiar metaphor by which to characterize the cumulating surplus in the German federal budget, but it was a symbol of a much wider experience (Ohkawa and Rosovsky 1972, Chs 6 and 8, Wallich and Wallich 1976, Ch. 4, Carré *et al.* 1975, Ch. 9).

Government support for investment

Private firms were the dominant agents of capital formation in all the advancing countries, but governments participated in different ways and in different degrees. Government was less prominent in Germany, perhaps because large-scale industry was better established there than in other European countries. Also, German industry had enjoyed a recent period of profitable expansion in the 1930s and during much of the war under the stimuli of Nazi military preparation and war production. Elsewhere, large-scale industry was less developed, and France and, to a lesser degree, Italy, had suffered periods of stagnation more recently. These countries, as well as Japan, had traditions of regulation and protection that gave their governments postwar roles of great importance.

To appreciate that influence, one should recall that, as late as the early 1950s, expectations of rapid growth were not common. Few people in Japan or Europe yet appreciated the growth potentials of their countries (Carré *et al.*, pp. 278–9, 471, Ohkawa and Rosovsky, p. 232). In this atmosphere of uncertainty and indecision, governments acted to give an impetus to investment. By analogy with Schumpeter's 'New Men', the dynamic innovators to whom he attributed recurrent expansions, there were again 'New Men' after the war, who got their chance in the train of war and defeat and who operated in and through government.

In these respects, France is the type case. Spurred by Jean Monnet and the group who founded the Plan, the government undertook unprecedentedly large programmes to modernize transport, power and heavy industry generally. The government's ability to act was the stronger because postwar nationalizations had enlarged the scope of state-owned industry and because it had enough control over finance and trade to give effective priority to heavy industry not owned directly (Carré *et al.*, pp. 477, 274–6, and, on French 'planning' and its influence, Ch. 14). In Italy, too, government take-overs under Fascism and after the war had enlarged the public sector. Grouped in umbrella organizations like ENI and IRI and led by forceful new personalities, these government-directed corporations also took an early lead in postwar capital investment.

In Japan, the government made itself felt partly through its own large investments in infrastructure and partly through the Ministry of International Trade and Industry. The Ministry's purpose and effect were to provide guidance to private firms and to reduce the risks of innovation and investment in business on a large scale. It operated by selecting sectors for development, by supporting tariff protection, by choosing firms for the controlled importation and exploitation of foreign technology, and by helping to arrange the industrial combinations needed to ensure a proper scale of operation. Its activities served to raise the sights of private business (Ohkawa and Rosovsky, Ch. 9).

The early importance of governments helps to explain one of the otherwise puzzling features of the postwar catch-up process. Gaps in technology and capital intensity were significantly reduced during the decade of the 1950s. Yet the pace of convergence and catch-up did not decline in the 1960s as one might have expected; rather it accelerated. The paradox is at least partly resolved if we consider that private business was at first hesitant and went forward more boldly only as the growth potential of the postwar economy became clearly apparent. It was government that provided much of the early impetus, and this was carried forward only later by the rising confidence of private business. The same considerations meant that investment in the earlier years was more particularly concentrated in the sectors under government ownership and special influence, that is, power, transportation, communications and heavy industry generally. These demanded very large forward-looking investment which yielded its returns slowly. The private investment of the 1960s could be more largely applied to equipment, the operation of which both raised the utilization rate of infrastructure and yielded more immediate returns to its owners and to the economy.

Payments balances and supplies of money

The investment boom had a monetary, as well as a real, side. Nominal income and, therefore, money supply must normally grow at least as rapidly as the real output that an investment boom supports. In the postwar years, the conceivable alternative that a long-term price decline might provide was neither practical economics nor practical politics. In the USA itself, the release of wartime suppressed inflation made a large postwar price rise inevitable, and inflation was then renewed by the Korean War and later by the Vietnam War.

The growth of nominal income and money stock in the rest of the industrialized world, however, was necessarily more rapid than in the USA. Not only was real output growth faster than in the USA, so was the rate of inflation. The reason is that in a fixed exchange-rate system, the process of balance-of-payments adjustment, forces up money wages faster, although with a lag, in countries with relatively rapid productivity growth than in countries with slower productivity growth, like the USA. Prices, therefore, rose faster than in the USA, not so much in tradable goods where productivity growth is relatively rapid and international competition rules, but in the less progressive, non-tradables (McKinnon 1971).

The implied growth of money stock involved a rapid but by no means equal growth of reserve assets. And given the commitment to fixed exchange rates, a large part of those reserves had to have international currency. Under the Bretton Woods dollar-exchange system, that meant gold or short-term claims on dollars. When the war ended, however, the world's monetary gold stock was disproportionately concentrated in the USA, and foreign short-term claims on dollars were extremely small. Monetary growth in Japan and Europe, therefore, required a redistribution of the American gold stock and the accumulation in these countries of dollar claims.

Monetary growth in the industrialized world, therefore, came to depend on an arrangement of great delicacy, one that called for the simultaneous fulfilment of two basically contradictory conditions. The continuing redistribution of gold and acquisition of dollar claims required a chronic US balance-of-payments deficit and a cumulative deterioration of the US reserve position. But it also required continued faith in the ability of the USA to maintain convertibility and the gold par of exchange, failing which a flight from the dollar and a tight US monetary policy would have halted American capital exports and produced business contraction, first in the USA, and secondarily, in the rest of the industrialized world.

The USA did maintain a chronic balance-of-payments deficit. By 1970, the USA had lost $13.5 billion in gold, $2.5 billion in other international reserves, and accepted some $41 billion of additional short-term liabilities.

Meanwhile, the international reserves of other countries had risen by some $52 billion and those of developed countries alone by $42 billion – a quadrupling of their 1949 holdings (Abramovitz 1979, p. 29 and footnote).

The world's success in maintaining this process for two decades in the face of the cumulative deterioration of the US reserve position constitutes a basic difference between the money-growth experience after the war and in earlier times. Before 1914, when investment booms and growth spurts overseas drew large capital exports from Britain, they had to be sustained in part by slower growth in Britain and, to some extent, in other parts of Europe, which limited their loss of reserves. This, therefore, is a reason why concerted growth both in Europe and the USA in pre-World War I years was difficult. Moreover, when Britain was the monetary leader, losses of exchange reserves even a fraction as large as those of the USA during the postwar boom, would have caused the Bank of England to impose severe checks on monetary expansion and capital exports. The dollar basis of the postwar boom proved as durable as it did because of several transitory peculiarities of the postwar economy:

- The dollar was initially extremely strong. The USA at first had an enormous stock of gold and other international reserves and few liquid liabilities. The limited production capabilities of Europe and Japan in the early 1950s and their needs for imports tended to generate an excess demand for dollars. The actual US deficit, due to unilateral transfers, was discretionary, in a sense deliberate, and it was so perceived.
- Short-term claims on the USA cumulated but some part of them was willingly held as working balances to support a growing trade denominated in dollars.
- The USA proved to be politically capable of exercising monetary and fiscal restraint for a dozen years after the Korean War. This reduced its own rate of inflation to a practical minimum and thereby limited the rate of inflation and demand for money in the rest of the world.
- When, at last, the US international position and prospects came to be viewed unfavourably, other countries faced a difficult choice. They might continue to amass dollar claims and thereby accept an increasing risk of loss by dollar devaluation. Or they might demand gold at once and so precipitate immediate devaluation and US disfavour as well. The two risks were about equally unattractive. Countries, therefore, chose to postpone rather than hasten the event. The life of the system was, in this way, extended for several years.

The system finally broke down when the deficit financing of the Vietnam War triggered a rise of American inflation. The deficit in the US international account then increased both for that reason and because of speculation against the dollar. Dollar devaluation and a realignment of exchange rates followed. The formation of OPEC and the 1973 oil crisis completed the downfall of the postwar system of monetary growth. But the underlying cause of its breakdown was the contradiction inherent in an arrangement that depended on a chronic US balance-of-payments deficit and continued faith in dollar–gold convertibility.

5. CONCLUDING REMARKS

The main purpose of this chapter is to direct attention to the importance of technological congruence and social capability as determinants of catch-up potential, along with the productivity gaps themselves. This is hardly a new idea. It has been an inescapable consideration in studies of the experience and prospects of less developed countries. The concept of technological congruence is akin to that of 'relevant' or 'appropriate' technology, familiar in the development literature. The emphasis of development economists on the need for social and political modernization is related to that of social capability as a condition for catching-up. I have tried to show that such considerations also have their place in the experience of the presently advanced nations of Western Europe, Japan and North America.

I have tried to do this, first by advancing an hypothesis to account for the failure of these countries to catch-up to the USA until after World War II. I did this, secondly, by considering the developments that gradually reduced the obstacles that inadequate technological congruence and laggard advances in social capability had earlier placed in the way of catch-up. It was the cumulative force of these developments that, after the disasters and disturbances of the years from 1913 to 1945, at last rendered effective the pent-up potential for catch-up that had persisted for so long and that was inherent in the large productivity gaps with which the postwar period opened. Even so, a strong and rapid catch-up process was dependent on the appearance of a new assemblage of factors that supported the realization of potential – new international institutions governing trade and money, new governmental policies supporting investment and new facilities for the diffusion of technology. It was the conjuncture of all these circumstances influencing both potential and realization that produced the unusually strong postwar catch-up and convergence boom.

Many of the elements of the conjuncture, beginning with the decline of the large initial gaps themselves, have now weakened or disappeared. The break-up of the conjuncture has slowed the rate of catch-up and brought convergence within the group of presently advanced countries to a virtual halt. Although not discussed in the present chapter (but see my 1993b), the weakening of the conjuncture was the result of developments largely inherent in the catch-up process itself.

The account that this chapter offers poses questions about both the present state of affairs and the future. In this account, the broad features of technology have been evolving and changing the relative growth potentials of nations. Low-cost access to raw materials has become a less important condition of growth; it therefore counts for less in handicapping some countries more than others. The emergence of an intangible capital-using bias in technical progress places emphasis on capital accumulation by education and R&D. The incentives at least for education, and perhaps for R&D as well, are less scale-dependent than those for tangible capital. In the older technology, America's demonstrated managerial competence in organizing, financing and conducting the mass production of standardized commodities counted heavily. The Japanese and German plans of organization, finance and personnel management now challenge the American doctrine and practice.

In this newer technological constellation, the social, political and economic characteristics of nations will define a new set of relative advantages in growth potential. This applies with particular force, first, to differing national abilities to generate the kinds of education and training that favour the absorption of new products and production methods. It applies, secondly, to their abilities to establish and support the legal, corporate, governmental and university institutions on which advances in practical knowledge and their diffusion rest. The possibility, therefore, arises that there may be a new surge to leadership, not only in industrial technology, but also in aggregate productivity. Nations that so far have lagged behind may forge ahead while old leaders fall back. The variance among the productivity levels of the present group of advanced countries may widen for some extended period and begin to narrow again only after difficult adaptations to the newer technological conditions and to others still emerging.

NOTES

1. The writer gratefully acknowledges the helpful comments of Paul David, Gavin Wright, Richard Nelson, Nathan Rosenberg and the editors of this volume.
2. The empirical findings that follow have been repeatedly confirmed, mainly on the basis of national statistical series collected by Maddison (1982 and 1991) and rendered comparable by purchasing power parity conversions (Abramovitz 1979 and 1986, Baumol 1986, Baumol, Batey Blackman and Wolff 1989). DeLong (1988) has argued persuasively that the findings suffer from sample-selection bias: hence the limited statement in the opening sentence of the text speaks of 'the growth of the *presently advanced* market economies ...'.

3. Abramovitz (1986), Baumol (1986) and Baumol, Batey Blackman and Wolff (1989, Ch. 5) present measures of the correlation between initial productivity levels and subsequent growth rates consistent with the observations in the text. Abramovitz (1986) argues that such measures tend to overstate the true degree of association, and Milton Friedman (1992) presents a systematic treatment of the same problem of bias in measures of regression. Convergence is more reliably depicted by measures of variance, as in Table 2.1.

4. This statement is based on the comparative figures of output per manhour as presented in Table 2.1. Even in 1870, however, the USA appears to have enjoyed a large advantage over the average of the other presently industrialized countries. Some estimates of gross domestic product per capita suggest that the American advantage may have been increasing even in earlier decades going back to 1820. That is the showing of Maddison's figures (1991, Table 1.1). But estimates for these early years are exceedingly rough, and other estimates, at least for the USA, would indicate that the American advantage increased little if at all between 1820 and 1870. In any event, industrialization in several of the European countries as well as in Canada, Australia and Japan had hardly begun before 1870.

5. TFP is the difference between the growth of total output and the part of that growth attributable to the growth of the inputs of all the measured factors of production. If labour input measured in manhours and capital measured uniformly at base-period cost are the two factors of production, the growth of total output can be decomposed into three sources, as follows:

$$\hat{Y} = \alpha \hat{L} + \beta \hat{K} + \hat{A}, \ (\alpha + \beta = 1)$$

where Y is total output, A is TFP, L is the input of labour and K the input of capital; α and β represent the shares of labour and capital earnings in the income counterpart of output; and a hat denotes a compound growth rate.

The equation yields a derivative formula for labour productivity, and it is this to which the text discussion refers:

$$(\hat{Y/L}) = \beta(\hat{K/L}) + \hat{A}$$

TFP appears in both equations, not as a directly measured component, but as a residual:

$$\hat{A} = (\hat{Y/L}) - \beta(\hat{K/L})$$

Although TFP is sometimes taken to be a measure of the contribution of technological progress, it is properly interpreted as reflecting the influence of all the unmeasured sources of growth. As such, it includes, besides technological advance, also changes in labour quality due to education or otherwise, gains from the better allocation of resources and those from the economies of scale – unless these are somehow measured.

6. With some amendment, much of this section and the next follows the argument and evidence of several earlier papers: Rosenberg (1980), Wright (1990), Nelson (1991), David and Wright (1992), and Nelson and Wright (1992).

7. As late as the 1920s, 'Ford UK faced steel input prices that were higher by 50 percent than those paid by the parent company' (Nelson and Wright 1992, p. 622, citing Foreman-Peck 1982, p. 874).

8. These statements are based on Maddison's tables (1991, GDP per capita Table 1.1; Population, Tables B–1, B–2 and B–3; GDP, Tables A–5, A–6, A–7). An alternative set of estimates for the USA in the period, 1870-1913, yields results different in some details but qualitatively similar (Abramovitz and David 1973).

9. Rosenberg (1980) treats these subjects in a more extended way and provides references to supporting materials.

10. Denison makes much of this process in his analysis of postwar progress in Europe and Japan (1967, Ch, 17, esp. pp. 234 ff., 1976, Ch. 10).
11. The Maddison figures in the text are probably representative of northwest Europe as a whole, but Italy lagged far behind until after the war (see Denison 1967, p. 107).
12. Some of the pages that follow are adapted from an earlier paper (Abramovitz 1993b).

REFERENCES

Abramovitz, M. (1979), 'Rapid Growth Potential and Its Realization: The Experience of the Capitalist Economics in the Postwar Period', in E. Malinvaud (ed.), *Economic Growth and Resources*, Vol. I, London and N.Y.: The Macmillan Press.

Abramovitz, M. (1986), 'Catching-Up, Forging Ahead and Falling Behind', *Journal of Economic History*, 46(2) (June), 385–406.

Abramovitz, M. (1993a), 'The Search for the Sources of Growth: Areas of Ignorance, Old and New', *Journal of Economic History*, 53(2) (June).

Abramovitz. M. (1993b), 'Catch-Up and Convergence in the Postwar Growth Boom and After', in W. Baumol, R.R. Nelson and E.N. Wolff (eds), *The Convergence of Productivity: Cross-national Studies and Historical Evidence*, Oxford and N.Y.: Oxford University Press.

Abramovitz, M. and P.A. David (1973), 'Reinterpreting Economic Growth: Parables and Realities', *American Economic Review*, 63(2) (May), 428–39.

Baumol, W. (1986), 'Productivity Growth, Convergence and Welfare: What the Long-Run Data Show', *American Economic Review*, 76(5) (December), 1072–85.

Baumol, W., S.A. Batey Blackman and E. Wolff (1989), *Productivity and American Leadership: The Long View*, Cambridge, MA and London: The MIT Press.

Berle, A.A. and G.C. Means (1934), *The Modern Corporation and Private Property*, N.Y.: Macmillan Press.

Carré, J.J., P. Dubois and E. Malinvaud (1975), *French Economic Growth*, Stanford, CA: Stanford University Press.

Chandler, A. (1990), *Scale and Scope*, Cambridge, MA and London: Harvard University Press.

David, P.A. (1975), *Technological Choice, Innovation and Economic Growth*, New York: Cambridge University Press.

David, P.A. (1977), 'Invention and Accumulation in America's Economic Growth', in K. Brunner and A.H. Meltzer (eds), *International Organization, National Policies and Economic Development*, Vol. 6, 179–228, Amsterdam: North Holland Publishing Company.

David, P.A. and G. Wright (1992), 'Resource Abundance and American Economic Leadership', Center for Economic Policy Research, Stanford University, No. 267 (August).

DeLong, J.B. (1988), 'Productivity Growth, Convergence and Welfare: Comment', *American Economic Review*, 78(5) (December), 1138–59.

Denison, E.F. (1967), *Why Growth Rates Differ*, Washington, D.C.: The Brookings Institution.

Denison, E.F. and W.K. Chung, (1976), *How Japan's Economy Grew So Fast*, Washington, D.C.: The Brookings Institution.

Dumke, R. (1990), 'Reassessing the Wirtschaftswunder: Reconstruction and Postwar Growth in an International Context', *Oxford Bulletin of Economics and Statistics*, 52(2), 452–91.

Earle, E.M. (ed.) (1951), *Modern France: Problems of the Third and Fourth Republics*, Princeton: Princeton University Press.

Englander, S. and A. Mittelstadt (1985), 'Total Factor Productivity: Macroeconomic and Structural Aspects of the Slowdown', *OECD Economic Studies*, Paris, OECD, 1988, 7–56.

Foreman-Peck, J. (1982), 'The American Challenge of the Twenties: Multinationals and the European Motor Industry', *Journal of Economic History*, 42 December.

Friedman, M. (1992), 'Do Old Fallacies Ever Die?', *Journal of Economic Literature*, XXX(4) (December).

Kindleberger, C. (1967), *Europe's Postwar Growth: The Role of Labor Supply*, Cambridge, MA: Harvard University Press.

Kravis, I., A. Heston and R. Summers (1982), *World Product and Income: International Comparisons of Real Gross Product*, Phase III, United Nations and World Bank, Baltimore and London: Johns Hopkins Press, and earlier and later volumes in the same series.

Kuznets, S.S. (1966), *Modern Economic Growth: Rate, Structure and Spread*, New Haven, Connecticut and London: Yale University Press.

Lewis, W.A. (1954), 'Development with Unlimited Supplies of Labour', *The Manchester School*, XXII (May), 130–91.

Maddison, A. (1982), *Phases of Capitalist Development*, Oxford, N.Y.: Oxford University Press.

Maddison, A. (1987), 'Growth and Slowdown in Advanced Capitalist Countries: Techniques of Quantitative Assessment', *Journal of Economic Literature*, XXV(2) (June), 649–98.

Maddison, A. (1989), *The World Economy in the 20th Century*, Paris: Development Centre of the Organization for Economic Cooperation and Development.

Maddison, A. (1991), *Dynamic Forces in Capitalist Development*, Oxford and N.Y.: Oxford University Press.

Maddison, A. (1993), 'Explaining the Economic Performance of Nations, 1820–1989', prepared for publication in W.J. Baumol, R.R. Nelson and E.N. Wolff (eds), *Convergence of Productivity: Cross-National Studies and Historical Evidence*, Oxford and N.Y.: Oxford University Press.

McKinnon, R.I. (1971), 'Monetary Theory and Controlled Flexibility in the Foreign Exchanges', *Studies in International Finance*, Princeton: Princeton University Press.

Mowery, D. and N. Rosenberg (1989), *Technology and the Pursuit of Economic Growth*, Cambridge: Cambridge University Press.

Nelson, R.R. (1991), 'Diffusion of Development, Post-World War II Convergence Among Advanced Industrial Nations', *American Economic Review*, 81(2), 271–5.

Nelson, R.R. and G. Wright (1992), 'The Rise and Fall of American Technological Leadership', *Journal of Economic Literature*, XXX(4), 1931–64.

Ohkawa, K. and H. Rosovsky (1972), *Japanese Economic Growth*, Stanford, CA: Stanford University Press.

Parker, W.N. (1972), 'Productivity Growth in American Grain Farming: An Analysis of Its Nineteenth Century Sources', in R.W. Fogel and S. Engerman (eds), *The Reinterpretation of American Economic History*, N.Y.: Harper & Row, 175–86.

Pellicelli, G. (1976), 'Management 1920–1970', in C.M. Cipolla (ed.), *The Fontana*

Economic History of Europe: The Twentieth Century–1, Collins/Fontana Books, Ch. 4.

Rosenberg, N. (1980), 'Why in America?', in O. Mayr and R. Post (eds), *Yankee Enterprise: The Rise of the American System of Manufactures*, Washington, D.C.: Smithsonian Institute Press, 49–81.

Schultz, T.W. (1951), 'The Declining Economic Importance of Agricultural Land Rents', *Economic Journal*, 725–40.

Wallich, H.C. and M. Wallich (1976), 'Banking and Finance', in H. Patrick and H. Rosovsky (eds), *Asia's New Giant*, Washington, D.C.: The Brookings Institution, 249–316.

Wolff, E.N. (1991), 'Capital Formation and Productivity: Convergence Over the Long-Term', *American Economic Review*, 81(3) (June), 565–79.

Wright, G. (1990), 'The Origins of American Industrial Success', *American Economic Review*, 80(4) (September), 651–68.

3. Technology, Capital Accumulation, and Long-Run Growth

Edward N. Wolff

1. INTRODUCTION

An extensive literature has now documented the convergence in average labour productivity levels among industrialized economies over the last century or so and particularly since the end of World War II (see, for example, Abramovitz 1986, Baumol 1986, Dowrick and Nguyen 1989, and Baumol *et al.* 1989). Baumol's 1986 results, in particular, highlight these trends. Using data from Maddison (1982), he reported an almost perfect inverse relation between initial labour productivity level (in 1870) and the rate of labour productivity growth between that year and 1979 among 16 OECD countries. However, other work has highlighted a more uneven pattern of convergence. Abramovitz (1986), using the same Maddison data, found that labour productivity convergence was much slower in the period before 1950 (particularly 1870–1913) than after, and productivity levels actually diverged between 1938 and 1950 (see also his chapter above).

In a 1991 article, I explored the role of capital formation in the process of productivity convergence. The empirical analysis covered the period from 1870 to 1979, but was limited to the Group of Seven, with data provided in Maddison (1982). I found that total factor productivity (TFP) levels (to be defined below) converged over the 1870–1979 period. However, the pattern is far from uniform, with convergence much stronger after World War II than before, as Abramovitz (1986) found for labour productivity. Second, aggregate capital–labour ratios showed convergence over the long period, though the process was much stronger after 1960. Before World War II, it is evident only when the US, which surged ahead of the other countries between 1900 and 1938, is excluded from the sample.

Third, I investigated whether there are positive interactions (complementarities) between capital accumulation and technological advance. This deserves some comment. There are several ways in which capital formation and total factor productivity growth may be associated. First, it is likely that substantial capital accumulation is necessary to put new inventions into practice and to effect their widespread employment. This association is often referred to as the 'embodiment effect', since it implies that at least some technological innovation is embodied in capital (see, for example, Kuznets 1973, Abramovitz and David 1973, or Solow 1988). It is also consistent with the 'vintage effect', which states that new capital is more productive than old capital per (constant) dollar of expenditure (see, for example, Nelson 1964, or, more recently, Hulten 1992). If the capital stock data do not correct for vintage effects, then a positive correlation should be observed between the rate of technological gain and the change in the growth rate of capital.

A second avenue is that the introduction of new capital may lead to better organization, management, and the like. This may be true even if no new technology is incorporated in the capital equipment. A third is through learning-by-doing, which would also imply a positive relation between technological advance and the accumulation of capital stock (see Arrow 1962). A fourth is that technological advance may stimulate capital formation, because the opportunity to modernize equipment promises a high rate of return to investment.

A fifth is through the so-called Verdoorn or Kaldor effect, whereby investment growth may lead to a growth in demand and thereby to the maintenance of a generally favourable economic climate for investment. Such positive feedbacks may act cumulatively. A sixth is through knowledge externalities associated with the acquisition of new capital stock. This differs from the embodiment effect in that the productivity gains associated with new capital accrue to society rather than to individual firms (see, Romer 1986). These last five arguments do not lead to a specific functional relation between TFP growth and the rate of capital or capital–labour growth but do suggest a positive correlation between the two sets of variables.

The results of my 1991 paper showed a positive correlation of 0.79 between the rate of TFP growth and that of the capital–labour ratio over the 1880–1979 period. Results, based on regression analysis, are somewhat mixed but generally support the existence of an interaction effect between technological advance and capital accumulation. The effect was strongest during the postwar period, when both capital–labour growth and the speed of technological catch-up were greatest. Overall, convergence in labour productivity levels was found to be a consequence of all three effects.

This chapter extends my 1991 analysis in four ways. First, I use new data provided in Maddison (1991, 1993) to update my previous analysis. Maddison's 1991 data contain standardized estimates of capital stock, both gross and net, across countries. Moreover, Maddison (1993) also provides estimates of the average age of capital (my original figures reproduced in Table 3.1 below, were derived from the capital stock estimates in Maddison's 1982 book).

Second, on the basis of the 1991 Maddison data, capital stock will be subdivided into two parts, structures and equipment, to determine whether interaction effects differ between these two forms of capital. This issue is motivated by the work of DeLong and Summers (1991), who found that machinery and equipment investment had a much stronger impact on GDP growth than did other forms of capital formation.[1]

Third, particular consideration will be given to vintage effects on measured labour productivity growth. Such a formulation does imply a specific functional relationship between productivity growth and the average age of the capital stock.

Fourth, changes in labour productivity growth over time will be decomposed into three components: (i) increasing capital intensity of production, (ii) a vintage effect, estimated by changes in the average age of capital; and (iii) the catch-up effect. Particular attention will be paid to the relative importance of each component in the fall-off of productivity growth observed among OECD countries in the 1970s and 1980s.

The remainder of the chapter is divided into three parts. In the next part (Section 2), I present basic statistics on trends in labour productivity, TFP, capital intensity, and the age of capital over the period from 1880 to 1987. In Section 3, I use regression analysis to try to account for the decline in labour productivity growth since 1970. Concluding remarks are made in the last section.

2. TRENDS IN PRODUCTIVITY AND CAPITAL INTENSITY, 1880 TO 1987

Table 3.1 shows the basic statistics for the entire economy from the period 1880 to 1979, based on data from Maddison (1982). Output is measured by GDP in 1970 US relative prices, the labour input by hours worked, and the capital input by gross non-residential fixed plant and equipment (net for Germany). The capital stock data in this Maddison work are basically drawn from national sources. The only standardization is to convert the capital stock figures of different nations into 1970 US relative prices.[2]

Cross-country average labour productivity growth remained fairly stable between 1870 and 1938, at about two percent per year, fell precipitously during World War II, to about one percent per year, climbed to 4 percent in the 1950s and then to 5 percent in the 1960s, and fell off to about 3.5 percent in the 1970s.[3]

Table 3.1.   *Basic statistics on labour productivity, TFP, and capital-labour growth, and average age of capital stock, drawn from Maddison (1982), 1880-1979*[a]

	1880 –1890	1890 –1900	1900 –1913	1913 –1929	1929 –1938	1938 –1950	1950 –1960	1960 –1970	1970 –1979
A. Average annual rate of labour productivity growth (%)									
Canada	1.24	1.71	2.71	1.21	–0.06	5.36	3.10	2.72	1.83
France	0.90	2.02	1.82	2.35	2.83	0.75	4.39	5.39	4.09
Germany	2.15	2.42	1.42	1.41	2.35	–0.41	6.64	5.30	4.51
Italy	0.43	1.20	2.36	1.93	2.97	0.57	4.27	6.69	3.91
Japan	1.72	1.88	1.88	3.42	3.41	–3.42	5.57	9.96	5.04
UK	1.20	1.24	0.91	1.44	0.88	2.21	2.20	3.56	2.77
USA	1.86	1.96	1.99	2.40	0.75	4.03	2.41	2.52	1.93
Arithmetic average (%)									
5-country sample[b]	1.47	1.74	1.71	2.12	2.07	0.63	4.22	5.61	3.63
7-country sample	1.36	1.78	1.87	2.02	1.87	1.33	4.08	5.16	3.44
Ratio of average labour productivity level of all countries except the US to the US level at the beginning of the period									
7-country sample	0.64	0.60	0.59	0.57	0.52	0.57	0.43	0.50	0.64 0.74

Also shown in Panel A is the ratio of the average labour productivity level of all countries except the US to that of the US. This is an index of catch-up, extensively discussed in my 1991 paper. There was no catch-up to the US level between 1880 and 1950, as, in fact, the US pulled further ahead of the other six countries. However, the years 1950 to 1979 showed marked catch-up by the other countries with the US.[4]

Similar patterns are evident for total factor productivity (TFP) growth. TFP here is defined as

$$\ln TFP_t^h = \ln Y_t^h - \bar{\alpha} \ln L_t^h - (1-\bar{\alpha}) \ln K_t^h, \qquad (3.1)$$

where Y^h is the total output of country h, L^h is labour input, K^h is capital

Table 3.1. (continued)

	1880 –1890	1890 –1900	1900 –1913	1913 –1929	1929 –1938	1938 –1950	1950 –1960	1960 –1970	1970 –1979	1979
B. Average annual rate of TFP growth (%)										
Canada					–0.45	4.49	1.48	1.74	0.88	
France						3.34	3.40	2.06		
Germany	1.27	1.53	0.67	1.02	2.26	–0.78	5.07	2.58	1.91	
Italy	–0.58	0.60	1.29	0.86	1.19	0.26	3.16	3.93	1.66	
Japan	1.38	1.14	0.75	1.72	2.45	–3.67	4.72	5.61	1.58	
UK	1.11	0.86	0.42	0.85	0.79	1.62	1.41	1.65	1.16	
USA	1.30	0.43	0.93	1.54	–0.23	3.64	1.33	1.49	1.10	
Arithmetic average (%)										
5-country sample[b]	0.89	0.91	0.81	1.20	1.29	0.21	3.14	3.05	1.48	
7-country sample							2.93	2.92	1.48	
Ratio of average TFP level of all countries except the US to the US level at the beginning of the period										
5-country sample[b]	0.77	0.73	0.78	0.76	0.70	0.83	0.52	0.63	0.75	0.78
7-country sample							0.58	0.68	0.79	0.82

input, and $\bar{\alpha}$ is the international average wage share. For the wage share, the only available data for the full 1880–1987 period are employee compensation (EC) and national income (NI) for the UK and the US, so that factor shares are based on the average ratio of EC to NI in the two countries.[5] It should be noted that the sample of countries diminishes as one goes further back in time because of data availability.[6]

TFP growth, ρ, is then defined as

$$\rho_t^h = \hat{Y}_t^h - \bar{\alpha} \, \hat{L}_t^h - (1-\bar{\alpha}) \, \hat{K}_t^h, \tag{3.2}$$

where a hat (^) indicates the rate of growth. The Tornqvist approximation

Table 3.1. (continued)

	1880 –1890	1890 –1900	1900 –1913	1913 –1929	1929 –1938	1938 –1950	1950 –1960	1960 –1970	1970 –1979	1979

C. Average annual rate of growth of gross capital to hours (%)

Canada					0.95	2.17	4.01	2.44	2.37	
France							2.62	4.95	5.04	
Germany	2.20	2.21	1.87	0.95	0.22	0.92	3.90	6.74	6.44	
Italy	2.51	1.48	2.65	2.64	4.41	0.75	2.76	6.85	5.60	
Japan	0.85	1.85	2.81	4.23	2.38	1.08	2.11	10.82	8.58	
UK	0.23	0.94	1.21	1.47	0.23	1.47	1.96	4.75	4.01	
USA	1.40	3.81	2.62	2.12	2.42	0.98	2.68	2.54	2.05	

Arithmetic average (%)

5-country sample[b]	1.44	2.06	2.23	2.28	1.93	1.04	2.68	6.34	5.34	
7-country sample							2.86	5.58	4.87	

D. Average age of capital stock at the beginning of the period (in years)[c]

Germany	23.0	21.9	20.4	20.0	27.3	28.7	30.9	19.4	14.4	15.3
Italy	24.3	22.9	24.2	21.9	22.8	21.5	25.9	21.2	16.4	15.8
Japan	24.6	25.9	24.3	20.5	16.9	18.4	23.4	19.6	10.7	10.0
UK	25.6	27.1	27.0	25.7	28.5	30.1	31.4	24.8	19.3	19.2
USA	19.5	18.4	15.8	16.5	20.3	25.5	26.7	22.7	19.0	17.3

Arithmetic average (in years)

5-country sample[b]	23.4	23.2	22.3	20.9	23.2	24.8	27.7	21.5	16.0	15.5

a. Output is measured by GDP, labour by hours worked, and capital by gross non-residential fixed plant and equipment (net for Germany). Factor shares are based on the average ratio of employee compensation to national income for the UK and the US over the 1880-1979 period. TFP levels are computed according to Equation (3.1) and standardized so that TFP in the US is equal to unity in 1950. See the text for data sources and methods.
b. Germany, Italy, Japan, UK, and US.
c. Average age is estimated from capital stock data for 1870, 1880, 1890, 1900, 1913, 1929, 1938, 1950, 1960, 1970, and 1979. It is assumed that the service life is 50 years and that the average age of the capital stock was 25 years in 1870.

based on average period shares is employed. It also follows directly that

$$\hat{\pi}_t^h = \rho_t^h + (1-\overline{\alpha})\,\hat{k}_t^h, \tag{3.3}$$

where $\pi \equiv Y/L$, the level of labour productivity; and $k \equiv K/L$, the ratio of the capital stock to labour. This will be of use later.

Average TFP growth remained rather steady at about one percent per year from 1880 to 1938 (Panel B).[7] World War II, not unexpectedly, caused severe damage to the three Axis powers – Germany, Italy, and Japan – and, for Japan and Germany, TFP growth was actually negative between 1938 and 1950. However, the Allied powers did well. Both Canada and the US enjoyed their highest TFP growth ever (4.5 and 3.6 percent per year, respectively), while the UK averaged 1.6 percent per year, its second highest level. The 1950s and 1960s were the boom years, with TFP growth averaging around three percent per year. The 1970s showed a substantial fall-off in TFP growth among OECD countries. Perhaps most dramatic was Japan, whose annual rate of TFP growth fell from 5.6 percent in the 1960s to 1.6 percent in the 1970s. However, overall the pattern over time was quite similar to that for labour productivity growth.

Also shown in Panel B is the ratio of the average TFP level of all countries except the US to the TFP level of the US – a crude index of the technology gap with respect to the leader. There was moderate catch-up on the US level between 1890 and 1938 (the US became the TFP leader in 1900), a significant setback between 1938 and 1950, as the US surged ahead and Germany and Japan fell back in absolute terms, and then substantial catch-up between 1950 and 1979.

Between 1880 and 1938, the international average annual growth in capital intensity tended to remain relatively stable, at about two percent per year (Panel C). During the war and war recovery years, 1938–50, it fell to about one percent, and then increased to 2.7 percent during the 1950s. The 1960–70 period thus represents an unusual departure from the long-term historical trend, with an average annual rate of 5.6 percent. The average rate then declined to 4.9 percent in 1970–79.

It is of interest to note that countries with higher capital–labour growth generally had higher TFP growth. The rank order is identical for the 1950–79 period: Japan (annual capital–labour growth of 7.1 percent), Germany (5.7 percent), Italy (5.1 percent), France (4.2 percent), UK (3.6 percent), Canada (3.0 percent), and the US (2.4 percent). For the whole 1880–1979 period, Japan was first in capital–labour growth, followed by Italy, Germany, the US, and the UK. Except for a reversal between Italy and Germany, the rank order is identical to that of TFP growth. These empirical findings suggest the existence of interaction effects between capital growth and technology growth.

I derived estimates of the average age of the capital stock from capital stock data for 1870, 1880, 1890, 1900, 1913, 1929, 1938, 1950, 1960, 1970, and 1979. I assumed that the service life is 50 years and that the average age of the capital stock was 25 years in 1870. Estimates are not provided for Canada or France, because the capital stock series are not long enough. (Maddison provides estimates of average ages in his 1993 worksheets.)

Results on average age are shown in Panel D. The average age for the five countries declined from 23 years in 1880 to 21 years in 1913, rose steadily to 28 years in 1950, then rapidly declined to 15 years in 1979. Perhaps, the most telling result is the extreme rejuvenation of the capital stock during the 1950s and 1960s, during which the average age fell by 6.1 and 5.6 years, respectively. Germany during the 1950s and Japan during the 1960s experienced extremely sharp drops in the age of their capital stock. In contrast, the average age of capital remained virtually unchanged during the 1970s. Changes were also relatively modest in the periods before 1938.

The US had by far the newest capital stock from 1880 to 1913 (a third younger than the other four countries in 1900), a consequence of its high rate of capital growth. US capital stock aged relative to the other countries from 1900 onward, and by 1979, it was 13 percent older than the other countries. From 1929 onward, Japan had the youngest capital stock; in 1979, its average age was two-thirds of its nearest rival, Germany, and 0.58 that of the US. In contrast, the UK had the oldest capital stock, a position it maintained for 100 years. In fact, in 1900, the UK capital stock was 70 percent older than that of the US.

Table 3.2 shows a similar set of results based on the Maddison (1991) data. In this case, capital stock estimates are standardized across countries by using the same service lives (a 39-year life for non-residential structures and a 14-year life for machinery and equipment), as well as the same (US) prices, and figures are provided separately for both plant and machinery and equipment. Moreover, estimates of the average age for both non-residential structures and non-residential machinery and equipment are shown in the table. Angus Maddison graciously supplied me with the underlying estimates for these figures (cited as Maddison, 1993). The data are also now updated to 1987, and the period 1973–87 is highlighted. The new country sample now includes the Netherlands but excludes Canada and Italy.

Results are similar to Table 3.1. According to the new data, average annual labour productivity growth fell from a peak of 5.0 percent in 1960–73 to 2.4 percent in 1973–87, close to its historical average; TFP growth from 2.8 percent in 1950–60 to 2.4 percent in 1960–73 and then to

Table 3.2. Basic statistics on labour productivity, TFP, and capital-labour growth, and average age of capital stock, drawn from Maddison (1991,1993), 1890-1987[a]

	1890 –1913	1913 –1929	1929 –1938	1938 –1950	1950 –1960	1960 –1973	1973 –1986	1987

A. Average annual rate of labour productivity growth (%)

France	1.74	2.35	2.82	0.64	4.46	5.15	3.11	
Germany	1.85	1.37	2.36	–0.39	6.65	5.09	2.56	
Japan	1.74	3.38	2.34	–0.67	5.54	8.70	3.08	
Netherlands	1.13	2.84	–0.12	0.32	4.08	5.12	2.35	
UK	1.04	1.44	0.92	2.22	2.27	3.82	2.30	
USA	2.20	2.40	1.42	3.14	2.44	2.42	1.04	
Arithmetic average (%)	1.62	2.30	1.62	0.88	4.24	5.05	2.41	

Ratio of average labour productivity level of all countries except the US to the US level at the beginning of the period

	0.64	0.53	0.50	0.50	0.38	0.45	0.65	0.81

B. Average annual rate of TFP growth (%)

France					2.95	2.73	0.92	
Germany					4.79	1.95	0.88	
Japan	0.84	1.49	1.42	–1.65	5.00	4.02	0.49	
Netherlands					2.08	2.58	0.80	
UK	0.52	0.54	0.43	1.63	0.54	1.50	0.92	
USA	0.73	1.49	0.19	3.14	1.56	1.65	0.32	
Arithmetic average (%)					2.82	2.41	0.72	

Ratio of average TFP level of all countries except the US to the US level at the beginning of the period

					0.50	0.63	0.71	0.79	0.85

Table 3.2. (continued)

	1890 –1913	1913 –1929	1929 –1938	1938 –1950	1950 –1960	1960 –1973	1973 –1986	1987

C. Average annual rate of growth of gross structures to hours (%)

France					2.04	4.57	5.36	
Germany					3.69	7.19	4.50	
Japan	1.94	4.09	3.21	1.08	2.76	11.16	7.18	
Netherlands					3.45	5.79	3.77	
UK	0.64	1.23	0.30	0.66	3.56	6.33	4.08	
USA	3.16	2.10	3.45	−1.11	1.88	1.69	1.18	
Arithmetic average (%)					2.90	6.12	4.35	

D. Average annual rate of growth of gross machinery & equipment to hours (%)

France					8.96	8.38	5.50	
Germany					7.24	9.11	3.48	
Japan	2.93	5.91	0.48	4.79	−1.08	12.52	4.95	
Netherlands					10.51	7.46	4.05	
UK	2.99	3.88	2.32	2.31	4.94	5.30	2.76	
USA	7.72	3.01	1.15	4.32	3.03	2.47	3.02	
Arithmetic average (%)					5.60	7.54	3.96	

E. Average age of gross structures at the beginning of the period (in years)

France				19.9	18.8	12.6	14.8	
Germany			19.9	19.9	18.9	15.4	12.4	15.7
Japan			13.2	14.3	14.7	12.9	8.8	11.9
Netherlands				19.8	18.1	13.5	16.9	
UK	18.3	18.8	19.6	18.7	18.1	16.1	12.6	15.9
USA	14.7	15.1	16.9	19.0	19.3	17.3	14.8	17.0
Arithmetic average				18.4	16.4	12.4	15.3	

Table 3.2. (continued)

	1890 –1913	1913 –1929	1929 –1938	1938 –1950	1950 –1960	1960 –1973	1973 –1987	1987

F. Average age of gross plant & equipment at the beginning of the period (in years)

	1890 –1913	1913 –1929	1929 –1938	1938 –1950	1950 –1960	1960 –1973	1973 –1987	1987
France					6.32	6.39	6.15	7.19
Germany				7.54	8.02	5.57	6.61	7.11
Japan		5.87	7.86	6.08	8.40	5.58	5.59	6.43
Netherlands					6.36	6.26	6.75	7.03
UK	7.48	7.60	6.45	7.17	7.25	6.60	7.93	7.15
USA	7.20	6.85	7.14	7.93	6.35	7.30	6.48	7.04
Arithmetic average					7.12	6.28	6.42	6.99

a. Output is measured by GDP (1985 US$), labour by hours worked, and capital by gross non-residential fixed plant (structures) and machinery and equipment. Factor shares are based on the average ratio of employee compensation to national income for the UK and the US over the 1890–1987 period. TFP levels are computed according to Equation (3.1) and standardized so that TFP in the US is equal to unity in 1950. See the text for data sources and methods.

0.7 percent in 1973–87, also near its historical average; and (total) capital–labour growth from 6.9 percent in the 1960–73 to 3.7 percent in 1973–87 (results not shown). Japan also slowed down, with its rate of (total) capital–labour growth almost falling in half between 1960–73 and 1973–87 (from 9.3 to 4.9 percentage points).

Trends are similar in the growth rates of structures to hours worked and machinery and equipment (M&E) to hours worked. Both accelerated between the 1950s and the 1960–73 period and then fell off in the 1973–87 period. Interestingly, the rate of growth of M&E to hours worked was greater in the 1950–60 and 1960–73 periods than the growth of structures to hours, but in the 1973–87 period the growth rates were about the same.

The average age of the total gross capital stock declined from 15.3 years in 1950 to 10.2 years in 1973 but then rose to 12.2 years in 1987 (results not shown). The average age fell by 2.3 years between 1950 and 1960 and by 2.8 years between 1960 and 1973. However, this was followed by a substantial reversal in the 1973–87 period, when the average age *increased by 2.1 years*. Indeed, this change occurred for each of the six countries in the sample (for the US, the age declined by 3.7 years in 1950–73 and then rose by 1.2 years in 1973–87).

The postwar trends for the age of structures are similar to those for the total capital stock (structures comprise over 75 percent of total capital stock). The average age of structures fell in every country between 1960 and 1973 but then increased between 1973 and 1987. By 1987, the US had the oldest plant. The age was 11 percent higher than the average age of the structures of other countries. Japan had the youngest non-residential structures throughout the postwar period.

Trends in the average age of M&E are surprisingly different. The average age fell between 1950 and 1960 and then increased somewhat between 1960 and 1973 and more significantly between 1973 and 1987. US M&E aged relative to the other countries between 1950 and 1960, from 11 percent younger to 16 percent older, but by 1987 its average age was just about equal to that of other countries. In 1973 and 1987, Japan had the youngest machinery and equipment but the differences between Japan and its rivals were relatively small (a 9 percent difference with the US in 1987).

The data already point to a dramatic turnaround in the aging of the capital stock before and after 1973. In order to gauge the contribution of this phenomenon to the productivity slowdown, we now turn to a regression analysis to measure the vintage effect.

3. REGRESSION ANALYSIS OF LABOUR PRODUCTIVITY TRENDS

Following Hulten (1992), I can first distinguish between capital stock measured in natural units (constant prices), K, and capital stock measured in 'efficiency units', K^*. To simplify, suppose that this year's capital investment is s percent more productive than last year's, and the parameter s is constant over time. To simplify further, suppose that investment occurs for a single year. Then, K^* measured in today's efficiency units is given by $K^* = Ke^{-sA}$, where A is the age of the capital stock (investment). In the more general case, where investment occurs yearly and (gross) capital stock is accumulated investment over the service life, there is no simple relation between K^* and K, since it depends on the pattern of investment over time. However, one can very loosely approximate the relation as

$$K^* = Ke^{-s\bar{A}}, \qquad (3.4)$$

where $\bar{A}$ is the average age of the capital stock (see Nelson 1964).

Assuming a Cobb–Douglas aggregate production function, with capital measured in efficiency units, we then obtain

$$\ln Y_t^h = \zeta^h + \bar{\alpha} \ln L_t^h + (1-\bar{\alpha}) \ln K_t^h - (1-\bar{\alpha}) s^h \bar{A}_t^h. \quad (3.5)$$

From (3.3) and (3.5) and with the added assumption that s is equal across countries, it follows that

$$\hat{\pi}_t^h = \rho_t^h + (1-\bar{\alpha}) \hat{k}_t^h - (1-\bar{\alpha}) s \Lambda_t^h, \quad (3.6)$$

where $\Lambda^h \equiv d\bar{A}^h/dt$, the *rate of change* in capital stock age in country h (again, see Nelson 1964).

3.1. Regression Analysis

From (3.6), the basic estimating form is

$$LPRGRT_t^h = b_0 + b_1 \, RELTFP_t^h + b_2 \, KLGRT_t^h + \quad (3.7)$$
$$b_3 \, AGEKCHG_t^h + \varepsilon_t^h,$$

where $LPRGRT_t^h$ is country h's annual rate of labour productivity growth, $RELTFP_t^h$ is country h's (Translog) TFP relative to the US at the start of each period, $KLGRT_t^h$ is country h's rate of capital–labour growth, $AGEKCHG_t^h$ is the (annual) change in the average age of country h's capital stock, and ε is a stochastic error term. The RELTFP term is included as a crude index of technology gap with respect to the US and hence of the catch-up potential.[8] Where appropriate, the total capital stock is also divided into structures (S) and machinery and equipment (ME).

Columns 1 and 2 of Table 3.3 show the results based on the 1982 Maddison data. The first column shows results without the vintage effect for purposes of comparison. The catch-up effect (the initial relative TFP level) is significant at the one percent level in explaining labour productivity growth and its coefficient has the expected negative sign. Capital-labour growth is also significant at the one percent level and has the expected positive sign.

When the vintage variable is included (column 2), these two variables remain significant at the one percent level, but both the absolute value of their coefficients and their *t*-values decline. The coefficient value of RELTFP is now –0.04. Thus a 50 percent difference between a country's initial TFP and that of the US is associated with about a 2 percentage point per year (half of –0.04) growth in labour productivity. A one percentage point increase in capital–labour growth is associated with a 0.4 percentage point increase in labour productivity growth. The constant term

Table 3.3.   Regression of annual labour productivity growth (LPGRT) on relative TFP level, capital–labour growth and the change in the average age of capital[a]

Independent variables	Maddison (1982) data[b]		Maddison (1991, 93) data[c]	
	(1)	(2)	(3)	(4)
Constant	0.004 (1.40)	0.005 (1.80)	0.008 (1.94)	0.009** (2.80)
RELTFP	−0.050** (4.05)	−0.039** (2.94)	−0.041** (3.05)	−0.018* (2.39)
KLGRT	0.485** (4.86)	0.428** (4.21)		
KSLGRT			0.135 (1.03)	0.279** (3.11)
KMELGRT			0.212* (2.42)	0.156* (2.32)
AGEKCHG		−0.0138* (2.05)		
AGESCHG				−0.0261** (2.95)
AGEMECHG				−0.0711** (4.02)
R^2	0.67	0.72	0.65	0.88
Adj. R^2	0.66	0.70	0.61	0.85
Standard error	0.012	0.012	0.012	0.008
Sample size	53	45	30	28
Degrees of freedom	50	41	26	22

a. t-ratios are shown in parentheses below the coefficient estimate.
Key: RELTFP: percentage difference of country's TFP from US TFP at the beginning of the period; KLGRT: country's annual rate of capital–labour growth; KSLGRT: country's annual rate of structures to labour growth; KMELGRT: country's annual rate of machinery and equipment to labour growth; AGEKCHG: annualized change in the average age of country's capital stock over the period; AGESCHG: annualized change in the average age of country's structures over the period; AGEMECHG: annualized change in the average age of country's machinery and equipment over the period.
b. For regression 1, observations are for Germany, Italy, Japan, the UK, and the US for nine periods: 1880–90, 1890–1900, 1900–13, 1913–29, 1929–38, 1938–50, 1950–60, 1960–70, and 1970–79; Canada for 1929–38, 1938–50, 1950–60, 1960–70, and 1970–79; and France for 1950–60, 1960–70, and 1970–79. For regression 2, the sample is identical except that data for Canada and France are excluded.
c. For regression 3, observations are for Japan, the UK and the US for seven time periods: 1890–1913, 1913–29, 1929–38, 1938–50, 1950–60, 1960–73, and 1973–87; and France, Germany, and the Netherlands for 1950–60, 1960–73, and 1973–87. For regression 4, the sample is identical, except that observations for Japan in 1890–1913 and 1913–29 are excluded.
* significant at the 5 percent level. ** significant at the 1 percent level.

is 0.005, suggesting an average growth of TFP of about one-half a percentage point per year.

The change in the average age of the capital stock has the expected negative sign and the variable is significant at the five percent level. The effect is surprisingly large: a one-year reduction in the average age of capital is associated with about a *one* percentage point increase in labour productivity growth.

There are several other results of note. First, the data reject the hypothesis that there is a statistically different size of the catch-up effect (coefficient of RELTFP) in the postwar period (1950–79) in comparison to the 1880–1950 period; moreover, the data reject that the coefficient of KLGRT is different after 1950 than before 1950 (results not shown).

Second, as noted above, including the change in the age of capital reduces the coefficient on capital–labour growth, by about 0.06. This is due to the fact that capital stock age moves inversely with changes in the rate of growth of the capital stock. If growth accelerates, the average age of the capital stock declines. Moreover, changes in the rate of growth of the capital stock are positively associated with the actual rates of growth of the capital stock (the correlation coefficient is 0.60). Thus, part of the effect normally attributed to capital–labour growth is actually the vintage effect, which results in an upward bias in the coefficient of capital–labour growth (an omitted variable effect).

Third, the goodness of fit, as measured by the adjusted-R^2 statistic, increases when the vintage effect is included in the model.

Results on the basis of the 1991 and 1993 Maddison data, with capital broken down into structures and machinery and equipment, are shown in columns 3 and 4 of Table 3.3. Regression 3 shows the results without the vintage effects included. The catch-up effect has the expected negative sign and is significant at the one percent level, as before. Both capital growth variables have the expected positive sign. However, interestingly, the growth in the ratio of structures to hours worked is not significant, while that of M&E to hours is significant at the five percent level.

When the vintage effects are included (column 4), the growth in the ratio of structures to hours worked now becomes significant at the one percent level, while that of M&E to hours remains significant at the five percent level. The coefficient of RELTFP remains negative, but its value drops in half and it is now significant at only the five percent level. Both vintage effect variables have the expected negative coefficient. That for structures (AGESCHG) is significant at the one percent level, as is that for machinery and equipment (AGEMECHG).

Comparing regressions 2 and 4 (both with vintage effects), we see that the sum of the coefficients on the two capital–labour growth variables from the 1991 and 1993 Maddison data is almost identical to the coefficient of (total) capital–labour growth in the regression based on the 1982 Maddison data. However, the vintage effects appear substantially larger on the basis of the more recent Maddison data. The coefficient on the change in the average age of structures is –0.026 in regression 4 and that on the change in the average age of machinery and equipment is –0.071, compared to a coefficient of –0.014 on the change in the age of total capital in regression 2.

The constant term from the 1991 and 1993 Maddison data is 0.009, compared to 0.005 from the 1982 Maddison data. This suggests a 'natural' rate of technological advance of 0.9 percent per year, rather than 0.5 percent per year. The difference, however, may simply reflect the fact that the observations from the more recent Maddison data are more heavily weighted toward the postwar period.

The catch-up effect is smaller on the basis of the newer Maddison data, about half the value of that based on the 1982 Maddison data. Here, I suspect, the difference in results is largely attributable to the disaggregation of the capital stock into structures and M&E, since the vintage effects are, as indicated above, substantially stronger. The goodness of fit, as measured by the adjusted-R^2 statistic and the standard error of the regression, is substantially higher on the basis of the more recent Maddison data. Disaggregating capital into structures and M&E thus appears to improve significantly the performance of the vintage model.

A final point of interest is that with vintage effects included (regression 4), the coefficient of machinery and equipment to labour growth is no larger than the share of machinery and equipment in total capital. Moreover, the annual rate of machinery and equipment to labour growth (KMELGRT) is statistically significant at the five percent level whereas the change in the average age of structures (AGESCH) is significant at the one percent level. These results conflict directly with the Summers and DeLong (1991) finding that the coefficient of machinery and equipment was significantly greater than its share in total capital. The reason for the difference in results becomes apparent in comparing regressions 3 and 4. Without vintage effects, the coefficient of M&E to hours growth is greater than its share in total capital (and, indeed, greater than the coefficient of structures to hours growth). Thus, controlling for vintage effects seems to cast doubt on the argument that machinery and equipment play a more important role in economic growth than structures.

3.2. Sources of Declining Productivity Growth

We are now in a position to understand some of the factors behind the slowdown in labour productivity growth in the 1970s and 1980s. A decomposition, based on the regression results of Table 3.3, is shown in Table 3.4. For example, on the basis of the 1982 Maddison data, for the 1880–90 period, of the 1.5 percent per year average growth in labour productivity, 0.3 percentage points can be attributed to the catch-up effect (RELTFP), 0.6 percentage points to the growth in the capital–labour ratio, 0.02 percentage points to the vintage effect (the decline in the average age of the capital stock), and 0.5 percentage points to general technological advance (with 0.04 points unexplained).

Between 1880 and 1938, average annual labour productivity growth increased from 1.5 to 2.1 percentage points, mainly because of an increasing catch-up effect (as US technology advanced relative to other OECD countries) and rising growth in the capital–labour ratio. Between 1929–38 and 1950–60, labour productivity growth doubled, to 4.2 percent per year. Of this *increase*, 42 percent ((1.51-0.62)/(4.22-2.07)) can be attributed to the increasing catch-up effect from the rising technological advantage of the US, as the TFP of other OECD countries slipped to 39 percent below the US level; 15 percent to increased capital–labour growth; and *50 percent* to the increasing vintage effect, as the average age of capital stock declined at an annual rate of *0.6 years* over this period.

During the 1960s, labour productivity growth increased to 5.6 percent per year, due exclusively to rising capital–labour growth (as it reached its highest point over the century), and despite a slight diminution of both the catch-up effect and vintage effect. Over a third (35 percent) of the fall-off in productivity growth during the 1970–79 period, to 3.6 percent per year, is attributable to the reduction in the vintage effect, as the average age of capital remained almost constant over the 1970s; 15 percent is attributable to the continued diminution of the catch-up effect, as the average TFP of other countries approached 26 percent of the US level; and 22 percent to a slowdown in capital–labour growth.

The results from the newer Maddison data for the postwar period are shown in Panel B, with separate terms for structures and machinery and equipment. As with the 1982 Maddison data, the contribution of the catch-up effect diminished over time, from 0.57 percentage points in 1950–60 to 0.48 percentage points in 1973–87, as other countries' TFP converged on the US level. The total contribution of capital–labour growth (the sum of KSLGRT and KMELGRT) is similar on the basis of the newer Maddison data. Also, as with the 1982 Maddison data, the contribution of capital-labour growth increased from the 1950–60 to the 1960–73 period and then declined in 1973–87.

The vintage effect from structures (AGESCHG) was quite strong and positive between 1950 and 1973, averaging about two-thirds of a percentage point, but then fell to –0.54 during the 1973–87 period, reflecting the

Table 3.4.   Contribution by component to average labour productivity growth by period (on the basis of the Maddison data)

A. Maddison (1982) data: five-country summary statistics[a]

	1880–1890	1890–1900	1900–1913	1913–1929	1929–1938	1938–1950	1950–1960	1960–1970	1970–1979
1. Average value of explanatory variables									
RELTFP	–0.07	–0.09	–0.08	–0.10	–0.16	–0.09	–0.39	–0.34	–0.26
KLGRT (% pts)	1.44	2.06	2.23	2.28	1.93	1.04	2.68	6.34	5.34
AGEKCHG	–0.02	–0.09	–0.11	0.14	0.19	0.24	–0.61	–0.56	–0.05
2. Percentage point contribution of each variable to average labour productivity growth[b]									
Constant	0.52	0.52	0.52	0.52	0.52	0.52	0.52	0.52	0.52
RELTFP	0.27	0.37	0.32	0.39	0.62	0.35	1.51	1.32	1.03
KLGRT	0.62	0.88	0.95	0.98	0.83	0.45	1.15	2.71	2.28
AGEKCHG	0.02	0.13	0.15	–0.20	–0.26	–0.33	0.85	0.77	0.07
Sum	1.43	1.90	1.95	1.70	1.71	0.99	4.03	5.33	3.91
Unexplained	0.04	–0.16	–0.24	0.42	0.36	–0.36	0.19	0.27	-0.28
LPGRT	1.47	1.74	1.71	2.12	2.07	0.63	4.22	5.61	3.63

aging of structures in OECD countries. The vintage effect from machinery and equipment (AGEMECHG) contributed almost half a percentage point to labour productivity growth during the 1950s, about zero during 1960–73, and actually reduced productivity growth by more than a quarter of a percentage point during the 1973–87 period.

Comparing the 1960–73 and 1973–87 periods, we can understand some of the reasons for the fall-off in labour productivity growth between these two periods of 2.6 percentage points. The slowdown in total capital–labour growth accounted for 40 percent of the decline in labour productivity growth, coming about equally from reduced investment in structures and machinery and equipment; the aging of structures accounted for 51 percent and that of machinery and equipment for 8 percent; while the diminution of the catch-up effect had a negligible impact (as did the change in the unexplained portion).

Table 3.4. (continued)

B. Maddison (1991, 1993) data: 6-country statistics[c]

	1950 –1960	1960 –1973	1973 –1987
1. Average value of explanatory variables			
RELTFP	−0.31	−0.28	−0.26
KSLGRT (% pts)	2.90	6.12	4.35
KMELGRT (% pts)	5.60	7.54	3.96
AGESCHG	−0.20	−0.30	0.21
AGEMECHG	−0.08	0.01	0.04
2. Percentage point contribution of each variable to average labour productivity growth[b]			
constant	0.88	0.88	0.88
RELTFP	0.57	0.53	0.48
KSLGRT	0.81	1.71	1.21
KMELGRT	0.87	1.18	0.62
AGESCHG	0.53	0.80	−0.54
AGEMECHG	0.59	−0.07	−0.29
Sum	4.25	5.02	2.35
Unexplained	−0.01	0.03	0.05
LPGRT	4.24	5.05	2.41

a. Coefficients from regression 2 in Table 3.3. See Footnote a to Table 3.3 for variable definitions.
b. Defined as coefficient value multiplied by the average value of the variable by period.
c. Coefficients from regression 4 in Table 3.3.

4. SUMMARY AND CONCLUDING REMARKS

The period before World War II was one of moderate growth in TFP (about one percent per year), capital intensity (about two percent per year), and labour productivity (also about two percent per year). There was moderate catch-up and convergence in TFP and labour productivity levels during this period, though both processes accelerated during the Depression years. However, there was no convergence in capital intensity (indeed, increasing disparity). The average age of the capital stock increased slightly between 1880 and 1938.

The war and war recovery years, 1938–50, saw a sharp increase in dispersion in TFP, capital intensity, and labour productivity, as well as TFP growth. Moreover, the rate of labour productivity growth and capital-labour growth fell to one percent per year, and TFP growth close to zero.

The postwar period was characterized by rapid convergence in all three dimensions (for capital intensity, after 1960). However, a sharp break in growth is evident around the early 1970s. The 1950s and 1960s were the boom years, with TFP growth averaging around three percent per year. The 1970s and 1980s showed a substantial fall-off in TFP growth among OECD countries, with average TFP growth returning to about one percent per year in the 1980s. Cross-country average labour productivity growth climbed to 4 percent in the 1950s and then to 5 percent in the 1960s, fell off to about 3.5 percent in the 1970s and thence to 2.4 percent in the 1973–87 period, close to its long-run historical average.

The international average annual growth in capital intensity was 3 percent during the 1950s, 6 percent during the 1960s, 5 percent in 1970–79 and then 3.7 percent in 1973–87 on the basis of the newer Maddison data. Postwar trends are very similar for the growth of the ratio of structures to labour and that of machinery and equipment capital to labour. The average age of structures declined from 18 years in 1950 to 12 in 1973 but then rose to 15 years in 1987, while the average age of machinery and equipment fell from 7.1 years in 1950 to 6.4 years in 1973 and then increased to 7.0 years in 1987.

From these results, one can piece together the following story. Over the last century or so, the average rate of TFP growth for OECD countries has been about one percent per year. Capital–labour growth has averaged about two percent per year, and as a result, the average rate of labour productivity growth has also been about two percent per year.

The Great Depression in the US exerted a severe retardant effect on its technology gains, with negative TFP growth recorded for the 1929–38 period. World War II was a period of very rapid technology gains for the US, which in part reflected the implementation of a backlog of technology developed but not implemented during the 1930s. In contrast, both continental Europe and Japan suffered severe economic losses during World War II. As a result, by 1950, the gap between US TFP and that of other OECD countries was at its highest point over the century.

The exceptionally high labour productivity growth rates of the 1950s and 1960s among OECD countries was thus due to a concurrence of three very favourable factors. First, the extremely high technology gap caused very high rates of TFP growth in continental Europe and Japan during the 1950s and 1960s, from the catch-up effect. Second, investment was very strong. Third, the *acceleration* in the rate of capital growth caused the average age of capital to decline sharply, thus creating a very favourable vintage effect.

However, by the early 1970s, most of the gains from catch-up had been exhausted, leading to a return of TFP growth to its historical norm. Moreover, capital–labour growth slowed down, causing a direct drag on labour productivity growth. The deceleration of capital growth also caused the average age of capital to increase, creating a negative vintage effect on labour productivity growth. The 1980s thus appears to represent a return to 'normalcy', with TFP and capital–labour growth returning to their historical average, and the vintage effect becoming close to zero again.

NOTES

1. In a follow-up article, de Long (1992) concluded on the basis of cross-national data that each additional percentage point of total output devoted to gross investment in machinery and equipment raised the growth in output per worker by one-third of a percentage point per year over the postwar period and by more than half a percentage point per year over the past century.
2. Problems of comparability of measures across countries are extensively discussed in Maddison (1982), Abramovitz (1986), and Wolff (1991).
3. It should be stressed that this sample is by no means representative and is subject to many of the same criticisms De Long (1988) makes of OECD samples.
4. The coefficient of variation in labour productivity levels, a measure of convergence, shows a slightly different pattern before 1950. There was very little convergence in labour productivity levels between 1870 and 1929, some convergence during the Great Depression of the 1930s, but this was followed by widening dispersion during the 1938–50 war and recovery period. However, the years 1950–89 show marked convergence in labour productivity levels.
5. Data on wage shares are computed from the following sources: (1) Data for 1950–87 are from the United Nations' *Yearbook of National Accounts Statistics*, selected years. (2) Data for 1937–50 are from the International Labour Organization's *Yearbook of Labour Statistics*, various years. (3) For the United Kingdom, data for 1870–1938 are from Deane and Cole (1964), p. 247. (4) For the US, data for 1870–1938 are from Johnson (1954).
6. For the postwar period, data availability is much greater and TFP was also computed using country-specific factor shares. Results did not materially differ from those reported here and are not shown.
7. It should be noted that the results for Panel B differ somewhat from those reported in Wolff (1991) because of the use of the Translog index here (and what I called a 'crude TFP' measure in that paper).
8. Though there are endogeneity problems associated with the use of relative TFP as the measure of catch-up potential, it appears to be a better index of the 'technology gap' than a country's relative labour productivity level, since the latter reflects both technology differences and differences in the capital intensity of production.

REFERENCES

Abramovitz, M. (1986), 'Catching Up, Forging Ahead, and Falling Behind', *Journal of Economic History*, 46 (2), June, pp. 385–406.

Abramovitz, M. and P.A. David (1973), 'Reinterpreting Economic Growth: Parables and Realities', *American Economic Review*, 63 (2), May, pp. 428–39.

Arrow, K. (1962), 'The Economic Implications of Learning by Doing', *Review of Economic Studies*, 29, June, pp. 155–73.

Baumol, W.J. (1986), 'Productivity Growth, Convergence, and Welfare: What do the Long-Run Data Show?', *American Economic Review*, 76 (5), December, pp. 1072–85.

Baumol, W.J., S.A. Batey Blackman and E.N. Wolff (1989), *Productivity and American Leadership: The Long View*, Cambridge, Mass.: MIT Press.

Deane, P. and W.A. Cole (1964), *British Economic Growth, 1688–1959: Trends and Structure*, Cambridge: Cambridge University Press.

DeLong, J.B. (1988), 'Productivity Growth, Convergence, and Welfare: Comment', *American Economic Review*, 78 (5), December, pp. 1138–54.

DeLong, J.B. (1992), 'Machinery Investment as a Key to American Economic Growth', in *Tools for American Workers: The Role of Machinery and Equipment in Economic Growth*, Washington, D.C.: American Council for Capital Formation, Center for Policy Research, pp. 1–31.

De Long, J.B. and L.H. Summers (1991), 'Equipment Investment and Economic Growth', *Quarterly Journal of Economics*, 151 (2), May, pp. 445–502.

Dowrick, S. and D.-T. Nguyen (1989), 'OECD Comparative Economic Growth 1950–85: Catch-Up and Convergence', *American Economic Review*, 79 (5), December, pp. 1010–31.

Hulten, C.R. (1992), 'Growth Accounting When Technical Change is Embodied in Capital', *American Economic Review*, 82 (4), September, pp. 964–80.

Johnson, D.G. (1954), 'The Functional Distribution of Income in the United States, 1850–1952, *Review of Economics and Statistics*, 36 (2), May, pp. 175–82.

Kuznets, S. (1973), *Population, Capital, and Growth: Selected Essays*, New York: W.W. Norton Company.

Maddison, A. (1982), *Phases of Capitalist Development*, Oxford: Oxford University Press.

Maddison, A. (1991), *Dynamic Forces in Capitalist Development*, Oxford: Oxford University Press.

Maddison, A. (1993), 'Average Age Gross Stock of Non Residential Structures and of Machinery and Equipment', Worksheet data supplied to the author by Angus Maddison, November 16.

Nelson, R.R. (1964), 'Aggregate Production Functions and Medium-Range Growth Projections', *American Economic Review*, 54 (5), September, pp. 575–605.

Romer, P.M. (1986), 'Increasing Returns and Long-Run Growth', *Journal of Political Economy*, 94, October, pp. 1002–37.

Solow, R.M. (1988), 'Growth Theory and After', *American Economic Review*, 78 (3), June, pp. 307–17.

Wolff, E.N. (1991), 'Capital Formation and Productivity Convergence over the Long-Term', *American Economic Review*, 81 (3), June, pp. 565–79.

4. The Role of Convergence in Trade and Sectoral Growth

Erik Beelen and Bart Verspagen[1]

1. INTRODUCTION

The title of this volume refers to catching-up, forging ahead, and falling behind. The first of these three descriptions of growth trends has gained much attention recently. The last two, however, have received far less attention. This is an unfortunate tendency, since the problems facing the poorest countries are more adequately described by falling behind from *their* perspective, and forging ahead from the *first world* perspective.

This chapter will therefore look at catching-up *and* falling behind (or convergence and divergence, alternatively). Its aim will be to apply a theoretical framework that can account for catching-up and falling behind, thereby attempting to build a bridge between the two different 'crafts' that have emerged in modern economics: development theory and growth theory. As this is quite an ambitious aim, the reader should not expect to find a complete framework that can be used to solve the most pressing problems with regard to development gaps. The level of expectations should rather be set to an exploratory analysis of some recent ideas.

The analysis will start from a description of some empirical trends, outlining where convergence applies, and where it is not a relevant concept. This will be conducted in Section 2, where some well-known datasets will be used to outline some general trends at the aggregate level.

Section 3 will then use a sectoral dataset to explore some of the sectoral dimensions of the convergence process. Although there are a lot of drawbacks with regard to the data used, some stylized facts clearly emerge from the analysis. Section 4 will then look at the interaction between convergence in growth rates (at the sectoral level) and specialization patterns. This is where the main theoretical framework will be outlined, and where some additional empirical results with regard to specialization will be presented. Section 5 will summarize the main line of thought and the main conclusions.

2. CATCHING-UP AND CONVERGENCE: WHERE IT APPLIES, AND WHERE NOT

With the advent of 'new growth theory', the issue of converging per capita income levels has gained much attention from mainstream economists recently (see Levine and Renelt 1992 for an overview of some recent empirical work). While this stream of literature on an 'old' topic has revealed many interesting findings, its narrow focus on convergence of per capita income levels also gives the reader a fairly one-sided interpretation of the facts of international growth rates.[2] This section is aimed at outlining some of the limitations of the usefulness of the notion of convergence in describing growth trends. It will do this mainly by summarizing some empirical trends known long before the recent interest in the topic.

The first limitation lies in the geographical dimension. In its simplest form, a theory of convergence would predict that the (initially) poorest countries expand most rapidly in the subsequent period. Such a conclusion could be reached from a simple argument based on the international diffusion of knowledge, or from a more neoclassical framework based on decreasing marginal returns to capital. However, the empirical facts on international growth in the postwar period do not support this simple interpretation of the convergence hypothesis.

Figure 4.1 shows convergence trends for different groups of countries.[3] The indicator is taken from Soete and Verspagen (1993a), and is defined as $(1/n)\sum_i |\ln Y_i - \ln Y^*|$. Y denotes per capita income, a subscript i $(1...n)$ denotes a country, and a * denotes a (weighted) sample mean of some reference group of countries ($Y^* = \sum Q/\sum N$, where Q is GDP and N is population). Thus, the indicator gives the average (logarithmic) deviation from the per capita income in the reference group of countries. A declining (increasing) trend indicates convergence (divergence) to (from) the target. The data used are taken from Summers and Heston (1991). GDP is measured in PPPs relative to the USA. In Figure 4.1, the reference group are the richest countries of the sample (OECD), so that the lines measure convergence to the *global* (rather than some local) frontier.

The figure clearly indicates that convergence is relevant for isolated groups of countries, but not for the world as a whole. The groups for which convergence is present over most of the period are the OECD countries and the oil-exporting countries. In the OECD, the convergence trend reverses to a weak divergence trend from 1975 onwards. For the Asian countries, convergence starts around 1973, and goes on into the 1980s. In Latin-America and Africa, divergence takes place rather than convergence.

Figure 4.1.   Per capita income differences relative to the OECD, 5 groups of countries, 1960–1985

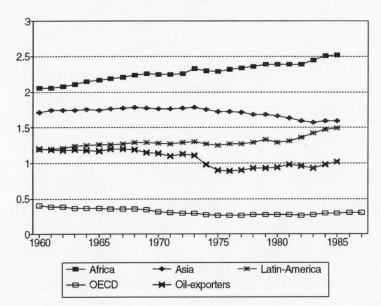

Thus, these results support Baumol's (1986) conclusion about 'convergence-clubs' (i.e., a group of countries converging to each other), and point against the simple interpretation of convergence on a global scale introduced above. The key concept explaining the existence of these convergence-clubs seems to be Abramovitz' (1979) 'social capability'. Rather than automatically assimilating knowledge spillovers, countries have to invest in a capacity to do so. This involves, among many other things, training of the labour force, political stability, building of financial institutions, and the development of a proper infrastructure. A model that attempts to take some of these factors into account is developed and tested in Verspagen (1991, 1993).[4]

Another element of the geographical specificity of convergence trends has been pointed to in a paper by Durlauf and Johnson (1992). They introduce the notion of local versus global convergence. The idea of local convergence may build upon the notion that spillovers and imitation are mainly taking place between similar, or nearby, countries. In terms of the indicator above, one could capture this by substituting the global frontier Y^* by a local average Y', which is defined as the intra-group (weighted)

*Figure 4.2.   Differences in per capita income relative to group-average
5 groups of countries, 1960–1987*

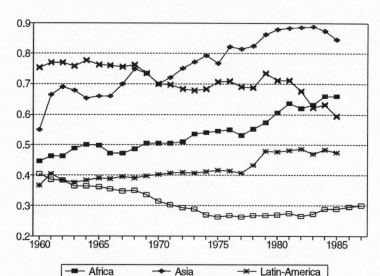

mean value of per capita income.

The trends for this new indicator are depicted in Figure 4.2. For the case of Asia, the differences with the previous figure are striking. The local trend points to divergence rather than convergence. This is mainly due to the strong expansion of the Japanese economy over the 1960s and 1970s, which was too rapid for the other countries to catch up to, and the strong expansion of some of the NICs during the 1970s and 1980s. However, Asia as a whole was able to catch up to the global trend, which was somewhat slower. In the case of Latin-America, the OECD, the oil-exporters and Africa, the trend does not change so much.

The conclusion from Figures 4.1 and 4.2 is therefore that convergence has a strong geographical dimension. In other words, whether or not one finds convergence between countries depends both on the group of countries under consideration, and to which frontier convergence is assumed to take place. In any case, convergence seems strong among developed market economies, and less strong among less developed countries.

A second point about convergence is that it is highly time-specific. Figure 4.3 serves to illustrate this. The figure applies the same indicator as above to Maddison's (1991) sample of 16 countries (the weighted mean value used is also for these 16 countries).[5] Clearly, convergence is taking place only in the period directly before and after the second world war. In the period before (mainly the Great Depression), the convergence trend is weak, as is indicated by a statistical test on the same data in Soete and Verspagen (1993a). For the first 30 years of the century, the trend is mainly flat. During the most recent period (from the 1980s onwards), the convergence trend also flattens.

Figure 4.3.   Convergence and divergence in 16 OECD countries, 1900–1989

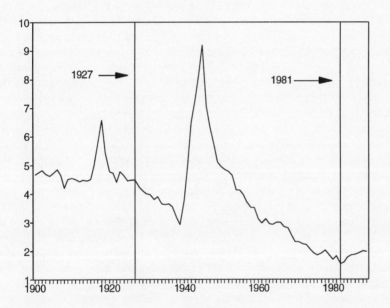

Abramovitz (1992) has given a detailed historical explanation of why convergence was so strong in the postwar period. Maddison (1992) and Nelson (1991) also provide useful elements of such an explanation. This point is not pursued any further here. For the present purpose, it is sufficient to point out that besides being specific in the geographical dimension, convergence is also specific in time.

The last observation about convergence that will be made in this section regards the scope of the process. Most authors have focused on per capita income when looking at convergence trends. However, convergence of per capita income levels is realized by an economic mechanism which is not limited to this variable only. Starting from a convergence theory that takes into account interactions between different parts of the economic system (such as knowledge production, international markets, and governmental policies), convergence can be expected to take place in other fields, such as production structure or technology efforts, too. Again, research in the institutional and historical tradition (see for example the contributions by Abramovitz and Freeman to this volume) has highlighted these interactions.

In the more empirical tradition that this chapter is written in, among others Fagerberg (1988) and Soete and Verspagen (1993a) have shown that convergence takes place in other fields too. They have, for example, looked at convergence in the field of technology, by applying patent and R&D indicators to the topic, and find similar trends as in the case of per capita income. Using an indicator directly linked to international growth, Soete and Verspagen (1993b) have looked at convergence or divergence in the field of international trade and specialization patterns, approaching the issue of convergence from the 'structural side'. They found that for the period 1970–85, specialization patterns in the OECD countries were strongly converging.

Although there are many more specific empirical observations worth making about convergence, the present chapter will not attempt to do so. This task is left for other contributors to this volume (see for example, the chapters by Dowrick and Wolff). The rest of the chapter will instead pick up the analysis along the lines of Soete and Verspagen (1993b), i.e., from a structural perspective. Structural change over time and structural differences between countries have been an important element in the theory of growth based on the work of Pasinetti (1981) (see Soete and Verspagen 1993b and Verspagen 1993 for some applications). By linking this literature to the work in the field of convergence, the remainder of this chapter will attempt to present a 'structuralist' explanation for the dynamics of catching-up, forging ahead and falling behind.

3. THE SECTORAL DIMENSION OF CATCHING-UP AND CONVERGENCE

A number of studies have looked at the sectoral dimension of catching up. Hansson and Henrekson (1991) consider nine manufacturing industries, and seven non-manufacturing industries in a sample of 14 OECD countries for the period 1970–85. While their tests based on coefficients of variation and mean levels of total factor productivity give ambiguous results, they find in a more sophisticated regression analysis that catching-up has been relevant in the nontradables sectors, but not in the tradable sectors.

Dollar and Wolff (1988) consider a sample of thirteen countries and 28 manufacturing industries. They look only at labour productivity, and come to the conclusion that convergence has taken place in each of the industries over the 1963–82 period, although at different paces. They put forward two different explanations for this convergence trend: international diffusion of technological change, and changes in international differences in the capital–output ratio. They also compare sectoral convergence trends with aggregate (i.e., total manufacturing) trends, and come to the conclusion that differences in the employment mix (i.e., differences in employment structure over sectors) between countries cannot explain aggregate convergence.

The hypothesis that changes in the employment mix are a factor in explaining aggregate convergence is also tested in Dowrick (1989). He applies a Cobb–Douglas-based model to a sample of 23 OECD countries, and distinguishes between agriculture, services and manufacturing. His conclusion is that changes in the employment mix cannot explain the observed catching-up, which supports the finding of Dollar and Wolff for manufacturing.

The hypothesis that has been investigated by Dowrick and Dollar and Wolff provides a direct link to the structuralist view on convergence that has been introduced above. However, as these authors have shown, the empirical case for such a direct interpretation does not seem to be very strong. Therefore, a convincing argument for the empirical and theoretical significance of the production and specialization structure will have to be based on a more elaborate line of thought.

The present chapter will try to develop such a theoretical approach along two different lines. The first one concerns the sectoral dimension of convergence, and is pursued in this section. The second line concerns the aspect of international trade and specialization, and is presented in the next section.

In order to study the sectoral dimension of catching-up, this section will use a dataset with 14 sectors. The principal breakdown of sectors is by the ISIC classification, revision 2. The level of aggregation is two or three digit. The sectors used are the following (numbers between brackets are the codes used to reference the sectors, total manufacturing is indicated by 3):

food, drinks and tobacco (31); textiles and leather (32); wood and products (33); paper and publishing (34); industrial chemicals (35A); rubber and plastic products (35B); glass, stone and clay (36); basic metals (37); fabricated metal (381); nonelectrical machinery (382);

electricals (383), transport equipment (384); instruments (385); other manufacturing (39).

The first analysis carried out looks at sectoral trends in catching up or convergence. Following some of the work summarized above, an indicator is constructed which summarizes the differences in labour productivity in a group of OECD countries. The principal set of countries consists of Belgium, Germany,[6] Denmark, Spain, France, the United Kingdom, Greece, Italy, the Netherlands, Portugal, Austria, Australia, Canada, Finland, Japan, Norway, New Zealand, Sweden, Turkey, the USA and Yugoslavia. However, because the dataset is not altogether complete, the statistics presented for specific sectors might exclude some of these countries.

The indicator is based on sector-wise labour productivity. The data are taken from the UNIDO industrial statistics database. Labour productivity is defined as value added (in 1980 dollars) per employee. No correction for purchasing power parities or hours worked is made, mainly because of a lack of adequate data in this large sample of countries (see among others Van Ark 1993, for a more adequate procedure in a smaller country sample). The indicator is again defined as $(1/n)\sum |\ln y_i - \ln y^*|$, where y is labour productivity, and i and $*$ denote a country and a (weighted) sample average, respectively.

Figure 4.4 summarizes the findings for the movement in this indicator. Each point in the figure gives a combination of an initial value of the coefficient (horizontal axis) and a subsequent one (vertical axis). Thus, if any point is below the 45-degrees line (indicated by the dashed line), this means the sector in question has displayed a convergence tendency over the period under consideration. A point above the 45-degrees line indicates divergence. For each sector, there are two points. One of them corresponds to the period 1963–73, and the other one to the period 1973–88. The two points are connected by an arrow, with the one for the last period at the arrow-head, and the one for the first period at the base.

In general, there is a tendency for the points to be below the 45-degrees line, which indicates that convergence is a more common phenomenon than divergence. There are 17 points in the convergence area of the graph, versus 11 points in the divergence area.[7] Distinguishing between periods, it is clear that convergence is more common in the first period. Out of a total of 14 points referring to the first period, there are 10 located in the convergence area. For the second period, exactly half of the points, i.e., seven, are in the convergence area.

The tendencies displayed in the graph can be summarized by forming four different categories of sectors. The first category consists of sectors which have been in a situation of convergence for the whole period 1963-

Figure 4.4. The evolution of sectoral technology gaps, 1963–1973 and 1973–1988

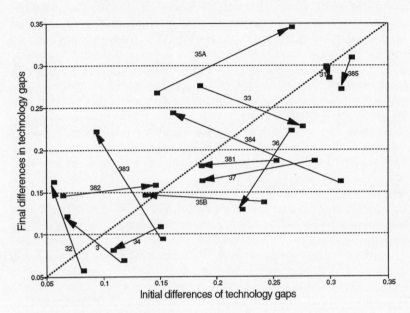

88. These sectors are:

paper and publishing; glass, stone and clay; basic metals; fabricated metals; instruments.

Second, there is a group of sectors showing convergence in the first period, but divergence afterwards. These sectors are

total manufacturing; textiles; rubber and plastic products; electricals; transport equipment.

Third, there are two sectors which transformed from diverging to converging:

wood and products; food, drinks and tobacco.

Finally, there are two sectors which have shown divergence over the total period 1963–88:

industrial chemicals; machinery.

These results show that the slowdown in aggregate convergence that was found in the first section, can only be confirmed for some manufacturing sectors (four out of 13 sectors, as well as manufacturing as a whole). Looking in more detail at the sectors in which divergence has occurred over (a subset of) the 63–1988 period, it is found that most 'high-tech' sectors are found in this set: chemicals; rubber and plastic, machinery; electricals; transport equipment. In fact, instruments is the only sector in which technology plays a large role, and convergence has occurred over the whole 1963–88 period.

In order to explain the sector-wise differences in the coefficients of variation over the long period 1963–88, a simple linear model is applied, which is based on the catching-up approach. The equation is as follows

$$\Delta G_{ij} = c_i + \alpha_j \, P_{ij} + \beta_j \, G_{ij}. \tag{4.1}$$

G is the technology gap, and is defined as the log of the ratio of labour productivity in the leading country and the follower country (i), P is the number of patents per employee, and j denotes a sector. This model takes an essentially dynamic approach, in which the motion of one variable (G) is assumed to depend on the level of others (c, P), as well as its own level. It thus assumes that the change in the technological gap is a function of a country-specific constant, sector-specific influences related to technological activities in the follower country (P), and technological spillovers (G), which are also sector-specific.

The constant is assumed to be positive, and α and β are assumed to be negative. This means that catching-up and falling behind are both possible. However, the case of falling behind is limited to countries which have a 'too small' technology gap. In fact, falling behind occurs when the initial technology gap is smaller than the *equilibrium technology gap*, which is a positive value found at $-(\alpha_j P_{ij} + c_i)/\beta_j$. As is argued in Verspagen (1991), it seems to be the case that a 'too large' technology gap can also be a reason for falling behind, something which is relevant for most of the developing countries.

The speed of catching-up, or the range of technology gaps for which catching-up will take place, can be increased in three ways. The first is by increasing β, which will bring the equilibrium value of the technology gap down. The model here assumes that β cannot be influenced by policy, but is a function of the specific technology underlying the production process in the sector.

The remaining two possibilities for speeding up the catching-up process are assumed to be subject to domestic effort, either by government or by private initiative. The second way is by bringing c_i down, which also reduces the equilibrium gap. It is assumed that this country-specific constant is related to the social capability to catch up, so one would typically expect bringing down c_i involves government policies such as improving the education of the labour force. Finally, the equilibrium value of the technology gap can be decreased by expanding the domestic technological efforts, or in terms of the model, by increasing P.

The model is estimated for a pooled sample of eleven manufacturing industries and sixteen countries. The first difference of G is calculated over the 1963–88 period, and the value of G for 1963 appears on the rhs. P is measured by the number of patents issued in the USA per employee, averaged over the 1963–88 period. The USA is left out of the regressions, because a bias in the patenting variable can be expected (due to a 'home advantage').

The results of the estimation are documented in Table 4.1. The results for the social capability variable (i.e., the country-wise constant) are quite plausible. The relatively backward countries in the sample almost all turn up with high values of the constant, which indicates their limited social capability to assimilate technology spillovers (the countries are listed in descending order of the constant). The disparity between the country with the largest constant (Portugal) and the one with the lowest value (Belgium), is a factor 3.5, which is quite large.

Turning to the sectoral estimates, it turns out that the catching-up variable is negative and significant in each sector. Thus, although some of the sectors have shown a net diverging trend, it seems to be the case that even for diverging cases spillovers are relevant, they are just counteracted by other forces, and/or the value of the catching-up parameter is too small.

Looking at the magnitude of the estimates, it turns out that the sectors with low technological content (such as textiles, glass etc., fabricated metal) are characterized by high values of the catching-up coefficient. Instruments, and to a lesser extent electricals, are exceptions to this rule. Chemicals ranks as the sector with the lowest spillover rate. The economic interpretation of this ordering seems to be that in sectors where the technological content is high, there is less scope for imitation, whereas if the technology in question is well established, imitation is easier.

Turning, finally, to the patent variable, it turns out that it is significant only in a number of cases. These sectors are textiles, glass etc., fabricated metal, and electricals. With the exception of the last, these are all low-tech sectors. This is consistent with the results in Soete (1987), who has also found that technological competition is important in some of the low-tech sectors. These results indicate that technological improvements in low-tech sectors might form a window of opportunity (Perez and Soete 1988).

Table 4.1.   Estimation results for equation (4.1)

Country	D_c	t	Sector	G_0	t	P	t
Portugal	0.093	8.144	Textiles	-0.065	-5.338	-0.376	-2.702
Yugoslavia	0.080	7.778	Glass etc.	-0.063	-7.826	-0.054	-2.399
Greece	0.076	10.135	Fabricated metal	-0.063	-8.071	-0.019	-1.647
New Zealand	0.059	3.406	Instruments	-0.058	-10.583	-0.003	-2.120
Turkey	0.053	6.066	Electrical	-0.048	-5.131	-0.013	-1.932
Austria	0.052	6.639	Food	-0.047	-8.499	-0.215	-1.356
Australia	0.047	6.798	Transport	-0.047	-6.105	-0.019	-0.848
Norway	0.045	6.896	Machinery	-0.044	-5.087	-0.005	-1.056
Italy	0.040	6.330	Basic metals	-0.043	-5.701	-0.054	-1.191
Sweden	0.039	3.810	Refined Oil	-0.039	-3.699	0.007	0.621
Netherlands	0.038	4.264	Chemicals	-0.035	-5.261	-0.003	-0.587
Spain	0.037	5.349					
Canada	0.036	4.313					
France	0.033	4.647					
Finland	0.030	3.978					
United Kingdom	0.029	4.054					
Germany	0.029	3.376					
Denmark	0.028	3.943					
Japan	0.027	2.891					
Belgium	0.026	3.582					

Summarizing, the regression shows that there are indeed significant differences between sectors and countries with regard to their catching-up behaviour. Although difficult to catch in any statistical relationship, this is an indication that the growth performance of a country is related to an interconnected set of factors, such as the structural mix of its production and its social capability to assimilate knowledge spillovers.

The outcomes of this analysis show that in addition to the geographical and historical specificity of the convergence process, there is also an element of sector-specificity, even within manufacturing. From a theoretical point of view, this conclusion underlines the importance of the sectoral mix of a country for its catching-up potential. This is true even if one abstracts from dynamic aspects such as shifts in the employment mix (as tested for by Dowrick and Dollar and Wolff).

4. CATCHING-UP, TRADE AND SPECIALIZATION

The facts about catching-up and growth are by now fairly well established. Some of these facts have been summarized above, or have been given a specific interpretation in a sectoral context. However, catching-up is a phenomenon that has mostly been addressed in the area of growth. Nevertheless, in a world where countries which are interacting heavily by means of international trade and mobility of production factors (labour, capital and knowledge), one could expect to see the convergence trends in the field of growth to be reflected in other areas too.

The work on the interaction between catching-up and trade has mainly focused on the question to what extent the volume of trade relative to domestic production facilitates the working of spillovers (see for example Helliwell and Chung 1991, Helliwell 1992, Nelson 1991). Soete and Verspagen (1993b) have also looked at convergence trends in the field of international specialization. The evidence in that paper seemed to be quite strong from a statistical point of view, but the approach lacked a clear theoretical foundation.

This section will modestly attempt to provide such an explanation, along with the presentation of some additional evidence concerning convergence of specialization patterns. Pasinetti (1981) has argued that the extent to which the specialization structure of a country is similar to that of the countries operating at the technological frontier, determines the degree to which this country can catch up.[8] This is a clear and intuitive notion, which concerns the relevance of the knowledge developed in the leading country for the follower country. The regressions in the previous section look at this point in a slightly different way, by showing that the extent to which a follower country's sectoral mix is concentrated in sectors with high rates of technology spillovers, determines the catching-up potential.

However, there is also a reverse causation effect. Under the influence of knowledge spillovers, a country might change its specialization structure in such a way as to become more similar to the structure found in the frontier country. There are supply-side factors as well as demand-side factors which accommodate such a shift. On the supply side, it seems obvious to reverse the Pasinetti argument, stating that in order to absorb knowledge spillovers, a country should change its production structure, so that it becomes more adapted to receiving spillovers. Although the evidence (Dollar and Wolff, Dowrick) discussed above seems to indicate that this effect is not relevant, it is clear that many so-called industrialization policies (for example in the NICs), have been aimed at least partially at this effect. One reason why one does not find this effect in the data might be that studies aimed at measuring sectoral convergence have mainly been performed for a limited sample of countries, which already have quite similar production structures.

An additional supply-side argument is that the high-tech industries (or alternatively, the ones in which the frontier countries are specialized) generally seem to be the ones which yield higher value added per unit of production. This is consistent with the view that in high-tech production activities, there is more scope for monopoly rents (see Soete and Verspagen 1993b). This would provide an incentive for followers to develop capabilities in these activities, thereby implying convergence of specialization structures. Of course, the entrance of new groups of producers in these high value-added activities implies the erosion of the monopoly rents of the leaders. This in turn might imply rent-seeking activities of the most advanced firms (countries) in the form of new innovative efforts, giving rise to forging ahead. This would imply a diverging world economy, and give the whole theory the flavour of long-wave theory (see for example Kleinknecht 1987, Kleinknecht *et al.* 1992).

The demand-side effect that leads to convergence in specialization patterns can also be found in Pasinetti's (1981) book. Starting from a dynamic theory of consumption (building on the work by Engel) Pasinetti shows that the emergence of important structural changes is unavoidable for an economy increasing its per capita income. The reason for this is that income elasticities of consumption change with the value of per capita income itself. With the level of per capita income growing, the importance of luxury goods will become higher and higher, and there will be an incentive for economies to produce these goods domestically instead of importing them.

So far, the analysis has mainly focused on catching-up and convergence. There is, however, a natural way in which falling behind enters the theory. In an evolutionary interpretation (see Nelson and Winter 1982, Silverberg 1988), the struggle for market shares can be represented as a process in which agents (countries) learn, and realize growing or declining market shares depending on their relative competitiveness. In such an interpretation, the market would no longer be regarded as a mechanism leading to some (optimal) allocation of production factors, but rather as a selection environment that imposes some tendency for the economy to change. This tendency does not necessarily have some optimal direction, just as biological evolution does not have a specific aim.

In fact, at the individual (firm) level, the selection process will yield winners as well as losers. Interpreted in this way, the above theory could be interpreted as a struggle for market share in which at some stage some agents may benefit from knowledge spillovers, and thereby realize relatively high competitiveness, and thus high growth rates. This process, initially induced by short-run increases in market shares, may lead to intertemporal economies of scale in the form of learning effects, and thereby lead to cumulative causation in a 'Kaldor-style'. In an evolutionary setting, this might be interpreted as a manifestation of the local character of evolutionary improvements.

However, the success of entry into the initially high-tech markets will be dependent on a number of issues. Clearly, not all countries will be able to make this entry. The concept of social capability is highly relevant here, but there are also specific historical circumstances or coincidences which might play a role in this respect. In any case, the evolutionary view of the market as a selection environment clearly suggests that there are, besides the winners, also losers. These losers might be found among the initially leading countries, but also, and foremost, among the initially very backward countries. The reason for this is that the initially weak position of these countries prevents them from competing successfully with other imitators which are closer to the frontier-technology. Due to the local character of evolutionary improvements, this might lead to a lock-in of low growth paths.

Thus, an initial 'small' backlog of knowledge might prove to be an advantage, since it provides an opportunity for imitation. However, an initially very large backlog of knowledge is likely to provide a less strong starting position, both with regard to the leading countries, and with regard to the other imitators, which are closer to the frontier. This provides an interpretation of why South Korea was able to make an entrance into the chip-market in the 1980s, but Uganda would not be.

All these arguments show the relevance of looking at the postwar convergence trend from a broad view, including not only growth, but also

other economic trends, as well as social and political factors. In fact, much
of the work in the convergence area has taken such a broad perspective
(for example, Abramovitz 1992, Maddison 1992, Nelson 1991, Dosi and
Freeman 1992). This chapter does not attempt to take such an overall
view. Instead, it tries to look in a systematic way at one aspect of convergence that has not caught so much attention: convergence in specialization
patterns and its relation to overall growth performance.

Soete and Verspagen (1993b) have found that for almost all manufacturing sectors (food products and textiles were the exceptions), specialization patterns have been converging. Their approach was to look at
Revealed Comparative Advantage (RCA) indices over the period 1970–88,
and to see whether or not the intercountry dispersion of these indices
within one sector has grown. Their main result was that for the period
1970–88 as a whole, intercountry dispersion has declined, although this
trend may vary for different subperiods within particular sectors. They did
not find any general trend for convergence in specialization to slowdown
over the 1980s.

Figure 4.5.   Convergence of specialization patterns, 1970–1988

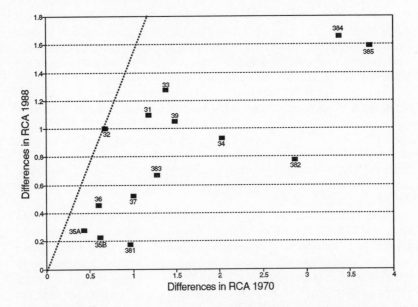

The approach here consists of comparing the results derived by Soete
and Verspagen (1993b) with the sectoral catching-up trends presented in
the previous section. Thus, we start by setting up Figure 4.5 which

illustrates the convergence trends in the field of specialization. The graph is similar to Figure 4.1 above, but it includes only one point per sector. The reason for this is that, like Soete and Verspagen (1993b), the analysis concentrates on a single period (1970–88). The indicator used in the graph measures the intercountry dispersion of specialization patterns within one sector. The exact definition is $(1/n)\Sigma(\ln R)^2$, where R is RCA, defined as the country's export share in sector j over its export share in total manufacturing exports.

As before, converging sectors occur below the 45-degrees line, which is again drawn as the dashed line. This time, it is clear that all sectors have been converging over the period under consideration. Textiles, which is on the edge of convergence and divergence, might be called the only exception to this rule. There are four sectors in which the initial cross-country disparity was quite large. These are paper and publishing, machinery, transport equipment, and instruments. Only the last two of these are still characterized by relatively high dispersion in 1988, although even these sectors have shown a sharp tendency for convergence.

Thus, in spite of the fact that in terms of labour productivity catching-up trends have weakened over the 1970–88 period, convergence in specialization seems not to have lost pace over this period. In theoretical terms, this might be explained by the following reasoning.[9] Interpreted along the lines set out above, the catching-up process has at least two different, although strongly complementary, modes. One is by means of the mechanism of technology spillovers, while the other one is by means of structural change. International specialization trends are an important component of the latter.

These two different modes of convergence are not likely to be synchronized in time. Before any convergence in terms of specialization structure can take place, the follower country must first catch up in terms of competitiveness. Therefore, one would expect technology spillovers to be most important initially. Once the catching up process has gained momentum, a convergence trend with regard to specialization structures sets in.

Naturally, catching-up comes to an end when the gap is at its equilibrium level. Thus, when productivity in the follower country has reached a level close to that of the leader, technology spillovers cease. The available evidence (Section 2) suggests that this has been an important factor behind the slowdown of convergence witnessed at the aggregate level from the early 1980s onwards (see Abramovitz 1992, Soete and Verspagen 1993a).

However, there is no reason at all why the process of convergence of specialization structures should come to an end simultaneously with the slowing down of technology spillovers. In fact, due to the time lags that have been discussed, the cessation of spillovers occurs before a full convergence of specialization structures has occurred. This view seems to be consistent with the evidence presented here. Extrapolating the argument, one might expect that at some stage, convergence in specialization structures would come to an end, as it loses its momentum in the form of productivity convergence. It is hard, however, to predict how long the period would be before such a trend would become visible. In any case, due to the slow speed at which specialization patterns tend to adjust, this would seem to be a matter of decades rather than years.

In an attempt to provide a somewhat more systematic treatment of the convergence in specialization patterns, a regression approach is adopted. The model for the regression looks as follows.

$$\Delta R_{ij} = c_i + \alpha_{rj} R_{ij} \qquad (4.2)$$

In order to underline the lag between convergence trends in productivity (per capita income) and specialization patterns, the equation is estimated for the 1973–88 period, for which it has been shown above that per capita GDP convergence began to slow down. Just as in the previous regression, there is a country-wise constant, which means that countries might show an inherent tendency to increase (positive constant) or decrease (negative constant) specialization. The results of the estimation are in Table 4.2.[10]

With regard to the country constants, there are only a few significant ones. These are Yugoslavia and Turkey (positive) and Sweden (negative). This means that there do not seem to be many country-specific tendencies to specialize or despecialize, but that these trends rather depend on general mechanisms. With regard to the estimated coefficients on initial RCA, almost all sectors have a significantly negative sign, which points to convergence. Textiles (insignificantly negative) and wood (insignificantly positive) are the two exceptions to this. Chemicals, oil, and low-tech metal sectors are among the ones with high coefficients (0.03–0.02), and the more high-tech sectors (electricals and instruments) as well as food are among the ones with low coefficients. Comparing this ordering with the one obtained in the regression on productivity gaps, it appears that they are quite different. This points to the fact that convergence in productivity levels and specialization structures are indeed two processes which are not straightforwardly connected.

The results of the regression analysis, as the previous results in Soete and Verspagen (1993b), have some obvious relations to other parts of the literature. First, the work by Archibugi and Pianta (1992) has examined a similar convergence model in the context of technological specialization of the most advanced OECD countries. Contrary to the results here, they found a divergence trend over the last decades.

Table 4.2. Estimation results for equation (4.2)

Country	D_c	t	Sector	α_{rj}	t
Australia	0.005	0.697	Food	-0.009	-1.657
Austria	0.003	0.408	Textiles	-0.002	-0.306
Belgium	0.003	0.443	Wood	0.000	0.040
Canada	0.000	0.039	Paper and printing	-0.012	-2.569
Germany	0.001	0.127	Chemicals	-0.021	-2.874
Denmark	0.000	0.040	Refined Oil	-0.030	-4.570
Spain	0.009	1.255	Glass etc.	-0.014	-1.873
Finland	0.005	0.704	Basic metals	-0.027	-3.839
France	0.001	0.094	Fabricated metal	-0.025	-3.195
United Kingdom	-0.011	-1.593	Machinery	-0.021	-5.080
Italy	0.000	0.020	Electrical	-0.011	-1.926
Japan	0.001	0.147	Transport	-0.013	-3.679
Netherlands	-0.003	-0.439	Instruments	-0.011	-2.942
Norway	-0.000	-0.011	Other manufacturing	-0.012	-2.544
New Zealand	-0.020	-3.020			
Portugal	-0.000	-0.040			
Sweden	0.027	3.428			
Turkey	0.039	4.777			
USA	-0.005	-0.746			
Yugoslavia	0.012	1.749			

The interpretation of such a result in the present context is that among these advanced nations, a process of forging ahead of some of the frontier-countries is (again) taking place in the technology field. Along the theoretical lines set out here, this could (eventually) give rise to a new convergence process some time in the long-run future.

Another part of the literature that is related to the results here is the part of trade theory that deals with the (increasing) importance of intra-industry trade (see for example Deardorff 1984). The implication of convergence of specialization is the growth of intra-industry trade, a phenomenon which poses large difficulties for 'traditional' trade theory. Although it is beyond the scope of this chapter to present a framework rich enough to add to this literature, the results do point out that the idea of convergence in trade and technology might provide some useful insights in this field too.

5. SUMMARY AND CONCLUSIONS

The above analysis leads to a somewhat ambivalent conclusion. On the one hand, the summary of convergence trends at the aggregate level has shown that convergence is a highly specific phenomenon, both in time and geography. Additionally, the sectoral breakdown of convergence trends has shown that there is also a sector-specific convergence element. On the other hand, the analysis with regard to other variables than just per capita income has shown that convergence is a process that affects other parts of the economic system than just growth performance.

This empirical conclusion calls for a convergence theory that is broader than just the 'standard' frameworks in the neoclassical or 'Gerschenkron' tradition. These theories can basically be reduced to one equation, either a production function with decreasing marginal returns to capital, or a catching-up equation dealing with knowledge spillovers.

The analysis has presented a 'structuralist' theory as a candidate for such an integrated theoretical framework. This theory starts from the observation that international high-tech markets, which are dominated by technologically leading countries, yield relatively high monopoly rents. Imitation by backward countries tends to destroy these monopoly rents over time, and causes the backward countries to converge to the international frontier.

Of course, this convergence is not unconditional, but depends crucially on variables generally captured under the heading 'social capability', something which also comes out of the above regressions. The imitation tendency not only brings converging per capita income levels, but also converging specialization structures. It has been argued that these two convergence processes will generally not synchronize in time. Convergence of specialization structures is expected to be slow, and may lag behind considerably relative to convergence in per capita income levels.

Forging ahead may occur when erosion of monopoly profits induces firms in the advanced countries to search for new products and technologies. This process might induce, after a new time lag, a new process of convergence. However, the institutional context of the international economy plays an important role in this process. The specific historical and institutional context might well provide important brakes or incentives for this process to take place. For example, the opening up of world markets after the second world war was an essential 'background-element' in order for the above theoretical framework to work out.

Also, there are reasons to expect that the very backward countries are less able to compete successfully in such a process. The reason for this is twofold. First, their social capability is usually low. Second, their initial position relative to other imitators (starting closer to the frontier) gives them an initial disadvantage hard to overcome in the subsequent period.

Although this framework is based upon an interpretation of some empirical trends, it should certainly be made subject to more robust (econometric) tests. This is a subject that is left for future research.

NOTES

1. The authors thank Luc Soete for stimulating discussions on the topics covered in this chapter, and Jan Fagerberg, Nick von Tunzelmann and the participants at the Oslo–conference for helpful comments. The usual disclaimer applies. The research of Bart Verspagen is made possible by a fellowship of the Royal Netherlands Academy of Arts and Sciences.
2. Notable exceptions to this rule are among others Dosi and Freeman (1992) and Maddison (1992).
3. The grouping is as follows. OECD: Australia, Austria, Belgium, Canada, Switzerland, West–Germany, Denmark, Spain, Finland, France, United Kingdom, Greece, Ireland, Iceland, Italy, Japan, Luxembourg, Netherlands, Norway, New Zealand, Portugal, Sweden, Turkey, USA, Yugoslavia. Asia: Burma, China, Hong Kong, India, Israel, Afghanistan, Jordan, South Korea, Sri Lanka, Malaysia, Nepal, Taiwan, Pakistan, Philippines, Singapore, Thailand. Latin–America: Bolivia, Brazil, Barbados, Chile, Colombia, Costa Rica, Dominican Republic, Guatemala, Guyana, Honduras, Haiti, Argentina, Jamaica, Mexico, Nicaragua, Panama, Peru, Paraguay, El Salvador, Surinam, Uruguay. Oil–exporters: Congo, Ecuador, Iran, Iraq, Gabon, Kuwait, Nigeria, Saudi Arabia, Syria, Trinidad and Tobago, Venezuela. Africa: Cape Verdian Islands, Cameroon, Kenya, Egypt, Ethiopia, Guinea, Angola, Burundi, Benin, Central African Republic, Ghana, Gambia, Liberia, Mauritius, Mali, Mauritania, Morocco, Malawi, Niger, Sudan, Senegal, Tanzania, Tunisia, Madagascar, Mozambique, Rwanda, SLE, Somalia, Swaziland, Togo, Tanzania, Uganda, South Africa, Zaire, Zambia, Zimbabwe.

4. The latter provides evidence that Amable's (1993) conclusion with regard to the first is not entirely valid.
5. These countries are: Australia, Austria, Belgium, Canada, Denmark, Finland, France, Germany, Italy, Japan, Netherlands, Norway, Sweden, Switzerland, UK, USA.
6. Germany always refers to West–Germany, since our analysis will only deal with the period before the re-unification.
7. No data are available for other manufacturing, but total manufacturing is included as a separate sector.
8. This argument also bears great similarity to Abramovitz's concept of technological congruence (see his chapter in this volume).
9. There are also many factors influencing specialization, such as country–size, comparative advantages, etc., which play a role in the explanation of the observed trends. These are left out of the analysis here.
10. Regressions with additional explanatory variables have also been run. These are not documented for space considerations. In general, the results for the initial RCA variable remained the same, although the significance of (some of) the country–constants was larger under some specifications. Using patenting as an additional explanatory variable did not yield any significant sector-wise coefficients. The wage rate showed significantly positive estimations, something which is hard to explain from a theoretical point of view. See also Soete and Verspagen (1993b). It is also true that the relatively high sectoral aggregation here covers up more disaggregated trends, which might indeed point in opposite directions in some cases.

REFERENCES

Abramovitz, M. (1979), 'Rapid Growth Potential and its Realisation: The Experience of Capitalist Economies in the Postwar Period', in Malinvaud, E. (ed.), *Economic Growth and Resources, vol. 1 The major Issues*, Proceedings of the fifth World Congress of the International Economic Association, London: Macmillan, 1–51.

Abramovitz, M. (1992), 'Catch-up and Convergence in the Postwar Growth Boom and After', Paper presented at the Workshop on Historical Perspectives on the International Convergence of Productivity, New York, April 23–24.

Amable, B. (1993), 'Catch-up and Convergence: a Model of Cumulative Growth', *International Review of Applied Economics*, 7(1), 1–25.

Archibugi, D. and Pianta, M. (1992), *The Technological Specialization of Advanced Countries*, Boston: Kluwer.

Baumol, W.J. (1986), 'Productivity Growth, Convergence, and Welfare: What do the Long-Run Data Show?', *American Economic Review*, 76 (5), December, pp. 1072–85.

Deardorff, A.V. (1984), 'Testing Trade Theories and Predicting Trade Flows', in Jones, R.W. and P.B. Kenen (eds), *Handbook of International Economics*, Vol. I, Amsterdam: North Holland, 467–517.

Dollar, D. and Wolff, E.N. (1988), 'Convergence of Industry Labor Productivity Among Advanced Economies 1963–1982', *Review of Economics and Statistics*, LXX, 549–58.

Dosi, G. and Freeman, C. (1992), 'The Diversity of Development Patterns: On the Processes of Catching-up, Forging Ahead and Falling Behind', Paper presented at the IEA conference on Economic Growth and the Structure of Long-Term Development, Varenna, Italy, 1–3 October.

Dosi, G., Freeman, C., Nelson, R.R., Silverberg, G. and Soete, L. (eds.) (1988), *Technical Change and Economic Theory*, London: Pinter.

Dowrick, S. (1989), 'Sectoral Change, Catching Up and Slowing Down. OECD Post-war Economic Growth Revisited', *Economics Letters*, 331-5.

Durlauf, S.N. and Johnson, P.A. (1992), 'Local versus Global Convergence across National Economies', *NBER Working Paper*, No. 3996.

Fagerberg, J. (1988), 'Why Growth Rates Differ', in Dosi *et al.* (1988), 432–57.

Hansson, P. and Henrekson, M. (1991), 'Catching Up in Industrialized Countries: A Disaggregated Study', *Working Paper Trade Union Institute for Economic Research*, No. 92.

Helliwell, J.F. (1992), 'Trade and Technical Progress', Paper presented at the IEA conference on Economic Growth and the Structure of Long-Term Development, Varenna, Italy, 1-3 October.

Helliwell, J.F. and Chung, A. (1991), 'Macroeconomic Convergence. International Transmission of Growth and Technical Progress', in Hooper, P. and J.D. Richardson (eds), *International Economic Transactions*, Chicago: The University of Chicago Press, 388–436.

Kleinknecht, A. (1987), *Innovation Patterns in Crisis and Prosperity. Schumpeter's Long Cycle Reconsidered*, New York: Macmillan.

Kleinknecht, A., Mandel, E. and Wallerstein, I. (eds) (1992), *New Findings in Long Wave Research*, London: Macmillan.

Levine, R. and Renelt, D. (1992), 'A Sensitivity Analysis of Cross-Country Growth Regressions', *American Economic Review*, 82(4), 942–63.

Maddison, A. (1991), *Dynamic Forces in Capitalist Development*, Oxford: Oxford University Press.

Maddison, A. (1992), 'Explaining the Economic Performance of Nations 1820–1989', Paper presented at the Workshop on Historical Perspectives on the International Convergence of Productivity, New York, April 23–24.

Nelson, R.R. (1991), 'Diffusion of Development: Post World War II Convergence Among Advanced Industrial Nations', *American Economic Review*, 81(2), 271–5.

Nelson, R.R. and Winter, S.G. (1982), *An Evolutionary Theory of Economic Change*, Cambridge, Mass.: Harvard University Press.

Pasinetti, L.L. (1981), *Structural Change and Economic Growth. A Theoretical Essay on the Dynamics of the Wealth of Nations*, Cambridge: Cambridge University Press.

Pasinetti, L.L. and Solow, R.M. (eds) (1994), *Economic Growth and the Structure of Long-Term Development*, London: Macmillan.

Perez, C. and Soete, L. (1988), 'Catching Up in Technology: Entry Barriers and Windows of Opportunity', in Dosi *et al.* (eds), 458–79.

Silverberg, G. (1988), 'Modelling Economic Dynamics and Technical Change: Mathematical Approaches to Self-Organisation and Evolution', in: Dosi *et al.* (eds.), 531–59.

Soete, L. (1987), 'The Impact of Technological Innovation on International Trade Patterns', *Research Policy*, 16: 101–30.

Soete, L. and Verspagen, B. (1993a), 'Technology and Growth: The Complex Dynamics of Catching Up, Falling Behind and Taking Over', in Szirmai, A., B. Van Ark and D. Pilat (eds), *Explaining Economic Growth*, Amsterdam: Elsevier Science Publishers, 101–27.

Soete, L. and Verspagen, B. (1993b), 'Competing for Growth: The Dynamics of

Technology Gaps', in Pasinetti and Solow (1994).

Summers, R. and Heston, A. (1991), 'The Penn World Table (Mark 5): An Expanded Set of International Comparisons, 1950–1988', *The Quarterly Journal of Economics*, CVI: 1–41.

Van Ark, B. (1993), 'International Comparisons of Output and Productivity. Manufacturing Productivity Performance of Ten Countries from 1950–1990', *Groningen Growth and Development Centre Monograph Series*, No. 1.

Verspagen, B. (1991), 'A New Empirical Approach to Catching Up or Falling Behind', *Structural Change and Economic Dynamics*, 2(2), 359–80.

Verspagen, B. (1993), *Uneven Growth Between Interdependent Economies. The Evolutionary Dynamics of Growth and Technology*, Aldershot: Avebury.

5. Investment and Resource Allocation as Sources of Long-Run Growth

Steve Dowrick

1. INTRODUCTION

In this chapter I will discuss some ideas about sources of economic growth related to the allocation of resources between different activities within the economy. I will address these under the broad headings of sectoral disequilibrium and sectoral technical change, then returns to scale and endogenous growth through investment.

There are two methodological lines running through the chapter. The first is that empirical investigation of the growth relationship can profitably take account of the recent theoretical developments which go under the broad heading of 'new growth theory' or, more aptly, 'endogenous growth theory'. Indeed, I shall argue that such theories have important implications for our interpretation of the causality lying behind empirical relationships. The second methodological line is to suggest that empirical work should utilize appropriate econometric techniques to take account of complex patterns of causation, and in particular that the time-series dimension of data sets should be used to supplement the cross-section information which predominates in the empirical examination of the causes of growth across countries.

A simple exercise in growth accounting suggests that transferring resources from one sector of the economy to another can influence aggregate growth in several ways. On the one hand, to the extent that factors have a higher marginal product in their new activities, then the aggregate growth rate is increased by the reallocation of resources. So, for instance, if labour's marginal product is higher in manufacturing than in agriculture because of some impediment to labour mobility, then an increase in mobility which allows a transfer of labour out of agriculture will increase aggregate growth. This is only a transitory shock to growth. Once the transfer is completed, perhaps because marginal products have been equalized, the aggregate rate of growth of output is no longer stimulated, although the level has been raised. Comparing growth rates across countries and across time, this marginal productivity approach suggests that we can look to rates of transfer of resources between different sectors of the economy – from agriculture to industry to services, from private to public, from domestic market production to exports – as explanations of differences in aggregate economic growth. But such comparisons give us only proximate explanations. What drives the model is the assumed disequilibrium in factor markets which allows a wedge to exist between marginal products in different sectors in the first place. It is the breaking down of the factors promoting disequilibrium which really lies behind the relationship between growth and sectoral transfers.

A second consideration is whether rates of technical progress are inherently different between sectors. It is possible that marginal products might be equalized across sectors, but that nevertheless technical progress, hence the rate of growth of average product, might be faster in, say, manufacturing than in services. If so, aggregate growth would be a function not of the rate of transfer of resources between manufacturing and services, but of the size of the manufacturing sector relative to the size of the service sector.

Under this scenario, technical progress is exogenous to each sector – a function perhaps of both the rate of expansion of the world technology frontier in that sphere of activity and also of the distance of the particular country from that frontier, i.e. its potential for catching-up. But if these rates of technical progress differ across sectors, then a country can increase its overall rate of growth by allocating resources to the sectors where exogenous progress is the fastest. It is in this sense of choosing to harness one's resources to the fastest horse that technical progress can be said to be quasi-endogenous, even though the speed of the various horses may be beyond the influence of any one particular country.

The notion that returns to scale may exert a systematic influence on countries' growth rates has a long history, from the pessimism of Malthus' decreasing returns model which predicts an inability to escape from subsistence, through the Kaldorian focus on Verdoorn's 'law' of scale economies in manufacturing and Arrow's intertemporal economies of learning by doing, through to the recent rediscovery by Romer and others of the importance of increasing returns in models of endogenous growth. The notion that there may be economies or diseconomies of scale at the aggregate level of the economy suggests that growth may depend not only on the allocation of resources between sectors but also on the overall rate of growth of resources, particularly the rate of increase of population and labour force.

An issue related to returns to scale is investment. This has been the focus of a re-awakened interest on the part of the neoclassical theorists who have discovered (or rediscovered) the possibility that long-run growth can be generated in an equilibrium model of decentralized decision-making by self-interested individuals. The key notion in these models is the deceptively simple premise that continued diversion of resources to investment can produce long-run growth, with an addendum that individuals will find it in their interests to continue to so divert resources from immediate consumption. To the non-economist, and probably to most non-neoclassical economists, the first of these notions is blindingly obvious, that investment in buildings, equipment, infrastructure, a store of knowledge, human skills, etc. is both a necessary and sufficient condition for economic growth. Yet the model of growth which has dominated mainstream economics over most of the past four decades has, in its usual interpretations, denied such a proposition. I would contend that despite his own best efforts, Robert Solow's 1956 growth model (allied to what was essentially the same model developed simultaneously in 1956 by Trevor Swan) led the economics profession, or perhaps was led by the profession, into an unproductive backwater.

The essential problem for the neoclassical growth model is that increasing returns to scale for individual producers are incompatible with the price-taking behaviour assumed in the neoclassical model of general equilibrium. Assuming constant returns to scale and a fixed input-output elasticity (Cobb–Douglas) then implies that the marginal product of investment must fall to zero as the capital–labour ratio rises, so even if investment is fixed at some positive rate the economy will grow only until it reaches a point of maximum output per head. In a framework of optimizing choice between current and future consumption, growth will stop earlier, at a point where the discounted utility of the marginal product of investment equals the marginal utility of current consumption. In either case, investment is a source of growth only in the short run, until it runs aground on the rock of decreasing marginal products. Long-run growth has to be tacked on to the model as manna from some technological heaven.

The escape route taken by the recent literature on endogenous growth follows Romer's 1986 title in returning to Kaldorian ideas of increasing returns to scale, made compatible with general equilibrium modelling by some mix of externalities and monopolistic competition. Given such assumptions, it follows that long-run growth is feasible (hurray!) as the outcome of decentralized and rational decision-making. It also follows from the existence of externalities and/or price-making behaviour that private costs and benefits do not capture the full social costs and benefits. So neoclassical luminaries of the profession such as Robert Lucas and Robert Barro are led to the conclusion that public intervention affecting investment, whether in education or industry policy or fiscal policy, has the potential to increase growth and welfare – although they warn that it also has the potential to lower them. Such conclusions are reached too, albeit via a very different route, by Scott (1989).

In fact the key condition for endogenous growth is not aggregate increasing returns. Jones and Manuelli identify the sufficient condition as some positive lower limit to the marginal product of investment. As long as that lower limit is less than the intertemporal discount rate, deferring current consumption will be perceived to be profitable and growth will continue. Such a limit is compatible with convex technologies. Indeed, the mainstream of the economics profession might profitably have learnt this point as long ago as 1960 when another of my Australian colleagues, John Pitchford, pointed out that long–run growth is feasible within the Solow-Swan framework of constant returns if one abandons the constant input-output elasticity formulation of technology and replaces it with a constant elasticity of factor substitution. The Cobb–Douglas formulation imposes a unitary elasticity of substitution, but within the more general framework of CES the elasticity of substitution may be greater than unity, in which case marginal products do not disappear to zero and long-run growth can occur.

It is perhaps ironic that the 'new growth theory' is neoclassical economics finally beginning to catch up on theories of growth which go back at least as far as Schumpeter and Kaldor. Nevertheless, the application of modern modelling techniques to venerable ideas can generate new results. I will proceed in the rest of this chapter to discuss some of the recent theoretical and empirical findings on the sectoral allocation of resources before going on to focus on the role of investment.

2. SECTORAL DISEQUILIBRIUM MODELS, QUASI-ENDOGENOUS TECHNICAL CHANGE AND CROSS-COUNTRY ESTIMATION BIAS

Recent attempts at estimating the effects of resource transfer from one sector to another have followed Feder's (1983) model. He imposes an assumption that there is a constant ratio between the marginal product of a factor in one sector to its marginal product in another sector. He also posits an external effect running from export activity to the rest of the economy. Some algebraic manipulation and simplifying assumptions yield an estimating equation which relates the rate of growth of aggregate output, Y, not only to the weighted sum of aggregate factor inputs, K and L, and to exogenous technical progress, g, but also to the rate of growth of the export sector, $\hat{X}$ (a hat represents a proportionate growth rate).

$$\hat{Y} = \alpha \, \hat{K} + \beta \, \hat{L} + \gamma + \delta \, \hat{X} \qquad (5.1)$$

His estimation on a cross-section of developing countries finds that the coefficient δ is positive which suggests that marginal products are higher in the export sector and/or that there are positive spillovers, implying that faster aggregate growth accrues to those countries which transfer resources to their export sectors.

Ram (1986) used an identical model, only he examined the transfer of resources between the government sector and the rest of the economy. He also found a positive coefficient δ, which he took as evidence of strong positive externalities emanating from government activity. In the case of Ram's analysis, however, there is considerable doubt about the validity of his econometric results because he does not allow for the possible endogeneity of government. We expect external shocks to output to affect national income, hence the demand for government services. This demand-side relationship implies an upward bias in single-equation estimation of the supply-side relationship. Rao's (1989) subsequent analysis of time-series data demonstrates that reverse causation is indeed a significant factor. My own cross-section analysis, Dowrick (1992b), controls for such endogeneity and suggests that Ram's original estimates of government externalities are indeed too high.

These criticisms are not intended to deny that government activity may have some positive external effects, only to point out that simple single-equation estimation may not provide reliable and robust evidence. This criticism of endogeneity can also be applied to the evidence of Feder and others on the positive externalities emanating from activity in the export sector. In the latter case the reverse causation, output growth directly causing export growth, is not particularly plausible. Rather, it is a case of potential missing variables. There may be some other factors such as business ethos or industrial relations which boost productivity growth, hence increasing both aggregate output and export competitiveness simultaneously. Such simultaneous causation can lead to a spurious correlation between export growth and output growth if the underlying factors are not identified.

The best solution to the missing variable problem would obviously be to obtain measures of business attitudes, etc. to include in the empirical analysis. In the absence of such direct measures, however, we can supplement the cross-country information which is typically used in growth regressions with time-series information to construct a panel of data. Analysis of changes over time allows us to control for missing variables, or at least for those such as history and culture which are invariant over time. Time-series data also make available lagged values which can be used as instruments for current endogenous variables.

Greene (1990) gives a good summary of the methods used with panel data to control for unobserved country-specific effects. If we believe that the important missing variables are constant over time within each country, which may well be approximately true over a period of several decades for institutional features such as the industrial relations system, then unbiased estimates of other relationships where variables do change over time may be obtained by taking first differences of the data. This corresponds to the Fixed Effects model where the regression on the panel of data includes a dummy variable for each country. Whilst this procedure yields unbiased estimates, it is inefficient in that it effectively discards all the information contained in the average cross-section data. Generalized Least Squares estimation, as described by Greene, provides more efficient estimation which may retain the desired property of unbiasedness.

I suggest that systems estimation and panel-data estimation are the way ahead for empirical investigation of the causes of growth. In their absence, single-equation cross-country regression results provide little more than a description of the partial correlations to be found in the data. Such correlations are of course of interest as stylized facts, but it is dangerous to use them as evidence of causation without further investigation using supplementary information such as that contained in time series.

Returning to the specification of the relationship between growth and sectoral allocation of resources, note that the relationship in (5.1) above is between output growth and sectoral growth. An alternative specification which has often been used in empirical work is to replace, or supplement, the sectoral growth term, $\hat{X}$, with a level term representing the share of that sector in aggregate output, X/Y:

$$\hat{Y} = \alpha \, \hat{K} + \beta \, \hat{L} + \gamma + \delta \, \hat{X} + \theta \, X/Y. \tag{5.2}$$

Dowrick and Gemmell (1991) show that the coefficient on this additional term can be interpreted as the difference in rates of technical progress between sector X and the rest of the economy. We found, for instance, that technical catch-up in industry was particularly important in explaining the high growth rates of many middle-income economies in the 1960s and 1970s. On the other hand such catching-up did not appear to be taking place in the industrial sectors of the poorest economies, principally located in sub-Saharan Africa, although there was some evidence of technical catch-up in agriculture.

These results highlight one of the additional sources of bias in cross-country growth regressions, bias due to the inappropriate aggregation of dissimilar groups of countries. Our results demonstrated that relationships which hold for the richest countries or the middle-income countries do not necessarily hold for the least developed economies. Indeed, it would be surprising if they did given the plethora of variables such as culture, institutional structure, wars, climate, etc. which undoubtedly do affect growth but are typically missing from our cross-country growth regressions. The appropriate response to this problem is, I suggest, to use standard statistical tests of parameter stability across various sub-groups of countries. The sub-groups might be defined by some measure of level of development or by continent.

Returning to the relationship between government and growth, it is interesting to note that although Ram and others have observed a strong positive correlation with the growth of government, $\hat{G}$, almost all studies report a negative correlation with the size of government, G/Y – see, for instance, Barro (1991). The simple interpretation of this negative correlation is that technical progress in the government sector lags behind that found in the private sector. This could reflect inefficiencies due to lack of market incentives within government, but it could equally well reflect the problems faced by national accounts statisticians in measuring the output of non-marketed government services. Accounting practices vary across countries, but I know that the response of the government statistician in Australia to this problem is to record such non-marketed government output as an index of the measurable inputs of capital and labour. This accounting practice defines away the possibility of any technical progress in government and is one possible explanation of the observed negative correlation between economic growth and the size of government.

Another possible explanation is put up by Barro (1990). His simple model of endogenous growth has government size contributing to growth in a double-edged manner. Government activity is taken to be a productive input into private sector production, albeit with a decreasing effect on private sector marginal productivity. In other words, *ceteris paribus* an increase in government activity will increase the marginal product of capital, providing the incentive for increased private investment which produces higher long-run growth. Everything else is not, however, equal. In particular, government has to finance its activities. In Barro's model, financing requires distortionary taxation. Tax drives a wedge between private returns to investment and social returns, reducing the incentive for private agents to invest and thus reducing the long-run growth rate of the economy. A country will find that it faces a hump-shaped relationship between government size and economic growth. If government is very small, the positive effect of government on private sector productivity dominates the distortionary tax effect, so the marginal net effect of government is positive. Beyond a certain point, however, the tax effect dominates and the net marginal effect of government is negative. Choice of government size to maximize the discounted utility of the representative consumer does not necessarily coincide with the size of government which maximizes growth, but optimal government size is certainly positive.

The Barro argument continues by noting that if government size were the result of a random draw, then we should expect to observe this hump-shaped relationship between government and growth. In practice, however, we observe a monotonic negative relationship. Rather than rejecting the Barro model, this evidence may be taken to suggest that government size is not chosen randomly, rather that it at least approximates the optimal size for each country. We expect countries to have different needs for government services, reflecting perhaps intercountry variation in the problems of public goods and externalities due to geographical, climatic and cultural factors. A country with, say, a high population density and an individualistic culture may need relatively more government intervention to overcome problems of externalities in interactions between individual consumers and producers. If so, it will have to rely more heavily on distortionary taxation which reduces incentives for private investment. A country which faces substantial market failure will exhibit both a large government sector and a slow growth rate relative to some other country with less need for public intervention.

In the Barro model, then, if all countries choose their level of government optimally, cross-section observation will find a negative correlation between government size and growth. But this will reflect an equilibrium relationship, not a direct causal relationship. The equilibrium relationship

Figure 5.1.   Economic growth and government size in the Barro–model

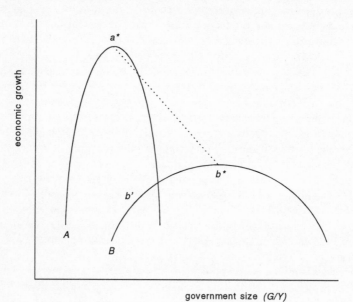

is driven by underlying and probably unobserved variation in the extent of market failure.

This argument is illustrated in Figure 5.1 where it is assumed for simplicity that welfare optimization equates with growth maximization. Country *A* faces a government/growth trade-off represented by the solid line *A*, and it chooses a level of government represented by the point *a**. Similarly for country *B*. The negative cross-section relationship, illustrated by the dotted line *a*b**, should not be interpreted to imply that government in *B* is too large – indeed a reduction in government to the level found in country *A*, moving to the point *b'*, would actually reduce growth and welfare in country *B*.

In some recent work, Dowrick (1992b), I have attempted to test this model of the relationship between government and growth. I note that the price of government services relative to GDP varies considerably over time and across countries, so it is possible to distinguish empirically between the real level of government activity and the size of the financing requirement. I also use panel data to control for fixed country effects, allowing for unobserved differences in the underlying extent of market failure. The results give support for the Barro model, at least amongst the more advanced capitalist economies, finding that *ceteris paribus* government activity does indeed stimulate growth, whilst *ceteris paribus* taxation reduces growth. These results serve as another warning against over-simplistic inference of causation from observation of partial correlations in single-equation regressions.

3. RETURNS TO SCALE AND ENDOGENOUS GROWTH THROUGH INVESTMENT

One of the puzzles of the standard growth-accounting literature has been the observation that physical investment appears to account for only a small part of observed variation in growth rates, whether the variation is examined across time or across countries. Compared with the magnitude of differences in rates of technological progress, the impact of physical investment appears small. This finding is puzzling in the face of the popular view amongst economic historians and others that it is the development of new physical means of production that impelled the first, and subsequent, industrial revolutions.

In the conventional growth-accounting approach where the elasticity of output with respect to capital stock is assumed to equal the share of profits in national income, the marginal effect of a one percent rise in the stock of capital is to increase output by only 0.3 percent or so. Putting it another way, if the real rate of return on capital is ten percent and the capital-output ratio is three, then a rise in the share of GDP devoted to investment from 20 percent to 21 percent would increase the growth rate of the capital stock by one-third of one percentage point and raise annual GDP growth by only 0.1 percentage points. These growth-accounting estimates are supported by econometric estimates of cross-country aggregate production functions as in Barro (1991) and Dowrick (1992a) where real annual rates of return to physical investment are found to be between seven and ten percent. Differences in rates of aggregate investment across countries and across time go some way to explaining differences in GDP growth, but the unaccounted differences are apparently much greater.

There is, however, some recent evidence that the contribution of capital to growth may be severely underestimated by failing to distinguish between different types of investment. DeLong and Summers (1991) argue forcefully that the key to growth is investment in equipment rather than investment in structures and transport. They find evidence that the real rate of return on equipment may be as high as 30 percent. They suggest that much of this return is in the form of external effects on productivity growth in related sectors, citing studies by Jorgenson as supporting evidence. Their evidence is impressive, involving tests for the influence of many other factors including reverse causation.

The main problem with the DeLong and Summers results is that their estimates seem implausibly high. If the annual real rate of return on equipment investment really is over 30 per cent, why are rational agents not busy exploiting such phenomenal returns when real interest rates are typically under five percent. I guess that the authors would reply that private returns are not necessarily so high. But such an answer still requires us to believe that the spillovers are at least as high as the private returns. I find it hard to believe that spillovers are quite so high, but I certainly find their results fascinating and suggest that their findings should be taken seriously – albeit subjected to further rigorous testing.

One plausible interpretation of the DeLong and Summers results is that equipment investment is the principal channel through which advances in technology are diffused both within a country but also, perhaps more importantly, across countries. This interpretation is strongly supported by the finding in their Table V that amongst the high productivity group of 25 countries the impact of equipment investment is strongest in those countries lagging furthest behind the technological leaders. DeLong and Summers are, however, reluctant to come to such a conclusion because such a relationship does not appear to hold for their larger sample of 63 countries. But that failure to hold across a sample of high and low productivity countries is perfectly consistent with the findings of Dowrick and Gemmell (1991) who find evidence to support the 'disadvantage of backwardness' or 'social capability' arguments of Abramovitz (1986). These studies suggest that technological diffusion does not extend to the poorest economies which lack the physical and human capital infrastructure to exploit new techniques and new products.

Another study which disaggregates investment and finds high returns to some parts is Aschauer (1989). He presents evidence that public investment in core non-military infrastructure is highly productive. The core of public investment includes streets and highways, airports, electrical and gas facilities, mass transit, water systems and sewers. Here, the nature of the investments suggests that spillover benefits are particularly important. His work has been subject to some important criticism, particularly with regard to the treatment of causality, but I agree with Munnell's (1992: 195) summing up: 'an even-handed reading of the evidence ... suggests that public infrastructure is a productive input which may have large payoffs.'

These studies by DeLong and Summers and Aschauer imply that the estimation of returns to aggregate investment may miss much that is important in disaggregating investment. Moreover, inappropriate aggregation in regression analysis has the effect not only of averaging out the effects of high return investment and low return investment, it is also likely to bias downwards the estimate of the average effect. For example, if investment in A has a five percent return and investment in B has a 15 percent return, econometric estimation of the return to aggregate investment AB is likely to yield a figure below ten percent.

While noting these important concerns about the use of aggregate investment data, I will nevertheless proceed with investigation of the productivity of aggregate national investment. My aim here is to investigate whether or not returns to capital are decreasing, and whether or not there are spillover effects between economies.

In the introductory section I indicated that increasing returns to scale or, more particularly, a non-diminishing marginal product of investment, are features which can help to explain long-run growth as the endogenous outcome of agents' decisions, rather than as the result of some exogenous force labelled technical progress. Here I will examine some preliminary evidence which can shed light on these relationships.

First, I look at some simple cross-country regressions of growth of real GDP on investment, workforce growth and initial labour productivity. The sample is 113 countries, excluding 25 from the full Summers and Heston (1991) sample of 138 because of gaps in the data coverage or because a country's output is dominated by oil. Growth, $\hat{Y}$, is measured as the annual compound growth rate between 1960–64 and 1985–88, where I take five-year averages at the beginning and end of the time series to minimize

Table 5.1.   Descriptive statistics – means (st. dev.)

		poor economies $n=42$	middle-income $n=32$	rich economies $n=39$
Growth of real GDP (% p.a.)	$\hat{Y}$	3.96 (2.21)	4.38 (1.91)	3.81 (1.49)
Investment share (%)	(I/Y)	12.4 (7.3)	20.1 (8.4)	22.6 (5.9)
Continental investment (%)	$(I/Y)^*$	14.2 (1.6)	17.6 (4.4)	20.4 (4.7)
Growth of workforce (% p.a.)	$\hat{L}$	2.06 (0.57)	2.34 (0.68)	1.75 (1.02)
Real GDP per worker 1960–64 (1985 $US)	y	1584 (667)	4261 (1083)	12238 (4816)

business cycle noise. Growth of the workforce, $\hat{W}$, is measured similarly. Investment, I/Y, is the average ratio of investment to GDP over the whole period at constant international prices. Initial labour productivity, y, is the natural logarithm of average real GDP per member of the workforce 1960–64. I also add a measure of per capita investment in the continent to which a country belongs to test for spillover effects between countries which are geographically related, and a set of dummy variables for each continent to capture unmeasured cultural and historic effects. The continental investment rates are as follows: Africa, 13.2 percent; South America, 17.0 percent; Asia, 16.9 percent; Europe, 25.9 percent; the rest of the world (North America and Pacific), 16.5 percent.

I assume an aggregate production function, $Y = e^{gt} f(K,K^*,L)$ where K is the domestic capital stock and K^* is the capital stock for the continent, L is labour input, and g is the exogenous rate of technical progress which contains a catch-up element. Differentiation tells us that growth in output is a function of the growth of the domestic capital–output ratio, which I assume to be a quadratic function of the gross investment rate, (I/Y). I assume that any spillovers from the foreign capital stock are a function of the change in the foreign capital–output ratio, proxied by $(I/Y)^*$. Furthermore, I take the rate of technical progress to be a linear function of the technology gap, where y is the log of labour productivity relative to the US:

$$\hat{Y} = \alpha_1 \, (I/Y) + \alpha_2 \, (I/Y)^2 + \alpha_3 \, (I/Y)^* + \beta \, \hat{L} + \gamma_1 + \gamma_2 \, y. \qquad (5.3)$$

We can interpret the coefficients as follows. The marginal product of domestic capital is:

$$f_K = \partial \hat{Y}/\partial(I/Y) = \alpha_1 + 2\alpha_2 \, (I/Y), \qquad (5.4)$$

that is to say, we have evidence of increasing or decreasing returns to investment as α_2 is greater than or less than zero.

The spillover from the external capital stock is:

$$(f_{K*} \, K^*/f)(Y^*/K^*) = \partial \hat{Y}/\partial(I/Y)^* = \alpha_3, \qquad (5.5)$$

and the elasticity of output with respect to labour is:

$$f_L L/f = \beta. \qquad (5.6)$$

The production function is homogeneous of degree λ, where λ is the sum of the factor elasticities. Assuming, conservatively, a capital–output ratio of 2, the returns to scale parameter can be calculated approximately as:

$$\lambda \cong \beta + 2[\alpha_1 + 2\alpha_2 \, (I/Y) + \alpha_3]. \qquad (5.7)$$

The regression results are summarized in Table 5.2 below. Descriptive statistics of the variables involved are in Table 5.1. Of course, the qualifications raised earlier about inferences based on single-equation correlations apply here. In particular, these results need to be tested for country-specific unobserved effects and for reverse causation between output growth and investment. So the discussion that follows should be taken as suggestive rather than conclusive.

The marginal productivity of investment appears to lie between nine and 11 percent per year. The insignificant coefficient on the squared investment term in regression 2 implies a lack of evidence of decreasing marginal productivity. Note that the sample contains a very wide range of investment rates, from three to 37 percent of GDP.

There is particularly interesting evidence that investment rates have spillover effects on other countries within the same continent. Regression 3 appears to suggest that productivity growth is above average in Asia and below average in Africa and South America. The African and South American effects disappear, however, when we control for continental investment rates in regression 4, leaving a significant 'Asian effect' of annual productivity growth some 1.3 percent higher than that found in the rest of the world. The implication is that poor performance in Africa and South American economies may be explained by low investment rates in individual countries compounded by low investment in neighbouring

Table 5.2.   Regression coefficients and t-statistics* explaining growth of real GDP 1960–64 to 1985–88

Sample = all countries, *n* = 113

	1.	2.	3.	4.
(*I/Y*)	0.11	0.12	0.095	0.089
	(4.2)	(1.5)	(3.0)	(2.6)
(*I/Y*)²		–0.060		
		(–0.25)		
(*I/Y*)*		0.11		0.11
		(2.0)		(2.4)
$\hat{L}$	0.88	1.11	0.87	1.00
	(4.6)	(4.4)	(4.6)	(4.5)
y	–0.006	–0.008	–0.006	–0.006
	(–3.1)	(–4.7)	(–2.9)	(–2.8)
constant	0.049	0.044	0.057	0.026
	(3.3)	(2.6)	(3.2)	(1.2)
Asia			0.007	0.013
			(1.5)	(3.0)
Africa			–0.006	0.004
			(–1.0)	(0.7)
South America			–0.006	0.000
			(–1.2)	(0.0)
s.e.	0.0163	0.0162	0.0158	0.0158
	0.2562	0.2685	0.3026	0.3082
λ	1.10	1.55	1.06	1.40

* using a heteroscedasticity-consistent covariance matrix.

countries.

Overall, there is some evidence of increasing returns to scale, especially when intra-continental spillovers are taken into account. But before taking these results too seriously, we should investigate whether parameters are stable across different levels of development. To this end, I have divided the sample into three groups based on rankings by average *per capita* real GDP over the period 1960–88 and I have re-estimated the models for each group. The results are summarized in Table 5.3 for two specifications, the first without the quadratic investment term and the second including it. The country groupings are listed in the appendix.

Table 5.3. *Regression coefficients and t-statistics* by development group*

	poor countries $n=42$		middle-income $n=32$		rich countries $n=39$	
(I/Y)	0.149	−0.071	0.008	0.169	0.056	0.056
	(4.0)	(−0.5)	(0.2)	(1.7)	(4.2)	(0.5)
$(I/Y)^2$		0.645		−0.424		0.002
		(1.7)		(−1.4)		(0.0)
$(I/Y)^*$	−0.244	−0.181	0.219	0.221	0.070	0.070
	(−1.3)	(−1.0)	(2.1)	(2.2)	(3.1)	(3.1)
$\hat{L}$	0.83	1.25	1.04	0.98	0.79	0.79
	(2.1)	(2.4)	(1.5)	(1.4)	(5.5)	(5.8)
y	−0.013	−0.013	0.012	0.011	−0.007	−0.007
	(−2.2)	(−2.2)	(1.1)	(1.0)	(−2.0)	(−1.8)
constant	0.129	0.123	−0.128	−0.127	0.061	0.061
	(3.0)	(3.0)	(−1.4)	(−1.5)	(1.9)	(2.0)
Asia	0.014	0.015	0.018	0.016	0.025	0.025
	(2.6)	(3.1)	(2.1)	(2.0)	(6.0)	(5.9)
s.e.	0.0190	0.0187	0.0165	0.0165	0.0064	0.0065
	0.2619	0.2862	0.2525	0.2566	0.8159	0.8102
λ	1.05	1.05	1.48	1.48	1.04	1.05

Parameter stability tests: specification 1, $F_{12,95} = 1.80$ ($p = 0.06$); specification 2, $F_{14,92} = 1.93$ ($p = 0.03$).

It is evident that parameters vary quite significantly across the three development groups. In particular, the marginal product of investment appears to be increasing in the investment rate for the poor countries, constant for the rich countries, and possibly decreasing for the middle-income economies. Although the increasing marginal product in the poor countries is significant only at the ten percent level on this quadratic specification, it is significant at the one percent level on a logarithmic specification not reported here. This evidence suggests that, with the possible exception of the middle-income economies, investment may indeed be an important source of long-run growth as its marginal product does not appear to diminish.

Investment spillovers within continents appear to be significant for the more advanced economies, but not so for the poorest group. This finding is consistent with the Abramovitz hypothesis that successful exploitation of the possibilities opened up by technological transfer depends on a minimum level of development of the domestic infrastructure. This infrastructure might consist of physical items such as transport, power supplies and telecommunications as well as intangible human capital, related to education and training. The poorest group of countries, located mainly in sub-Saharan Africa (see appendix for a listing) appear to be unable to capture spillovers from neighbours' investments.

Only the middle-income group shows evidence of increasing returns to scale, but I note that the overall explanatory power for this group of countries is low and that the standard errors of the coefficient estimates are large, so we cannot reject the hypothesis of constant returns to scale.

There is an interesting indication here that investment may be rather more important than previous studies of aggregate investment and growth accounting have suggested. If the marginal product of capital does not decline with increased capital intensity, we have some vindication for the recent interest amongst theorists in models of endogenous growth. If the spillovers to neighbouring countries are as large as these results suggest, then investment is indeed a major source of growth.

Before reaching any firm conclusions on the basis of these preliminary results, however, it is important to further investigate their robustness, particularly with respect to reverse causation and the effects of missing, country-specific variables. Table 5.4 presents summary results for a slightly smaller sample of 111 countries, again split up into three development groups. Here observations have been taken for each country for every available five-year period, 1950–54, 1955–59 ... 1985–88 (ending with a four-year period because that is all the data that are available). The first period is dropped from the sample in order to make available a full series of lagged investment variables to be used as instruments to control for simultaneous endogeneity.

Table 5.4 reports two sets of results for each development group, reporting the coefficients only for the investment variables which are the subject of interest here. First, the Two Stage Least Squares estimates are reported and then the Generalized Least Squares estimates. The former method of estimation controls for endogeneity, the latter for unobserved country-specific effects.

Diagnostic statistics are reported. They indicate that heteroscedasticity

Table 5.4.   *Panel estimation: instrumental variables and Generalized Least Squares*

	poor countries $n=179$		middle-income $n=282$		rich countries $n=230$	
	2SLS	GLS	2SLS	GLS	2SLS	GLS
(I/Y)	−0.08	−0.13	−0.12	−0.039	0.44	0.60
	(−0.6)	(−1.3)	(−1.1)	(−0.5)	(2.7)	(4.6)
$(I/Y)^2$	0.37	0.63	0.24	0.23	−0.82	−0.92
	(0.8)	(2.2)	(0.9)	(1.5)	(−2.5)	(−3.6)
$(I/Y)^*$	−0.03	−0.05	0.13	0.020	0.21	0.047
	(−0.4)	(−0.5)	(2.4)	(0.3)	(4.2)	(0.9)
s.e. (e_{it})	2.64	2.34	2.47	2.11	1.75	1.49
s.e. (u_i)		1.72		1.35		0.81
adj-R^2	0.176		0.374		0.497	
B–P–G	$X^2(11)=10.2$		$X^2(11)=14$		$X^2(11)=19$	
Reset 2	$t=1.5$		$t=1.0$		$t=1.3$	
Exo-geneity	$t=2.1$		$t=5.8$		$t=4.1$	
GLS vs OLS		$X^2(1)=11.1$		$X^2(1)=31$		$X^2(1)=3.4$

Observations are five-year averages, 1955–59 to 1985–88, for 111 countries. Coefficients and *t*-statistics are reported only for the investment variables. The unreported variables are workforce growth, productivity gap and period dummies.

2SLS is Two Stage Least Squares estimation using the following variables as instruments for investment: lagged investment, price of investment relative to GDP, real per capita GDP, continent dummies. GLS is the Generalized Least Squares regression with random country-specific effects (estimated using the LIMDEP package). The error term is $e_{it} + u_i$ where i indexes country and t time. B–P–G is the Breusch-Pagan test for heteroscedasticity.

Reset 2 is the Reset test for functional form (augmenting the OLS regression with the square of the predicted value). The Exogeneity test reports the *t*-statistic when the OLS regression is augmented by the residual from the instrumenting equation. GLS vs OLS is the Lagrange Multiplier test of the GLS model versus the OLS model.

is not a significant problem and that the functional form is not rejected (on the Reset 2 test). Exogeneity of investment is, however, rejected. Country-specific effects are found to be significant for the poor and middle-income groups but not for the rich countries.

We are now led to a rather more conservative assessment of the importance of investment in promoting medium-term growth. There is some weak evidence of increasing returns to investment in the poor and middle-income countries, but this effect is not statistically significant when simultaneous causation is taken into account. Nevertheless, there is no evidence of neoclassical decreasing returns to investment in these developing countries. Amongst the relatively rich countries, however, decreasing returns are strongly in evidence.

There is again evidence that spillover effects may be important for the middle-income and, in particular, the rich countries, though not for the least developed. These spillovers are not statistically significant when country-specific effects are allowed for in the GLS estimation for the middle-income countries. Nor are they significant in the GLS estimation for the rich countries, but here the GLS model is not preferred.

4. CONCLUDING COMMENTS

I have argued that it is important to look closely at questions of reverse causation and missing variable bias in any attempt to investigate the sources of long-run growth. I suggest that the effects of resource re-allocation have sometimes been mis-estimated in the familiar cross-country regressions, particularly with respect to the allocation of resources between the public and private sectors of the economy.

I have gone on to conduct a preliminary investigation into the question of whether or not physical investment runs into the neoclassical trap of decreasing returns, or whether there is any evidence of constant (or even increasing) returns to investment of the type which might support some of the recent models of endogenous growth. Using time-series variation in data on investment and growth to supplement the usual cross-section data, I have constructed a panel of observations which allow investigation of these issues whilst testing for, and taking account of, endogeneity and unobserved country-specific effects. One important result that emerges is that the growth process is significantly different across countries at different stages of economic development, and that therefore results derived from pooling broad cross-sections of countries are not necessarily robust and may be quite misleading.

The results on investment are broadly supportive of a conclusion that returns to domestic investment are constant in the poorer and middle-income countries, but decreasing in the richer countries of the sample. On the other hand, there is some evidence that for the richer countries there are significant positive spillovers from investment by other countries in the region. Whilst the former set of results suggest that endogenously generated long-run growth is possible for the less developed economies if they can generate sufficient domestic investment, for the richer economies we find the interesting suggestion that long-run growth is more likely to depend on spillover and catch-up effects. This latter finding fits with the Abramovitz hypothesis that there is a threshold level of development, related to both technological and social capability, which has to be reached before countries are able to benefit from the advances in technology of the most advanced economies.

These conclusions are necessarily very tentative, to be regarded as suggestions for further more detailed research. In particular, further investigation of the role of investment and spillovers in growth should take account of the distinction between equipment and other investment as suggested by DeLong and Summers, and also the distinction between private investment and public infrastructure investment, as emphasized by Aschauer.

REFERENCES

Abramovitz, M. (1986), 'Catching up, forging ahead and falling behind', *Journal of Economic History*, 46, 385–406.
Aschauer, D.A. (1989), 'Is public expenditure productive?', *Journal of Monetary Economics*, 23, 177–200.
Barro, R.J. (1990), 'Government spending in a simple model of endogenous growth', *Journal of Political Economy*, 98(2), S103–S125.
Barro, R.J. (1991), 'Economic growth in a cross-section of countries', *Quarterly Journal of Economics*, CVI: 407–43.
DeLong, J.B. and L.H. Summers (1991), 'Equipment investment and economic growth', *Quarterly Journal of Economics*, 106(2), 445–502.
Dowrick, S. and N. Gemmell (1991), 'Industrialisation, catching up and economic growth: a comparative study across the world's capitalist economies, *Economic Journal*, 101, 263–75.
Dowrick, S. (1992a), 'Technological catch up and diverging incomes: patterns of economic growth 1960–88', *Economic Journal*, 102, 600–10.
Dowrick, S. (1992b), 'Estimating the impact of government consumption on growth: growth accounting and optimising models', conference paper, National Bureau of Economic Research, October 1992.
Dowrick, S. and D.T. Nguyen (1989), 'OECD comparative economic growth 1950–85: catch-up and convergence', *American Economic Review*, 79(5), 1010–30.
Greene, W.H. (1990), *Econometric Analysis*, New York: Macmillan.
Jones, L.E. and R. Manuelli (1990), 'A convex model of equilibrium growth: theory and policy implications', *Journal of Political Economy*, 98(5), 1008–38.
Munnell, A. (1992), 'Policy Watch: Infrastructure Investment and Economic Growth', *Journal of Economic Perspectives*, 6(4), 189–98.
Pitchford, J. (1960), 'Growth and the elasticity of factor substitution', *Economic Record*,

36, December, 491–504.

Ram, R. (1986), 'Government size and economic growth: a new framework and some evidence from cross-section and time-series data', *American Economic Review*, 76(1), 191–203.

Rao, V.V.B. (1989), 'Government size and economic growth: comment', *American Economic Review*, 79(1), 272–84.

Romer, P.M. (1986), 'Increasing returns and long-run growth', *Journal of Political Economy*, 94, 1002–37.

Romer, P.M. (1990), 'Endogenous technological change', *Journal of Political Economy*, 98(2), S71–S102.

Scott, M.F. (1989), *A New View of Economic Growth*, Oxford: Clarendon Press.

Sharma, S.C., M. Norris and D. Cheung (1991), 'Exports and economic growth in industrialised countries', *Applied Economics*, 23(4A), 697–707.

Solow, R. (1956), 'A contribution to the theory of economic growth', *Quarterly Journal of Economics*, 70, 65–94.

Summers, R. and A. Heston (1991), 'The Penn World Table (Mark 5): an expanded set of international comparisons, 1950–88', *Quarterly Journal of Economics*, 106(2), 327–68.

Swan, T.W. (1956), 'Economic growth and capital accumulation', *Economic Record*, November, 334–61.

APPENDIX

ID = Summers and Heston (1991) identification number.
$\hat{Y}$ = annual growth rate of real GDP.
I/Y = average percentage share of investment in GDP, at constant international prices.
Countries are ranked by real GDP per worker, 1960–64.

ID	Country	$\hat{Y}$	I/Y (%)
poor countries			
41	Tanzania	0.055	18.8
14	Ethiopia	0.034	4.7
6	Burundi	0.032	7.9
22	Lesotho	0.076	10.8
44	Uganda	0.036	4.0
16	Gambia	0.056	3.2
33	Rwanda	0.049	4.5
45	Zaire	0.022	9.5
82	Burma	0.044	11.6
25	Malawi	0.041	11.8
42	Togo	0.046	16.7
18	Guinea	0.021	14.1
83	China	0.070	22.0
31	Niger	0.024	8.8
4	Botswana	0.099	23.9
95	Nepal	0.031	9.9
26	Mali	0.022	6.4
9	Cent.Af.Rp.	0.014	8.3
21	Kenya	0.053	14.4
85	India	0.029	16.5
7	Cameroon	0.062	10.3
57	Haiti	0.018	6.7
15	Gabon	0.077	37.2
86	Indonesia	0.060	19.8
3	Benin	0.025	5.5
81	Bangladesh	0.030	5.9

ID	Country	$\hat{Y}$	I/Y (%)
24	Madagascar	0.009	8.6
10	Chad	−0.004	15.1
104	Thailand	0.064	14.9
47	Zimbabwe	0.049	17.6
20	Ivory Coast	0.050	9.8
13	Egypt	0.070	6.2
36	Sierra Leone	0.017	2.2
79	Afghanistan	0.022	6.4
37	Somalia	0.025	10.0
12	Congo	0.064	14.3
8	Cape Verde I.	0.042	28.6
134	Papua N.G.	0.035	23.9
17	Ghana	0.016	7.6
27	Mauritania	0.024	13.3
97	Pakistan	0.049	15.5
30	Mozambique	0.006	12.4
middle-income countries			
2	Niger	0.002	11.8
23	Liberia	0.019	28.8
40	Swaziland	0.047	22.9
34	Senegal	0.022	7.2
92	S. Korea	0.081	24.7
58	Honduras	0.046	13.1
39	Sudan	0.023	1.8
46	Zambia	0.014	28.4
103	Taiwan	0.086	22.7
98	Philippines	0.043	19.1
68	Bolivia	0.033	1608
128	Turkey	0.051	21.0
101	Sri Lanka	0.033	21.2
74	Paraguay	0.055	11.4
29	Morocco	0.048	8.7
130	Yugoslavia	0.047	36.9

ID	Country	$\hat{Y}$	I/Y (%)
54	El Salvador	0.032	7.7
59	Jamaica	0.024	21.6
72	Ecuador	0.054	24.8
124	Portugal	0.046	23.7
53	Dominican R.	0.046	14.8
73	Guyana	0.007	31.1
120	Malta	0.060	27.3
62	Panama	0.057	24.8
43	Tunisia	0.052	14.9
1	Algeria	0.061	26.0
114	Greece	0.047	25.4
56	Guatemala	0.039	8.4
94	Malaysia	0.062	28.7
109	Cyprus	0.052	31.6
69	Brazil	0.058	19.9
91	Jordan	0.053	16.7
rich countries			
71	Colombia	0.046	17.2
61	Nicaragua	0.026	18.7
90	Japan	0.061	31.0
84	Hong Kong	0.083	20.9
51	Costa Rica	0.047	14.2
75	Peru	0.035	15.9
28	Mauritius	0.040	12.3
102	Syria	0.066	17.0
100	Singapore	0.080	29.2
76	Suriname	0.038	16.1
132	Fiji	0.038	22.4
38	South Africa	0.037	25.5
67	Argentina	0.022	11.8
125	Spain	0.039	26.2
49	Barbados	0.030	18.2
117	Ireland	0.032	26.4

ID	Country	$\hat{Y}$	I/Y (%)
70	Chile	0.024	13.3
107	Austria	0.035	27.5
60	Mexico	0.051	19.6
77	Uruguay	0.011	15.7
111	Finland	0.038	34.2
118	Italy	0.038	27.9
89	Israel	0.056	26.3
112	France	0.036	25.9
113	W. Germany	0.029	26.9
110	Denmark	0.030	27.8
116	Iceland	0.045	25.8
129	UK	0.024	18.1
65	Trinidad & T.	0.028	18.7
108	Belgium	0.030	23.0
122	Norway	0.042	32.8
126	Sweden	0.028	22.6
121	The Netherlands	0.035	24.0
119	Luxembourg	0.030	26.5
131	Australia	0.039	28.2
133	New Zealand	0.024	22.0
50	Canada	0.040	22.9
127	Switzerland	0.023	30.2
66	USA	0.032	17.2

6. Lock-in and Specialization (Dis)Advantages in a Structuralist Growth Model

Mario Cimoli

1. INTRODUCTION

The recent 'structuralist/evolutionary' models have paid increasing attention to uneven international technological change as an engine of growth, with emphasis on the dynamics of specialization (as for example in Metcalfe 1989, Amable 1992, 1993 and Soete and Verspagen 1992) and on the dynamics of catching-up (as for example in Verspagen (1993) and Dosi and Freeman 1992).

In this context, the formal approach developed in Dosi and Soete (1983), Cimoli (1988, 1991), Dosi, Pavitt and Soete (1990), Canter and Hanusch (1993) and Cimoli and Soete (1992) has pinpointed the importance of the interplay between absolute and comparative advantages as determinants of the participation of each country in world trade, the dominance of technological gaps in the process of international specialization, and the bounds imposed by the dynamics of innovation and trade on the 'growth possibility sets' of each economy.

On the determinants of absolute and comparative advantages, technological gaps – in terms of product and process innovation – and institutional asymmetries – in terms of the main form of organization of labour markets – contribute to determining the pattern of specialization and its evolution over time. On the demand side, on the other hand, the asymmetries in national consumption patterns, which relate to the price and income elasticities, play a crucial role for the interplay between specialization and the macroeconomic level of activity. Finally, the trade balance condition determines the growth-rate differential of trading economies, as has emerged in the well-known Kaldorian export-base models (Kaldor 1966, 1975, Kennedy and Thirlwall 1979, Thirlwall 1980, Dixon and Thirlwall 1975).

The main characteristics of these models can be viewed not only in terms of modelling methodologies, but also in the ways in which some of the empirical properties of the world economy are considered. Thus, as summarized in Dosi, Pavitt and Soete (1990), the structuralist/evolutionary approach has tried to account for what can reasonably be considered as some fundamental properties affecting the interplay between trade and growth: a) the different commodities show a wide range of price and income elasticities; b) the rate of growth of each economy is normally constrained by the need to balance the foreign account; c) wage rates are mainly determined by institutional factors which account for the mechanism that relates wage and productivity over time; and d) the interplay between technical change, trade, and growth has to be interpreted as a mechanism that generates a tendency to converge to an equilibrium in the world rate of growth only as a particular case.

In the following sections we shall adapt the model presented in Dosi *et al.* (1990), Cimoli (1991), and Cimoli and Soete (1992) to the analysis of the endogenous evolution of the pattern of trade. The dynamics of national productivity levels and comparative (dis)advantages will be determined by the dynamics of increasing returns and a cumulative learning mechanism.[1] The dynamics of specialization for the commodities produced in the home and foreign economies are explained by the differences in technological capabilities – approximated by the technological multiplier – and the evolution of wages and productivity levels over time.

In this context, we shall emphasize the interplay between dynamic endogenous changes of comparative advantages, specialization, and the national consumption patterns for the determination of growth possibilities. The national consumption patterns are determined by a mix of income and price elasticities, leading to endogenously-determined specialization. Thus, the sectoral distribution of specialization can bring about a divergence between the production and consumption pattern at the national level. In this context, as introduced in Pasinetti (1981), the asymmetry between domestic and foreign consumption patterns is considered as a key element in the explanation of convergence or divergence in the output rate of growth.

A stable pattern of specialization or its dynamics can give rise to a consumption pattern that determines whether convergence or divergence in output rates of growth will take place. In this context, we shall demonstrate that a balanced growth path exists, but this is a particular case among different scenarios dominated by forging-ahead and falling-behind perspectives.

The rest of this chapter is organized as follows. Section 2 introduces a basic model explaining the determination of comparative (dis)advantages and patterns of specialization. Section 3 describes the mechanism that explains the interaction between the Harrod foreign trade and technological gap multipliers. In Section 4 we introduce a mechanism that describes increasing returns and technological cumulative learning. In Section 5 we analyse the endogenous dynamics of comparative (dis)advantages and specialization. A solution of the model is introduced in Section 6.

2. COMPARATIVE (DIS)ADVANTAGES AND SPECIALIZATION

The model we shall use is a simplified version of Dosi, Pavitt and Soete (1990) and Cimoli and Soete (1992), which has been further analysed in the empirical analysis developed in Soete and Verspagen (1992), and Soete (1987). We start with the assumption of a continuum of goods which is ordered by a real index on an interval $[0, z_l]$, where z_l is the number of commodities produced in the world economy. A continuum of goods implies that each good corresponds to a real number on the interval. As many empirical studies[2] in trade and technology have shown, the assumption that products can be ranked by some proxy of technological intensity, to a large extent irrespective of the particular country, is very much supported by the available empirical evidence. Technological intensity can, in other words, be translated into empirical terms in a relatively straightforward manner; e.g. expenditures (direct and indirect) on R&D (David 1988), the number of patents granted (Pavitt and Patel 1988), the quality index of economic activities and the historical evolution of traditional and innovative commodities (for example the chapter in this volume by Reinert).

In the model which follows, we will assume that the technological intensity of the commodities is related to the technological gap in input efficiency independent of relative prices for the production of these commodities. The commodities are so-called Ricardian commodities, which can be produced both by the home and by the foreign country.[3]

Let w and w^* denote the wages in the foreign and home economies, $\omega = w/w^*$ denotes the relative wages measured in each common commodity; $\Pi(z) = \pi(z)/\pi^*(z)$ is the labour productivity function which ranks the produced commodities for the whole set in terms of an increasing technological gap. Thus, the borderline commodity $\tilde{z}$, which determines the pattern of specialization, can be written as the following function:[4]

$$\tilde{z} = \tilde{z}\left(\omega(t),\ \Pi(z,t)\right). \tag{6.1}$$

Differentiating equation (6.1) we obtain the changes of $\tilde{z}$ over time, under the assumption of exogenous technical progress in the production of existing commodities, which are described by the following equation (where hats denote proportionate growth rates):

$$\hat{\bar{z}} = \psi \left((\hat{w} - \hat{w}^*) + (\hat{\pi}^* - \hat{\pi}) \right),$$ (6.2)

Equation (6.2) can be considered as the basis for the analysis of the dynamics of comparative (dis)advantages, which are related to differences in the existing technological capabilities in the production of Ricardian commodities and the dynamics of relative wages and productivities. As introduced in Cimoli and Soete (1992), ψ is here called the technological gap multiplier which approximates the existing technological gap with respect to the Ricardian commodities.[5]

From equation (6.2) it emerges that the changes of $\bar{z}$ are a function of the percentage changes in wages and productivities, which are weighted by the technological gap multiplier. In fact, the technological gap multiplier defines a 'centre of gravity' around which the changes in wages and labour productivities determine the intensity of changes in specialization.

Thus, there is a limit as to how far the dynamics of comparative (dis)advantages can induce changes in specialization when the existing technological multiplier is already small. Conversely, in the case of a large technological multiplier, adjustments in the pattern of specialization will be very sensitive to changes in comparative (dis)advantages. Equation (6.2) illustrates, for example, that it is especially in the case of countries with a relatively small technological gap, that the technological gap multiplier will have its most significant effect on the pattern of specialization; i.e., in the case of North–North or South–South trade, rather than in the extreme North–South case.[6]

3. THE HARROD FOREIGN TRADE AND TECHNOLOGICAL GAP MULTIPLIERS

Let us analyse how the comparative advantages and the dynamics of specialization are introduced in an open macroeconomic framework. In general, the composition and dynamics of specialization flows are interpreted within a framework characterized by different sector-specific technological gaps between countries as introduced in the previous section, by generally non-clearing markets, and by Keynesian–Kaldorian links between international competitiveness and the process that explains the general stylized facts of uneven growth as opposed to the particular case of balanced growth.

We shall introduce an explanation that is the basis for a representation of the growth patterns determined by the international pattern of specialization and the national consumption patterns. Let us start by specifying the national consumption pattern. We choose to specify the foreign and home import demands, since in our model these are what counts in determining the balance of trade equilibrium condition. Then the demands for a commodity z are expressed in the following equations

$$\beta(z) = \frac{p^*(z)\ m\ (z,\ w,\ p^*(z))}{w}, \tag{6.3}$$

$$\beta^*(z) = \frac{p(z)\ m^*(z,\ w^*,\ p(z))}{w^*}, \tag{6.4}$$

where:

$\beta(z)$ and $\beta^*(z)$ are the foreign and home per capita import expenditure shares, respectively;

$m(z)$ and $m^*(z)$ are the foreign and home per capita import demands;

$p(z)$ and $p^*(z)$ are the prices of commodity z produced in the foreign and home country, which are defined respectively as $p(z) = w/p(z)$ and $p^* = w^*/p^*(z)$.

Thus the double factoral terms of trade will be given by $\omega = w/w^*$. Assuming $0 < \tilde{z} < z_l$, which defines the limit of changes in the pattern of specialization between foreign and the home country from changes in wages, we may write

$$\Gamma(\beta,\ \tilde{z}) = \int_0^{\tilde{z}} \beta(z)\,dz, \tag{6.5}$$

$$\Gamma^*(\beta^*,\ \tilde{z},\ z_l) = \int_{\tilde{z}}^{z_l} \beta^*(z)\,dz, \tag{6.6}$$

where:

Γ is the foreign share of wages spent on the commodities produced in the home country;

Γ^* is the home share of wages spent on the commodities produced in the foreign country.

In order to obtain an expression for the Balance of Trade Equilibrium Condition, we must specify the total home imports and exports. These can be expressed as:

$$M^* = Y^* \; \Gamma^*(\beta^*, \; \tilde{z}, \; z_l), \tag{6.7}$$

$$X^* = Y \; \Gamma(\beta, \; \tilde{z}), \tag{6.8}$$

where M^* is the total import demand in the home country, X^* is the home export (i.e., the import demand in the foreign country), Y^* and Y are the home and foreign incomes in which wages are the only component. Then the trade equilibrium condition is:

$$Y^* = \frac{\Gamma(\beta, \; \tilde{z})}{\Gamma^*(\beta^*, \; \tilde{z}, \; z_l)} \; Y. \tag{6.9}$$

At this point, we will be able to provide a link between the changes in international specialization and a 'Keynesian' determination of the level of activity. The corresponding trade equilibrium income is determined by: (a) the technological gap in the production of the existing commodities; (b) the composition of the import demand basket; and (c) the interdependence constraint via the trade balance.

It is clear that Γ and Γ^* can also be interpreted as the import propensities in the foreign and home economies respectively. In this sense, equation (6.9) can be taken as a static formalization of Harrod's foreign trade multiplier, as revived by Kaldor and Thirlwall.[7] The balance of payments approach followed here has shown its potentiality for the analysis of convergence and divergence in the trade-growth context when technological aspects such as the effect of catching-up effort, innovation variables (patents, R&D etc.) and learning mechanisms such as those found in Fagerberg (1988, 1993), are incorporated.

Our approach includes, however, the possibility of explicitly introducing the dynamics of comparative advantages and specialization. In order to obtain an expression for the growth rate differential, we now need to specify the percentage change in the share spent on imports.

$$\beta^*(z) = \hat{w}^*(\varepsilon^*(z) - 1) + \hat{p}(z) \; (1 - \eta^*(z)) \tag{6.10}$$

$$\beta(z) = \hat{w}(\varepsilon(z) - 1) + \hat{p}^*(z) \; (1 - \eta(z)) \tag{6.11}$$

ε^* and ε are the income elasticities, and η^* and η the price elasticities in the home and foreign country respectively. Equations (6.10) and (6.11) capture the demand absorption and price effects. Note that the changes in prices can be decomposed as $\hat{p} = \hat{w} - \hat{\pi}$ and $\hat{p}^* = \hat{w}^* - \hat{\pi}^*$.

In this respect, the changes in real wages affect the demand for imports, the impact of which is weighted by the price and income elasticities of each commodity, and the range of commodities produced and exported by both countries. The impact of the latter effect is itself determined by the relative differences in productivities, defined as the technological gap. By introducing the possibility of changes in the pattern of specialization, we will be able to link the technological gap and differences in demand structure, which will simultaneously explain the cases of uneven and balanced growth.

The percentage change in the domestic relative income then follows from the following equation:

$$\hat{Y}^* - \hat{Y} = \hat{w}\overline{\varepsilon} - \hat{w}^*\overline{\varepsilon}^* + \hat{w}^*\overline{\eta} - \hat{w}\overline{\eta}^* + \hat{\pi}\overline{\eta}^* - \hat{\pi}^*\overline{\eta} \qquad (6.12)$$
$$+ (\hat{\tilde{z}}/\psi) \, M,$$

where:

$$M = \psi \, \tilde{z} \, (\beta^*(z)/\Gamma^* + \beta(z)/\Gamma), \quad \overline{\varepsilon} = \frac{1}{\Gamma} \int_0^{\tilde{z}} (\varepsilon(z) - 1) \, \beta(z) \, dz,$$

$$\overline{\varepsilon}^* = \frac{1}{\Gamma^*} \int_{\tilde{z}}^{z_1} (\varepsilon^* - 1) \, \beta^*(z) \, dz,$$

$$\overline{\eta} = \frac{1}{\Gamma} \int_0^{\tilde{z}} (1 - \eta(z)) \, \beta(z) \, dz, \quad \overline{\eta}^* = \frac{1}{\Gamma^*} \int_{\tilde{z}}^{z_1} (\eta^* - 1) \, \beta^*(z) \, dz.$$

Equation (6.12) illustrates how the domestic relative rate of growth compatible with the trade balance constraint is a function of: (a) the difference in the consumption patterns between the two countries (i.e., the income and price elasticities in both economies); (b) the changes in the per capita demand absorption of imported commodities and the changes in relative prices and/or factoral terms of trade (i.e., β^* and $\hat{\beta}$); and (c) the technological multiplier and the relative changes in the pattern of specialization (i.e., ψ).[8] (The presence of the technological multiplier in the equation for the growth-rate differential can be seen by substituting 6.2 in 6.12.)

The net effect on domestic relative income will depend on how these changes are compensated. Changes in wages and productivities not only have an impact on prices and demand for imports, but also on the dynamics of comparative (dis)advantages and specialization. In this context, the technological gap multiplier assumes a multiplicative form which can amplify or reduce the effect of specialization on the growth-rate differential. This model can thus become an adequate representation of international differences in growth rates, whenever the technological capabilities, the regimes of national consumption formation, and the institutional set-ups that relate wages and productivities are asymmetric/symmetric and not stable over time.

Insofar as changes in wages and productivities also have an impact on the specialization pattern, most of the effects described above can be neutralized by changes in the pattern of specialization, which could move in favour of or against the domestic country. What emerges, in other words, is that the traditional income growth effects due to relative changes in prices and wages and differences in the demand structure are not so clear (let alone obvious) once the possibility of a feedback to the pattern of specialization is considered. An increase in the home wage will, for instance, reduce the range of commodities produced domestically and exported and will consequently change the pattern of specialization in favour of the foreign country. The rate of output growth will diverge proportionally with the technological gap multiplier. Thus, in the case of a large technology gap multiplier, a considerable number of commodities might be lost for the home country. By contrast, in the case of a small technological gap multiplier, the model will take the form of complete specialization and the differential rate of output growth will be primarily explained by the demand structure and price effects. In other words, and as emphasized in much of the trade and development literature, the effect of the asymmetry of national consumption patterns is associated with the 'type' and with the income elasticities of the commodities produced and exported in both countries (one can think of the case of primary and manufactured commodities or the different income elasticities associated with low- and high-tech products).

The emerging comparative (dis)advantages in favour of the home country, on the other hand, when the technological gap multiplier is small – with consequently little impact on the pattern of specialization – will affect the domestic rate of growth negatively via the worsening of the terms of trade. If the technological gap multiplier is large, however, the negative effect for the home country on the terms of trade can again be compensated by an increase in the amount of commodities exported by the home country.

4. DYNAMIC ECONOMIES OF SCALE AND CUMULATIVE LEARNING

The model introduced here can be considered a sort of 'theoretical abacus' which reproduces different scenarios characterized by specific linkages between technology gaps, dynamics of (dis)advantages, specialization and the growth-rate differential.

In a general view, different scenarios can be represented on the basis of how the dynamics of productivities, wages and their interplay are introduced. As set out in Vaglio (1988), we shall use a sort of cumulative Verdoorn–Kaldor law that explains the dynamics of productivity in both countries and introduces a clear mechanism of dynamic economies of scale. Labour productivity depends on the cumulative output and the learning capabilities over time creating a process of strong irreversibility which, moreover, is uniformly distributed among the producing sectors. Let us now introduce an explicit form of the Verdoorn–Kaldor law,[9]

$$\pi = \Omega^{\alpha}, \ 0 < \alpha < 1, \qquad (6.13)$$
$$\pi^* = \Omega^{*\gamma}, \ 0 < \gamma < 1,$$

where α and γ are the Verdoorn–Kaldor parameters in the foreign and home countries. Ω and Ω^* are the cumulative capabilities in each economy, which are defined as follows,

$$\Omega(t) = \int_0^t (Y(t) + \delta Y^*(t)) \, dt,$$

$$\qquad (6.14)$$

$$\Omega^*(t) = \int_0^t (Y^*(t) + \delta Y(t)) \, dt, \ 0 \le \delta \le 1.$$

δ can be considered as a parameter that indicates how much the cumulative capabilities are related to the internationalization of the learning process. In other words, the parameter δ can represent the international learning spillover which symmetrically influences the cumulative capabilities in both economies. $\delta = 0$ indicates that the cumulated and learning capabilities are related only to local effort or that the country does not assimilate international learning spillovers. $\delta = 1$ indicates that the capabilities are explained in terms of the world economy as a whole and that technology can easily be obtained from abroad; in this case the assimilated learning spillovers reach the maximum value.

As we indicated earlier, the productivities in both economies are related to a sort of cumulative-learning Verdoorn–Kaldor law which determines the following dynamics of relative productivity:

$$\frac{\hat{\pi}}{\hat{\pi}^*} = \frac{\alpha(\pi^*)^{1/\gamma} \, (Y + \delta \hat{Y}^*)}{\gamma(\pi)^{1/\alpha} \, (Y^* + \delta Y)}. \qquad (6.15)$$

The function $(\hat{\pi}/\hat{\pi}^*)$ (representing the relative dynamics of productivity) is a negatively-sloped function with respect to the relative productivities π/π^*. This equation is solvable for π/π^* on the basis of different values of relative incomes and the parameters indicated in the equation (α, γ and δ). Thus, there exists an equilibrium value of π/π^* for which the rate of productivity growth is the same in both economies, i.e., $\hat{\pi}/\hat{\pi}^* = 1$, and the equilibrium value will be reached in the domain of positive productivity in both economies.

Figure 6.1 shows a family of curves which emerges from equation (6.15) for different γ and fixed α and δ; thus, for each curve the relative productivities reach an equilibrium value for which $\hat{\pi}/\hat{\pi}^* = 1$. In Figure 6.1, when $\delta = 1$, there exists a family of curves which determines a sequence of equilibrium values of relative productivities in terms of the Verdoorn-Kaldor parameters in both economies. The curve characterized by $\alpha = 0.1$ and $\gamma = 0.2$ reaches an equilibrium value for $(\pi/\pi^*)^*$ which moves to the left side when γ increases and to the right side when γ decreases. In the particular case of a world characterized by perfect symmetric economies $\gamma = \alpha$, we found that the equilibrium value is $\pi/\pi^* = 1$. When $\gamma > \alpha$ the equilibrium value of relative productivities is lower with respect to the perfect symmetric economies, and conversely for $\gamma < \alpha$.

Moreover, the equilibrium value of (π/π^*) can be considered as a function of (Y/Y^*). Taking equation (6.15) and solving it for the equilibrium value of the productivities that guarantee the same rate in both

Figure 6.1.　Dynamics of comparative (dis)advantages and specialization

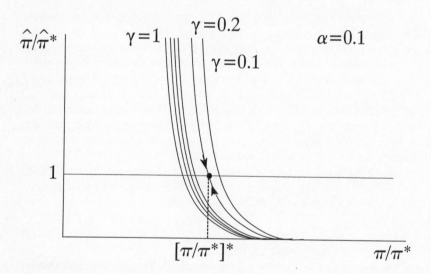

economies, we obtain the relative incomes:

$$\frac{Y}{Y^*} = \frac{\delta(\alpha/\gamma)\,\left(\pi/\pi^*\right)^{-1/\alpha}\,(\pi^*)^{(1/\gamma-1/\alpha)} \;-\; 1}{\delta \;-\; (\alpha/\gamma)\,\left(\pi/\pi^*\right)^{-1/\alpha}\,(\pi^*)^{(1/\gamma\,-\,1/\alpha)}}, \tag{6.16}$$

The two extreme cases that determine the domain of this function are:

$$(Y/Y^*) \to 0 \Rightarrow (\pi/\pi^*)^0 = (\delta\alpha/\gamma)^\alpha\,(\pi^*)^{(\alpha/\gamma-1)},$$
$$(Y/Y^*) \to \infty \Rightarrow (\pi/\pi^*)^1 = (\alpha/\delta\gamma)^\alpha\,(\pi^*)^{(\alpha/\gamma-1)},$$

which results for $\delta \neq 1$. Equation (6.16) describes a family of curves for different values of relative incomes (Y/Y^*), determining two extreme values of equilibrium for the relative productivities. Thus, when the relative incomes increase, the equilibrium value moves to $(\pi/\pi^*)^1$; when the relative incomes decrease, the value of equilibrium reached is $(\pi/\pi^*)^0$.

Equation (6.15) enables us to seek an equilibrium value of the relative productivities which determines a steady-state solution of comparative advantages for given relative wages ($\hat{w} = \hat{w}^* = 0$). Consequently, from equation (6.2), if an equilibrium is reached the result is that $\hat{z} = 0$ and, thus, a pattern of specialization is endogenously determined on the basis of the interaction of the learning mechanism that interacts between the trading economies.

Two cases can be emphasized. First, when the spillover effect reaches its maximum value $\delta = 1$, the world economy is characterized by the possibility that the technological knowledge and experience is easily transferred. In this case, the equilibrium solution of relative productivities and specialization is determined only by the differences in local learning effort of each country and its cumulative effect.

Second, when $0 \leq \delta < 1$, and, consequently, the world economy is characterized by an imperfect transfer of technological knowledge, the equilibrium solution and specialization pattern are determined by the local effort and the level of relative output of each economy. Thus, a country with a higher level of output will obtain a higher level of relative productivities and a pattern of specialization with increased export.

5. DYNAMICS OF COMPARATIVE (DIS)ADVANTAGES AND SPECIALIZATION

As emerges from equation (6.2), the dynamics of specialization and the differences in the output rate of growth depend crucially on the rate of increase in wages and the modes of how these are related to the increase in productivity. We shall assume that the changes in wages are related to productivity as follows

$$\hat{w} = \lambda\hat{\pi}, \; 0 \le \lambda \quad \text{and} \quad \hat{w}^* = \lambda^*\hat{\pi}^*, \; 0 \le \lambda^*, \tag{6.17}$$

where λ and λ^* can be interpreted as indicators of the wage–labour nexus that characterizes these economies. Following the results emerging in the theory of regulation developed in Coriat and Saboia (1987), Boyer (1988a, 1988b), and Aboites (1988), this parameter may reflect the following two extreme cases or others between them. First, is the case of an oligopolistic form of regulation, where the wage–labour nexus is characterized by tacit or statutory mechanisms of strong indexation of wages to labour productivity, as happens in the most advanced economies, hence λ and/or λ^* are near one. Second, is the case of a classical form of regulation, prevailing in the less developed economies, where the wage–labour nexus is determined by a weak indexation of wage to productivity in the larger part of the economy, hence λ and/or λ^* are near zero.[10]

Substituting (6.17) in equation (6.2) gives an expression for the specialization from which we can obtain the relative value of the dynamics of productivity that guarantees a stable pattern of specialization

$$\hat{\hat{z}} = \psi\left((\lambda\hat{\pi} - \lambda^*\hat{\pi}^*) + (\hat{\pi}^* - \hat{\pi})\right),$$

$$\hat{\hat{z}} = 0 \Rightarrow \left\{ \begin{array}{c} \psi = 0 \\ \hat{\pi}/\hat{\pi}^* = (\lambda^* - 1)/(\lambda - 1) \end{array} \right\}. \tag{6.18}$$

Changes in specialization are explained by: the existing technological gap multiplier, the dynamic increasing returns which determine the evolution of comparative advantages over time and the institutional wage–labour nexus prevailing in each economy. The pattern of specialization is stable in two cases: i) when the technological gap multiplier is zero, ii) when the wage–labour nexus is the same in both economies.

Now we may relate the mechanisms that explain the interplay between the endogenous dynamics of relative productivities, comparative advantage and specialization. Equation (6.15) determines an equilibrium solution of relative productivities, for example $(\pi/\pi^*)^*$ in Figure 6.2. Moreover, as emerges from equation (6.16), $(\pi/\pi^*)^*$ always lies between $(\pi/\pi^*)^0$ and $(\pi/\pi^*)^1$. For these extreme values of relative productivities indicated in Figure 6.2, which are determined by the Verdoorn–Kaldor and internationalization parameters, we found that the relative level of output will be radically in favour of one economy or the other.

The conditions that determine a stable pattern of specialization are not necessarily compatible with the equilibrium, in which the relative dynamics of productivities tend to converge. For each curve determined from equation (6.15), (π/π^*) will tend to converge towards an equilibrium value for which, however, the specialization pattern is not necessarily stable. Thus, as illustrated in Figure 6.2 and as emerges from equation

(6.18), the pattern of specialization is stable when $1 = (\lambda^* - 1)/(\lambda - 1)$ or $\lambda^* = \lambda$, i.e., when the wage–labour nexus is the same in both economies. The specialization is in favour of the home country when $1 > (\lambda^* - 1)/(\lambda - 1)$ or $\lambda^* < \lambda$, i.e., in the foreign economy the wage rises in line with productivity and the home wage is indexed more weakly; and, conversely, when the specialization is in favour of the foreign economy, i.e., $1 < (\lambda^* - 1)/(\lambda - 1)$ or $\lambda^* > \lambda$.

The dynamics of specialization are related both to the way in which the dynamics of increasing returns and the specific institutional wage-labour nexus operate in each economy. The equilibrium solution determined by the curves (Y/Y^*) in the range defined by $(\pi/\pi^*)^0$ and $(\pi/\pi^*)^1$ is compatible

Figure 6.2.   Dynamics of comparative (dis)advantages and specialization

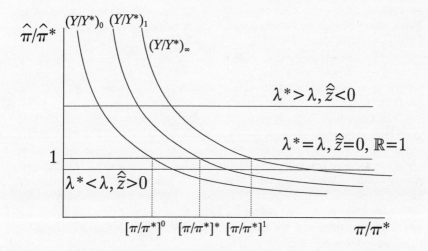

with a lock-in effect which reinforces the dynamics of the pattern of specialization in favour of one country or the other.

In general, what clearly emerges from the interaction of comparative advantages and specialization is that a stable pattern of specialization (and/or a stable solution for the comparative advantages) requires not only that the cumulative elements which explain the dynamics of increasing returns and cumulative learning reach a stable equilibrium, but also that the institutional factors that explain the wage–labour nexus must be symmetric.

6. A SOLUTION OF THE MODEL

Taking equation (6.12) and substituting (6.17) and (6.18) the growth-rate differential is defined as:

$$\hat{Y}^* - \hat{Y} = \hat{\pi}(\lambda\bar{\varepsilon} + (\lambda - 1)(M - \bar{\eta}^*)) - \hat{\pi}^*(\lambda^*\bar{\varepsilon}^* - (\lambda^* - 1)(\bar{\eta} - M)). \tag{6.19}$$

The growth-rate differential obtained is clearly related to dynamics of relative productivities, the changes in M, which include the technological gap multiplier, the wage–labour nexus prevailing in each country and the average value of income and price elasticities.

Equations (6.15) and (6.19) determine the interplay that exists between the dynamics of comparative (dis)advantages, specialization and the growth-rate differential. From equation (6.19) we can obtain the solution for which the growth rates of output are the same in both economies when both the consumption pattern and the wage–labour nexus differ,

$$\hat{Y}^* - \hat{Y} = 0 \Rightarrow \frac{\hat{\pi}}{\hat{\pi}^*} = \mathbb{R} = \frac{(\lambda^* - 1)(M - \bar{\eta}) + \lambda^*\bar{\varepsilon}^*}{(\lambda - 1)(M - \bar{\eta}^*) + \lambda\bar{\varepsilon}}, \tag{6.20}$$

where $\mathbb{R}$ is the curve that guarantees that the growth rates are balanced in both economies.

From equation (6.20) it emerges that the specialization pattern is stable and both economies grow at the same rate when $Y^* - Y = 0$ and $1 = \mathbb{R}$. To obtain the same rate of output growth it is not sufficient for the relative productivities to reach an equilibrium solution and the pattern of specialization not to change over time. Therefore, a stable pattern of comparative advantages and specialization is necessary but not sufficient to produce balanced growth. We can obtain balanced growth only when the specialization pattern does not change over time and the consumption pattern is perfectly symmetric.

As is illustrated in Figure 6.2, for a stable specialization pattern and balanced growth, $\hat{z} = 0$ and $1 = \mathbb{R}$, the equilibrium value of relative productivities always lies between the two extreme values of $(\pi/\pi^*)^0$ and $(\pi/\pi^*)^1$ and is determined by the curve (Y/Y^*); for example for $(Y/Y^*)_1$ we obtain $(\pi/\pi^*)^*$. Thus, when both economies are perfectly symmetric in consumption patterns and wage–labour nexus, the equilibrium solution is only explained by the mechanisms that describe the dynamics of increasing returns for a stable level of relative output.

In general, a process of divergence in the rate of growth can result under the general solution of equation (6.15), which shows that the dynamics of relative productivities will converge to an equilibrium. A pattern of divergence in the rate of growth is explained by the asymmetries in the consumption pattern at the national level, due to the pattern of specialization that has emerged ($\bar{\varepsilon} \neq \bar{\varepsilon}^*$, $\bar{\eta} \neq \bar{\eta}^*$, $\lambda = \lambda^*$). Another pattern of divergence in the rate of growth results when the consumption patterns are symmetric and the wage–labour nexus differs ($\bar{\varepsilon} = \bar{\varepsilon}^*$, $\bar{\eta} = \bar{\eta}^*$, $\lambda \neq \lambda^*$). In this case, the lock-in effect in the specialization pattern determines an increasing dynamic divergence in the rate of growth.

To solve the model, in the case of asymmetries in wage–labour nexus and national consumption patterns, we shall find the effective value of the specialization $\tilde{z}$ and $\mathbb{R}$. From differential equation (6.18), we obtain a

Figure 6.3.   Dynamics of comparative (dis)advantages and convergence vs divergence in the growth rate differential

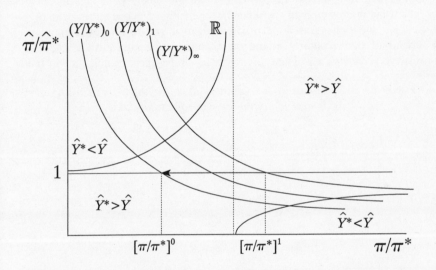

solution which determines the pattern of specialization expressed in (6.21) equation below. Then, substituting this in equation (6.20), results in the solution for $\mathbb{R}$. Thus, the specialization pattern and the condition that guarantees the same rate of growth can be rewritten as a function of relative productivities:

$$\tilde{z} = e^{\psi} \frac{(\pi^*)^{\psi(1-\lambda)}}{(\pi)^{\psi(1-\lambda)}}, \tag{6.21}$$

$$\mathbf{R} = \frac{(\lambda^* - 1)\left(\beta\psi e^{\psi}\dfrac{(\pi)^{\psi(\lambda-1)}}{(\pi^*)^{\psi(\lambda^*-1)}} - \overline{\eta}\right) + \lambda^*\overline{\varepsilon}^*}{(\lambda - 1)\left(\beta\psi e^{\psi}\dfrac{(\pi)^{\psi(\lambda-1)}}{(\pi^*)^{\psi(\lambda^*-1)}} - \overline{\eta}^*\right) + \lambda\overline{\varepsilon}}, \qquad (6.22)$$

where $\beta = (\beta^*(z)/\Gamma^* + \beta(z)/\Gamma)$. From equation (6.15), the relative productivity will converge to an equilibrium value for which $\hat{\pi}/\hat{\pi}^* = 1$. However, when there is some asymmetry in the wage–labour nexus or national consumption pattern, the rates of growth diverge and $\mathbf{R}$ changes. The curves $\mathbf{R}$, in Figures 6.3 and 6.4 indicate the areas where the growth-rate differential is in favour of one country or the other. $\mathbf{R}$ depicts the case where the only asymmetry is related to the national consumption pattern.

This situation starts up a process where a growth-rate differential in favour of one economy or the other changes the equilibrium value of relative productivities. There is a virtuous circle where output growth is a

Figure 6.4.   Dynamics of comparative (dis)advantages and convergence vs divergence in the growth-rate differential

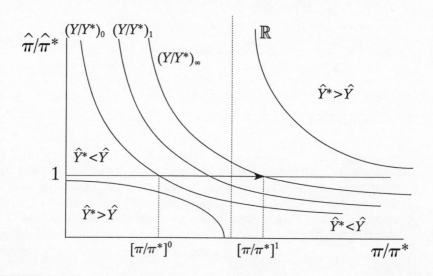

source which continuously moves the equilibrium solution for the relative productivities, and increases the divergence between the two countries. For example, this process moves the equilibrium solution to the left when $\eta < \overline{\eta}^*$ and the rate of income growth is higher in the home economy

(Figure 6.3); and, conversely, the equilibrium solution moves to the right when $\eta > \bar{\eta}^*$ and the growth-rate differential is in favour of the foreign economy (Figure 6.4). The cases depicted here represent the situation for which the country with exports characterized by higher price elasticities obtains a higher output rate of growth. This effect is due to the increasing price competitiveness when the exported commodities are elastic and the national consumption pattern asymmetric. The same can be applied for the differences in income elasticities and wage–labour nexus, i.e., $\bar{\varepsilon} \neq \bar{\varepsilon}^*$ and $\lambda \neq \lambda^*$.

These pictures describe a process of multiple equilibria which continuously moves the equilibrium solution to $(\pi/\pi^*)^0$ or $(\pi/\pi^*)^1$, as is shown in Figures 6.3 and 6.4. However, when the growth rate of output diverges, the equilibrium value will converge to one of the two extreme solutions which are determined mainly by the Verdoorn–Kaldor and internationalization parameters. For $(Y/Y^*) \rightarrow 0$ the value of relative productivities will tend to $(\pi/\pi^*)^0$ and, conversely, for $(Y/Y^*) \rightarrow \infty$ the solution will converge to $(\pi/\pi^*)^1$.

A solution for specialization and relative income, in the case of differences in price elasticities, is represented in Figure 6.5. Taking equations (6.19) and (6.21), we obtain:

$$\tilde{z} = e^{\psi}\left(\frac{\pi^*}{\pi}\right)^{\psi} \text{ and } \frac{Y^*}{Y} = \frac{(\pi)^{\eta^*}}{(\pi^*)^{\eta}} e^{(2\beta e^{\psi}(\pi^*/\pi)^{\psi})}.$$

The value of $\tilde{z}$ and (y/y^*) lies between the two extreme values of productivities determined by $(\pi/\pi^*)^0$ and $(\pi/\pi^*)^1$, or tends to one of the two extremes, whereas the shape of the curves is influenced by the technological gap multiplier. When both economies are perfectly symmetric, the equilibrium solution will be determined at a point within the interval. The two extreme cases will be reached when the growth rates of output diverge.

Thus, two scenarios emerge from this solution. The first scenario is associated with the case of perfectly symmetric economies in terms of the national consumption patterns and wage–labour nexus under conditions of stability dynamics in the relative dynamics of productivities and comparative advantages. The trade and growth pattern will reach an equilibrium solution which will be localized between $(\pi/\pi^*)^0$ and $(\pi/\pi^*)^1$ determining $\tilde{z}$ and (Y/Y^*). For example, in Figure 6.5, for $(\pi/\pi^*)^*$ we obtain $\tilde{z}^*$ and $(Y/Y^*)^*$.

The second scenario is related to a situation of forging ahead and falling behind under a stable situation in the dynamics of relative productivities (see Figures 6.3 and 6.4). The economies are asymmetric in the consumption patterns and wage–labour nexus. The process of uneven

Figure 6.5.   A solution for the model: specialization and output

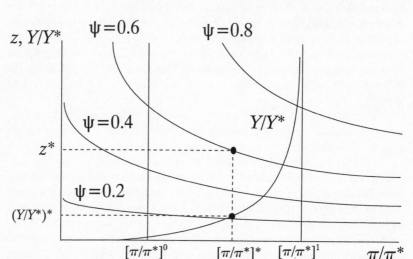

growth will move the equilibrium solution to $(\pi/\pi^*)^0$ or $(\pi/\pi^*)^1$ according to the differences in the output rate of growth. This rate can be in favour of one country or the other. As is indicated in Figure 6.5, if the growth differential is in favour of the home country, the equilibrium solution will reach $(\pi/\pi^*)^0$, and if the opposite happens the equilibrium solution will reach $(\pi/\pi^*)^1$.

7. CONCLUSIONS

The introduction of endogenous dynamic increasing returns in this model leads to a mechanism which produces a stable equilibrium solution. However, the dynamics of comparative (dis)advantages and specialization generated may lead to a steady-state solution, or to a lock-in situation in favour of one country or the other.

A stable pattern of specialization results in the case of a symmetric wage–labour nexus in trading economies. In this case, the equilibrium solution in comparative (dis)advantages and specialization will move in favour of one economy or the other according to the Verdoorn–Kaldor parameters and the internationalization in the technological transfer process. A scenario of lock-in in specialization patterns results when both trading economies are characterized by an asymmetric wage–labour nexus. However, a scenario of stable comparative (dis)advantages and patterns of specialization is not a sufficient condition to produce a balanced growth path. To obtain a path of balanced growth, the emerging pattern of specialization has to be associated with symmetric national patterns of consumption. Thus, while the mechanism of dynamic increasing returns and cumulative learning, on the one hand, could determine a stable pattern of specialization, the resulting pattern of specialization, on the other hand, may produce a national pattern of consumption which may or may not be compatible with a balanced path of growth.

A general outcome of the model is that a balanced and convergent path in the growth rates is a particular case where a stable equilibrium in the comparative (dis)advantages produces a stable pattern of specialization, and determines a symmetric national consumption pattern over time. A divergent path is related to a pattern of specialization associated with national consumption patterns which show structural asymmetries between countries. If the equilibrium solution in the specialization is associated with asymmetric patterns of national consumption, divergence in the rates of output growth will emerge. Thus, a stable pattern of specialization may determine a pattern of national consumption which gives rise to a process of lock-in and self-reinforcing mechanisms, leading to the divergence of the output rates of growth.

The model presents a paradoxical result with regard to falling-behind or forging-ahead perspectives, as technological learning and accumulation for the sectoral activities interact with the national consumption patterns. If a country shows high dynamic increasing returns and learning capabilities in the sectors where the consumption pattern is not favourable, it may result in a process of falling behind. In the case of low dynamic increasing returns and a favourable consumption pattern, a country may catch up or forge ahead. Thus, forging ahead and/or convergence take place if learning capabilities are taking place in those activities associated with a favourable national consumption pattern.

NOTES

1. In Cimoli (1991), the dynamics of comparative (dis)advantages are determined by the shares of the home and foreign commodities produced in the world economy; a similar dynamic approach in a more marked evolutionary context is developed in Metcalfe (1989) and Verspagen (1993).
2. For an overview, see Soete (1987) and Dosi, Pavitt and Soete (1990).
3. In this context the home country can be considered as a backward economy. The model can be extended to the introduction of innovative commodities which are produced only by the advanced economy. A different pattern of specialization emerges in this case: for a large

part of the innovative commodities the pattern of specialization is not sensitive to the comparative advantages; see Cimoli and Soete (1992) and Cimoli (1991).

4. As in Dornbusch, Fischer and Samuelson (1977), Wilson (1980) and Collins (1985).

5. Where ψ (the *technological multiplier*) is defined as: $\Psi = \omega/\bar{z}\ \partial\bar{z}/\partial\omega = -1/\Psi^{n\bar{z}}$ and $\Psi^{n\bar{z}} = z/\Pi\ \partial\Pi/\partial z$ which approximate the existing technology gap with respect to the produced commodities. Thus for a large ψ, an increase in relative wages (decrease in relative productivities) will considerably increase the amount of commodities exported by the home country. Conversely, if ψ is small, an increase in ω (decrease in relative productivities) implies smaller changes in specialization. Changes in relative wages and productivities thus have a significant effect on the share of commodities produced only when the technological multiplier is large, i.e., when the technological gap is small. For an increasing (decreasing) technological gap in Ricardian commodities, changes in relative wages produce a small (large) change in the specialization.

6. From equation (6.2), we can represent a situation of non-trade where $\psi = 0$. In this case a situation of autarky characterizes both economies. From these results, as obtained in Cimoli and Soete (1992), it is worth noting that the evidence with regard to the dominance of 'intra-industry' trade between advanced countries and the importance of product differentiation in such trade flows fits this result neatly.

7. As in Kaldor (1975), Kennedy and Thirlwall (1979), Thirlwall (1980, 1982), Thirlwall and Dixon (1979), Thirlwall and Hussain (1982).

8. A taxonomy of trade interdependence and the effects of the technological gap multiplier, income and price elasticities is developed in Cimoli and Soete (1992).

9. In a similar structuralist view of trade and growth, endogenous technical change and increasing returns to scale on the basis of the Kaldor–Verdoorn–type linear formula are introduced in Amable (1992, 1993) and Verspagen (1993).

10. The model can be extended to the case where wages are indexed with productivity in one of the two countries and fixed in the other. In this case the model introduced here can represent the traditional result on North–South models for the fundamental analysis developed in the Prebisch–Singer thesis and the Lewis approach, see Cimoli (1988).

REFERENCES

Aboites, J. (1988), 'Regimen de Acumulacion, Relacion Salarial y Crisis en Mexico', paper presented at the Conference on the Theory of Regulation, Barcelona, June 1988.

Amable, B. (1992), 'Effects d'apprentissage, compétitivité hors-prix et croissance cumulative', *Economie Appliqué*, 45(3), 5–31.

Amable, B. (1993), 'National effects of learning, international specialization and growth paths', in D. Foray and C. Freeman (eds), *Technology and the Wealth of Nations*, London: Pinter Publishers.

Boyer, R. (1988a), 'Technical Change and the Theory of Regulation', in G. Dosi, C. Freeman, R. Nelson and L. Soete (eds), *Technical Change and Economic Theory*, London: Pinter Publishers.

Boyer, R. (1988b), 'Formalizing Growth Regimes Within a Regulation Approach', in G. Dosi, C. Freeman, R. Nelson and L. Soete (eds), *Technical Change and Economic*

HD79.74
TEC

Theory, London: Pinter Publishers.

Canter, U. and H. Hanusch (1993), 'Process and Product Innovation in an International Trade Context', *Economics of Innovation and New Technology*, 2: 217-36.

Cimoli, M. (1988), 'Technological Gaps and Institutional Asymmetries in a North–South Model with a Continuum of Goods', *Metroeconomica*, 39, 245–74.

Cimoli, M. (1991), 'Innovation, Endogenous Comparative Advantages and Long-Run Growth', *Nota di lavoro* n. 8808, Dipartimento di Economia, Universitá di Venezia.

Cimoli, M. and L. Soete (1992), 'A Generalized Technological Gap Trade Model', *Economie Appliqué*, 45(3), 33–54.

Collins, S. (1985), 'Technical Progress in a Three-Country Ricardian Model with a Continuum of Goods', *Journal of International Economics*, 19, 171–9.

Coriat, B. and J. Saboia (1987), 'Régime D'Accumulation et Rapport Salarial au Brésil (des années 1950 au années 1980)', mimeo.

Cornwall, J. (1977), *Modern Capitalism: Its Growth and Transformation*, London: Martin Robertson.

David, L. (1988), *Technology Intensity of U.S., Canadian and Japanese Manufactures Output and Exports*, U.S. Department of Commerce International Trade Administration.

Dixon, R. and A. Thirlwall (1975), 'A Model of Regional Growth-Rate Differences on Kaldorian Lines', *Oxford Economic Papers*, 11, 1120–71.

Dornbusch, R., S. Fischer and P. Samuelson (1977), 'Comparative Advantage, Trade and Payments in a Ricardian Model with a Continuum of Goods', *American Economic Review*, 67, 823–39.

Dosi, G. and C. Freeman (1992), 'The Diversity of Development Patterns: On the Processes of Catching-up, Forging Ahead and Falling Behind', paper presented at the Conference on Economic Growth and the Structure of Long-term Development, Varenna 1–3 October.

Dosi, G., K. Pavitt and L. Soete (1990), *The Economics of Technical Change and International Trade*, Brighton: Harvester Wheatsheaf. HD45 1305

Dosi, G. and L. Soete (1983), 'Technological Gaps and Cost-based Adjustments: Some Explorations on the Determinants of International Competitiveness', *Metroeconomica*, 12, 357–82.

Fagerberg, J. (1988), 'Why growth rates differ', in G. Dosi, C. Freeman, R. Nelson and L. Soete (eds), *Technical Change and Economic Theory*, London: Pinter Publishers.

Fagerberg, J. (1993), 'The Role of Technology in Why Growth Rates Differ: An Overview', paper presented at the Conference on Catching up, Forging Ahead and Falling Behind, 14–16 May, Oslo.

Gomulka, S. (1971), 'Inventive Activity, Diffusion and the Stages of Economic Growth, Aarhus', *Skrifter fra Aarhus Universtets Okonomiske Institut*, 24.

Kaldor, N. (1966), *Causes of the Slow Rate of Economic Growth in the United Kingdom*, Cambridge: Cambridge University Press.

Kaldor, N. (1975), 'What is Wrong with the Economic Theory?', *Quarterly Journal of Economics*, 89, 347–57.

Kennedy, C. and A. Thirlwall (1979), 'Import Penetration, Export Performance and Harrod's Trade Multiplier', *Oxford Economic Papers*, 31, 303–22.

Metcalfe, S. (1989), 'Trade, Technology and Evolutionary Change', in R. Harrington *et al.* (eds), *Money, Trade and Payments*, MIT Press.

Pasinetti, L.L. (1981), *Structural Change and Economic Growth. A Theoretical Essay on the Dynamics of the Wealth of Nations*, Cambridge University Press: Cambridge.

Pavitt, K. and P. Patel (1988), 'The International Distribution and Determinants of Technological Activities', *Oxford Economic Papers*, 4.

Soete, L. (1987), 'The Impact of Technological Innovation on International Trade Patterns: The Evidence Reconsidered', *Research Policy*, 16, 101–30.

Soete, L. and B. Verspagen (1992), 'Competing for Growth: the Dynamics of Technology Gaps. Convergence and Imovation', paper presented at the Conference on Economic Growth and the Structure of Long-term Development, Varenna 1-3 October.

Thirlwall, A. (1980), *Balance of Payment Theory and the United Kingdom Experience*, London: Macmillan.

Thirlwall, A. (1982), 'The Harrod Trade Multiplier and the Importance of Export-Led Growth', *Pakistan Journal Of Applied Economics*, 1, 1–21.

Thirlwall, A. R. and Dixon (1979), 'A Model of Export-led Growth with Balance of Payments Constraint', in J. Bowers (ed.), *Inflation, Development and Integration*, Leeds: Leeds University Press.

Thirlwall, A. and M.N. Hussain (1982), 'The balance of payments constraint, capital flows and growth rate differences between developing countries', *Oxford Economic Papers*, 34, 498–510.

Vaglio, A. (1988), 'Statics and Dynamic Economies of Scale in Export-led growth', *Economics Notes*, 2, 61–81.

Verspagen, B. (1993), *Uneven Growth Between Interdependent Economies*, Aldershot: Avebury.

Wilson, C.A. (1980), 'On General Structure of Ricardian Models with a Continuum of Goods: Applications to Growth, Tariff Theory and Technical Change', *Econometrica*, 48, 1675–702.

7. Technological Change, Path Dependence and Growth: A Graph-Theoretic Approach

Fernando Vega-Redondo[1]

1. INTRODUCTION

Technological change has long been recognized as a fundamental force underlying sustained processes of economic growth. Only recently, however, has it become the focus of formal rigorous study by economic theory.

Despite substantial progress, most of the existing theoretical models in this area (both those belonging to the so-called New Growth Theory[2] as well as those of an evolutionary nature[3]) abstract from what I think should be an important consideration in the analysis of technological change. Namely, the fact that any process of technological development is a multidimensional phenomenon in which 'forwards' and 'backwards' cannot be taken as clearcut (one-dimensional) concepts. In general, different technological paths proceed along different lines, sometimes convergent, sometimes divergent, often 'parallel'.

In this chapter, I centre my analysis on this issue, modelling the technological development of two different economies as a joint stochastic process taking place on a directed graph of technologies.[4] Such a theoretical construct shall enable us to formalize precisely the following key notions:

- technological precedence,
- technological distance,
- technological convergence/divergence.

The preceding notions will be central to the analysis and discussion carried out in this chapter. Most of its results have been derived elsewhere.[5] Here, the main purpose is to provide an integrated summary of the approach, emphasizing its main implications. With this in mind, I present and discuss the different results somewhat informally when more careful discussion would become technical or notationally burdensome. Likewise, rather than providing formal proofs of the results, I convey only the main intuition underlying their logic.

The structure of the chapter is as follows. First, I shall start with a 'toy' model which already displays much of the main points. In it, two countries, each one of them identified with a single representative agent, evolve side by side, inventing and imitating with some lag as they go along. The key questions asked are: When will they technologically diverge? When may one stagnate? Will closer integration be beneficial for both countries? As it will turn out, the answer to these questions will crucially depend on both the parameters of the model (for example, the diffusion lag) and the features exhibited by the technological digraph (e.g. whether it exhibits 'branching', as well as its frequency and intensity).

In its second part, the chapter aims at adding some 'flesh' to the original simple model. I do this by replacing each artificial representative agent by a number of independent active firms operating in each economy. These firms compete with each other in the world arena. They are also subject to bankruptcy constraints and entry rules which determine their population dynamics. In this richer context, the gist of the analysis carried out for the simple model is essentially preserved. It will also be explained that, under our maintained assumptions on the technological structure, the process displays some further interesting implications at the microeconomic level. In particular, it will witness a continuous process of firm turnover. It will also exhibit a process of long-run technological specialization, by which the firms of each given economy eventually specialize in technologies which are, in relative terms, closely related.

2. THE BASIC MODEL

There are two countries, 1 and 2, each identified with a representative agent. Time is measured discretely ($t = 0,1,2,....$). For simplicity,[6] we assume that there is only one consumption good in the economy, which is produced every period with a single indivisible unit of labour available to each agent. Let Θ denote the set of all a priori possible technologies that can be used in production. It is called the technological space. At every point in time t, each economy $i = 1,2$ will have some subset of it available, denoted by $\Theta_i(t)$. The law of motion of this set represents the process of technological change in this economy.

Given the assumed indivisibility of labour, the production possibilities of each technology $\theta \in \Theta$ can be summarized by a certain associated scalar $\rho(\theta) \in \mathbb{R}$. It defines the amount of consumption good which may be produced by a unit of labour applied to technology θ. This formulation implies, in particular, that all technologies can be unambiguously ranked in terms of their productive potential.

As advanced, the set Θ will be endowed with a directed-graph (digraph) structure. This will permit the formalization of key notions such as technological precedence and technological gap which will be central to our approach. I describe this structure in the next subsection. In the subsequent one, I introduce the stochastic law of motion which models technological change. Finally, I shall end the description of the theoretical framework by presenting the intertemporal decision problem faced, at every point in time, by each of the two representative agents.

2.1. Technological Structure

The set Θ is endowed with a directed graph (digraph) structure (Θ, μ). That is, a binary relation μ is defined on Θ which is interpreted as reflecting 'directional bilateral links' among its elements. Conceptually, such relation μ is taken to formalize the notion of direct technological precedence, as presently explained.

When two technologies θ, θ' are consecutive points of Θ (i.e., $\theta \, \mu \, \theta'$) it is said that θ directly precedes θ' (technologically). Compositions of μ give rise to the notion of general (as opposed to direct or immediate) technological precedence. Specifically, when two technologies θ and θ' are joined by some μ-chain starting at θ and ending at θ' it will be simply said that θ technologically precedes θ' and we write $\theta \, \beta \, \theta'$. That is:

$$\theta \, \beta \, \theta' \Leftrightarrow \exists \, (\theta_1, \theta_2, ..., \theta_n) \; s.t. \; \theta_k \, \mu \, \theta_{k+1}, \qquad (7.1)$$
$$k = 1, 2, ..., n-1, \; \theta_1 = \theta, \; \theta_n = \theta'.$$

For any two technologies θ and θ' such that $\theta \, \beta \, \theta'$ (i.e., θ precedes θ'), the length of the *shortest chain* leading from θ to θ' will be denoted by $\lambda(\theta, \theta')$. For the sake of formal convenience, I shall use the conventions $\theta \, \beta \, \theta$ and $\lambda(\theta, \theta) = 0$ for all $\theta \in \Theta$, i.e., any technology θ 'precedes' itself and defines a μ-chain of length zero.

Motivated by the interpretation of β as reflecting technological precedence, it will be assumed that it is an ordering[7] (in general, a partial one) on Θ; or, in the language of Graph Theory, that (Θ, μ) is an acyclic digraph, i.e., one exhibiting 'no loops'. Such structure will be an essential component of both the innovation and imitation processes described in the next subsection. In particular, it permits to make precise the notion of technological gap between two technologies which is presently introduced.

Consider any two different technologies θ' and θ'' (not necessarily β-related) and define the set of their common predecessors by:[8]

$$Q(\theta',\theta'') = \{ \ \theta \in \Theta: \ \theta \ \beta \ \theta', \ \theta \ \beta \ \theta'' \ \}. \tag{7.2}$$

The technological gap from θ' to θ'' is defined as follows:

$$\gamma(\theta',\theta'') = \min \ \{ \ \lambda(\theta,\theta''): \ \theta \in Q(\theta',\theta'') \ \}, \tag{7.3}$$

where it will be recalled that $\lambda(\theta, \theta'')$ has been defined as the length of the shortest μ-chain leading from θ to θ''. The formulated concept of technological gap is reminiscent of biological contexts where the genetic ('information') differences between two species can be linked to their separate divergent evolution from a common ancestor. In a technological scenario, the motivation derives from the interpretation of every μ-step in (Θ, μ) as an homogeneous quantum of knowledge. Thus, if a shift from θ to θ' is performed, the 'knowledge gap' associated with it should count the number of μ-quanta in θ' *not* already incorporated in θ.

2.2. Technological Change

For each economy $i = 1$, 2, the set of currently available technologies $\Theta_i(t)$ will be assumed to change as time goes along through the operation of two phenomena: innovation and imitation.

Innovation at t is captured by the sets $N_i(t)$ of new invented technologies. Uncertainty and gradualness in innovation is incorporated by assuming that each $N_i(t)$ is composed of a number of *stochastic* draws from the set of *direct* technological successors (according to μ) of the technology *currently* adopted. For simplicity, we shall assume that these draws are costless and their (finite) number is fixed.[9] Thus, we may think of innovation here as the outcome of a stochastic process of learning by doing.

Imitation at t, on the other hand, is captured by the sets $M_i(t)$ which include those technologies that become available from imitation of the other economy. Very simply, it is postulated that technological know-how flows from one economy to the other with some lag $s \in \mathbf{N}$, a parameter of the model. Thus, more formally, we have:

$$\begin{aligned} M_i(t) &= \Theta_j(t-s), \text{ if } t \geq s; \\ &= \varnothing, \text{ if } t < s. \end{aligned} \tag{7.4}$$

Given any set $X \subset \Theta$ of technologies, denote by $H_\beta(X)$ the 'β-Hull' of A, i.e., $H_\beta(X) \equiv \{\theta \in \Theta: \theta \ \beta \ \theta' \text{ for some } \theta' \in X\}$. Under the interpretation that when one given technology is available, all of its predecessors become available as well, the described innovation and imitation processes are combined to give rise to the following law of motion:

$$\Theta_i(t) = H_\beta(\Theta_i(t-1) \cup N_i(t) \cup M_i(t)); \ t = 1,2,..., \ i = 1,2. \tag{7.5}$$

2.3. Decision Problem

The representative agents of each economy will be assumed fully myopic. This could be rationalized by identifying each of them with a given generation whose life ends with the period.

However, the decision problems faced by each agent have an intertemporal structure in the following two respects. The first obvious one is that current choice sets $\Theta_i(t)$ are obtained through the accumulation of past and present events (innovation and imitation) which are path (i.e., history) dependent.

There is a second sense, not yet discussed, in which the decision problems of the agents will be of an intertemporal nature. It is derived from the fact that any technological adjustment (i.e., change away from the currently adopted technology) will be assumed to involve switching costs. Quite naturally, these costs will be linked to the technological gap involved in the change. Thus, a function

$$C: \Theta \times \Theta \to \mathbb{R}_+ \tag{7.6}$$

is considered which, for each pair of technologies, $\theta, \theta' \in \Theta$, determines the cost $C(\theta, \theta')$ of switching from θ to θ' and admits the representation:

$$C(\theta,\theta') = \hat{C}(\gamma\,(\theta,\theta')), \tag{7.7}$$

for some strictly increasing function $\hat{C}\,(\cdot)$.

Let $U_i: \mathbb{R}_+ \to \mathbb{R}$ represent the ('instantaneous') utility function of agent $i = 1,2$ at every t. Given the current status-quo technology prevailing at t in economy $i = 1,2$ (denoted by $\theta_i(t-1)$), the choice $\theta_i(t)$ at t solves the following optimization problem:

$$\max_{\theta \,\in\, \Theta_i(t)} \quad U_i(\rho(\theta)) - C(\theta_i(t-1),\theta). \tag{7.8}$$

Starting from identical initial conditions for each economy, the purpose of our upcoming analysis may be succinctly described as follows: to explore the likely relative performance of both economies as the above described stochastic process unfolds. In particular, issues of convergence/-divergence and their effect on the 'world's' pace of technological development will be of special concern.

3. ANALYSIS OF THE BASIC MODEL

3.1. Assumptions

I first present some required assumptions.

> (A.1) $U(\cdot)$ is concave and $\hat{C}(\cdot)$ is convex.
>
> Furthermore, $\hat{C}(1) = 0$ and $\lim_{\gamma \to \infty} \hat{C}'(\gamma) = \infty$.

The first part of this assumption is standard. Its second part says that while gradual adjustment (one step at a time) is costless, further technological adjustments become progressively more costly without bound.

Our second assumption states that every technology has some better and no-better successors. By this assumption, the process of invention is genuinely uncertain, having always positive probability of both advancing or not the current productivity level.

> (A.2) Given any $\theta \in \Theta$, let $S(\theta) \equiv \{ \tilde{\theta} \in \Theta : \theta \, \mu \tilde{\theta} \}$. Then, there exist some θ', $\theta'' \in S(\theta)$ such that $\rho(\theta') > \rho(\theta)$ and $\rho(\theta'') \leq \rho(\theta)$.

The third final assumption is more involved. Verbally, it postulates that, along any technological path in Θ, some particular type of technologies called breakthroughs can be singled out. Let $\mathcal{L} \subset \Theta$ denote this set of technologies. They display (and are the only ones to do so) the following two-fold property. First, they are not too frequent and represent significantly larger productivity increases than 'normal' inventions.[10] Second, they represent 'branching points' in the technological structure (Θ, μ). The first of the distinguishing features of a breakthrough (its relatively large productivity increase) is obvious enough and requires no further explanation. As for the second (its induced branching), its precise formulation requires the introduction of some further notation.

Given any technology $\theta \in \Theta$, denote by $\vartheta(\theta)$ and $\Gamma(\theta)$ the sets of, respectively, (direct and indirect) predecessors and successors of θ. Thus, $B(\theta) \equiv \mathcal{L} \cap \vartheta(\theta)$ represents the set of preceding breakthroughs 'underlying' θ. We shall postulate the following assumption:

> (A.3) For all θ, $\theta' \in \Theta$:
>
> (i) $[B(\theta) \setminus B(\theta') \neq \varnothing]$ and $[B(\theta') \setminus B(\theta) \neq \varnothing] \Rightarrow \Gamma(\theta) \cap \Gamma(\theta') \neq \varnothing$.

(ii) There exist some $k \in \mathbb{N}$, $\zeta \in \mathbb{R}$, such that $\forall \theta$, $\theta' \in \Theta$:

$$[B(\theta) = B(\theta') \text{ and } \rho(\theta') \geq \zeta^k \rho(\theta)] \Rightarrow \theta \, \beta \, \theta'.$$

Part (i) states that if each of two given technologies incorporates a breakthrough that the other does not, then they belong to different 'technological lines', i.e., they induce a disjoint set of technological successors. On the other hand, part (ii) states that if two technologies share the same common set of breakthroughs, they also belong to a common technological line. (In particular, if one of them is sufficiently more advanced than the other, then the latter is a predecessor of the former.)

Admittedly, these assumptions (especially (A.3)) are quite special and too clearcut. They represent, however, a useful theoretical benchmark for discussing the issues that concern us here. Moreover, there is conclusive empirical research on particular technological scenarios which indicates that the sort of branching structures contemplated by our assumptions may be quite prevalent. For example, Foray and Grübler (1991) or Swan (1991) have reported such 'technological branching' in industries as diverse as ferrous casting or computer hardware. In the realm of economic history, the reader can find in Cardwell (1972) or Mokyr (1990) a number of interesting examples in this respect.[11] Finally, and in a similar vein, one must refer to the work of David (1985), Arthur (1989), or Freeman (1991), all of whom stress the empirical importance of this phenomenon in a variety of different contexts, not only technological but also institutional or cultural.

Before proceeding to the discussion of our first results, let me illustrate matters by presenting four different kinds of technological structures which satisfy (A.3). The first two digraphs in Figure 7.1 represent technological structures with no breakthroughs. (Notice that this does not violate (A.3); in this case, all technologies belong to the scenario contemplated by Part (ii) of this assumption.) The other two digraphs in Figure 7.2 do include breakthroughs. In fact, whereas in one of them breakthroughs appear 'occasionally', in the other digraph (a tree) every technology is a breakthrough.[12]

Figure 7.1a

Figure 7.1b

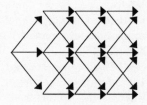

Figure 7.2a

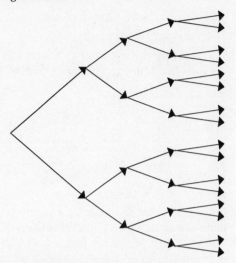

Figure 7.2b

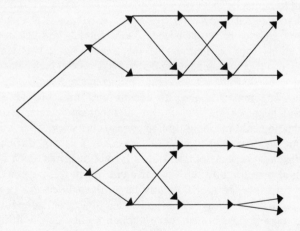

3.2. Basic Results

I start with the following result.

> *Theorem 1*: Assume $|\mathcal{L}| = \infty$. There exists some $\underline{s} \in \mathbb{N}$ such that if $s \geq \underline{s}$, then every technological path $\{\theta_1(t),\theta_2(t)\}_{t=1,2,\dots}$ satisfies, with probability one:
>
> (i) $\lim\limits_{t\to\infty} \gamma(\theta_i(t),\theta_j(t)) = \infty$, $i,j = 1,2$, $i \neq j$;
>
> (ii) $\text{Sup}_{t=1,2,\dots}\{\max [\dfrac{\rho(\theta_i(t))}{\rho(\theta_j(t))}, i,j = 1,2]\} = \infty$.

The former result establishes that, if the diffusion lag s is large enough and the possibility of future breakthroughs is never exhausted, our two-economy world will, almost surely, witness a path where the economies progressively diverge (technologically) from each other. Moreover, one of the economies will become arbitrarily underdeveloped relative to the other in the long run, the 'productivity gap' between them eventually becoming arbitrarily large with probability one.

Of course, the responsibility for such drastic conclusions lies on the extreme assumptions made; most essentially, on Assumption (A.3) and the 'irreversible branching' it allows. At this point, the theoretical nature of our conclusions should be emphasized. They should be regarded as clearcut illustrations (not predictions) of the trends which will tend to materialize when the environment under consideration matches, to a sufficient degree, the sharp theoretical assumptions made. Specifically, and with respect to Theorem 1 above, its conclusions must be viewed as indicating the tendencies present in an environment which exhibits substantial technological branching; not an implausible irreversible one.

The intuition underlying the proof of Theorem 1 is not difficult to convey.[13] If branching of technological lines is ever recurrent, each of the economies will also recurrently 'hit' one of them. When this happens, and as long as the diffusion lag is sufficiently large, there is always positive probability that each economy advances along divergent technological lines quite far enough. And then, even though technological diffusion gives each economy the option of readopting the technological line of the other, this is too costly to be done. Thus, both economies advance thereafter along separate and divergent technological lines. This leads to Part (i) of Theorem 1. As for Part (ii), it is a consequence of the fact that, from the moment in which each economy evolves independently, all arbitrarily large productivity gaps between them have positive probability.

In establishing Theorem 1, it is fully crucial that the diffusion lag is large enough. For, if this is not the case, we are led to the following alternative result.

Theorem 2: There exists some $\bar{s} \in \mathbb{N}$ such that if $s \leq \bar{s}$, then every technological path $\{\theta_1(t),\theta_2(t)\}_{t=1,2,...}$ satisfies:

(i) $\exists M \in \mathbb{R}$ s.t. $\text{Sup}_{t=1,2,...}\{\max\ [\gamma(\theta_i(t),\theta_j(t)),\ i,j = 1,2]\} \leq M$;

(ii) $\exists M' \in \mathbb{R}$ s.t. $\text{Sup}_{t=1,2,...}\{\max\ [\dfrac{\rho(\theta_i(t))}{\rho(\theta_j(t))},\ i,j = 1,2]\} \leq M'$;

(iii) $\forall t = 1,2,...,$ if $\rho(\theta_i(t)) \geq \rho(\theta_j(t))$ then, with probability one, there exists some $t'>t$ s.t. $\rho(\theta_i(t')) < \rho(\theta_j(t'))$.

Parts (i) and (ii) of Theorem 2 are the polar opposites of the respective ones in Theorem 1. On the other hand, Part (iii) states that, within the scenario considered, leadership in productivity is never more than an ephemeral state of affairs. In other words, along any technological path leader/follower reversals will continuously occur.

The essential rationale behind Theorem 2 may be explained as follows. Suppose that a 'branching off' occurs such that only one of the economies invents the corresponding breakthrough, say economy 1. Then, if the diffusion lag is relatively short, the fact that the breakthrough's productivity increase is significantly larger than that of normal inventions ensures that, before an irreversible divergence materializes, economy 2 will find it profitable to imitate it. A breakthrough, in other words, is always 'absorbing'. This precludes any technological divergence to ever grow beyond a certain bound. And then, given this continuous technological proximity, recurrent leader/follower reversals become a simple consequence of the facts that inventions are developed independently by each economy but only flow across them with some lag.

In view of the previous theorems, it becomes of some interest to investigate what is the dynamic evolution of the economies when no (further) breakthroughs are available. This should help clarify the key role played by such type of inventions in the former results. In this respect, the following Theorem can be established.

Theorem 3: Let $\mathfrak{L} = \varnothing$. Then Parts (i), (ii) and (iii) of Theorem 2 apply to every technological path $\{\theta_1(t),\theta_2(t)\}_{t=1,2,...}$.

This theorem points to the fact that, if the technological context contains no breakthroughs, the two economies will remain forever close (both in technologies and productivities), no matter what is the magnitude of the diffusion lag. (In general, of course, the bounds M and M' above will depend on s.)

The intuition for this result is straightforward. If no breakthroughs may ever arise, point (ii) of Assumption (A.3) always applies. But then, it implies that an economy cannot become too backwards without enjoying (through imitation) an available path through which it may approach the leader economy. This prevents the backwards economy from seeing the size of its gap (both technological and in productivity) increase any further.

3.3. On the Benefits and Drawbacks of Economic Integration

As established by Theorems 1 and 2, different degrees of economic integration (reflected by different magnitudes for the diffusion lag)[14] induce drastically different types of long-run behaviour. In the context with a large diffusion lag covered by Theorem 1, the economies eventually become technological isolates, thereafter evolving as essentially separate entities. On the contrary, in the context of Theorem 2 where the diffusion lag is small, the economies remain in genuine interaction throughout the whole process.

Motivated by these considerations, there arises the following natural question: Can it be established which of these two scenarios will be most conducive to growth? Intuitively, it seems that the process where interaction is maintained will display positive synergic effects that should stimulate growth. More specifically, the fact that, in this scenario, both economies may essentially pool their respective inventions should accelerate their joint rate of technological development. This intuition is indeed confirmed by the next result.

Theorem 4: Assume that $|\mathcal{L}| = \infty$ and (Θ,μ) is a stationary digraph.[15] Let $\underline{s}$, $\bar{s} \in \mathbf{N}$ be as in Theorems 1 and 2 and consider the (stochastic) paths $\{\tilde{\theta}_1(t), \tilde{\theta}_2(t)\}_{t=1,2,\dots}$, $\{\hat{\theta}_1(t), \hat{\theta}_2(t)\}_{t=1,2,\dots}$, starting from identical initial conditions but subject to diffusion lags $\tilde{s} \geq \underline{s}$, $\tilde{s} \leq \bar{s}$, respectively.[16] Then, $\exists T \in \mathbf{N}$, $\exists \alpha \in \mathbf{R}$, s.t. $\forall t \geq T$, $\forall i = 1,2$,
$$E[\ln \rho(\hat{\theta}_i(t)) - \ln \rho(\tilde{\theta}_i(t))] \geq \alpha(t-T).$$

On the basis of the previous theorem, one may be tempted to assert that, in general, it is always the case that the more integrated the economies become, the better off they are (i.e., the smaller the diffusion lag, the more enhanced are their expected long-run growth possibilities). This, however, would be a false extrapolation.

It is not difficult to construct examples where, despite the fact that the two economies are integrated enough to display synergic effects (as those described for the path $\{\hat{\theta}_1(t), \hat{\theta}_2(t)\}_{t=1,2,...}$ above), they are nevertheless 'too integrated'. That is, they would enjoy a higher expected growth rate if, maintaining their synergic interaction (and therefore, a diffusion lag not too large), the flow of information across them were not too fast. The intuition here is that, if the diffusion lag is very small, the two economies behave very much like a single one. Thus, they lack the desirable short-run heterogeneity which would allow them to explore, temporarily, alternative technological directions. They end up 'betting too often for the same horse', thus pooling a narrower wide of technologies than they otherwise could do if they maintained some (limited) extent of disintegration.

4. A RICHER CONTEXT: INDUSTRIAL COMPETITION AND TRADE

In this section, an elaboration on the former schematic model is proposed, which:

(i) expands on the former description of the economies, assuming that each of them is populated by a number of independent competing firms;

(ii) allows for trade and, therefore, market interaction across economies. As advanced, this modified theoretical framework reproduces, essentially unchanged, the main gist of our previous analysis. However, it also enriches our former analysis with some further insights on the 'microeconomics' of the process.

4.1. The General Model

The basic technological structure is inherited from the basic model, and is not repeated here. The presentation of the remaining new components now follows. When sufficient for our present purposes, the presentation is kept quite informal.

(i) Population

Let I_1 and I_2 denote the set of potentially active firms in each economy $i = 1,2$. They are assumed countably infinite and ordered according to potential entry, as described below.[17] At each $t = 0,1,2,...$, a subset of each I_i, $A_i(t)$, includes the active firms in economy i. This set evolves through time as the result of exit and entry, as presently described.

(ii) Exit

Every period, those firms whose profit is smaller than a certain fraction λ $\in (0,1)$ of the average profit in their respective economy are assumed to disappear (irreversibly). Different interpretations are possible here. One is that those firms which do not satisfy the survival requirement go bankrupt because they are unable to meet certain payments (say, capital services or wages) which are linked to the average performance in their own economy. (Thus, some implicit lack of mobility of resources across economies must be assumed in this respect.) A stochastic version of this scenario has been explored in Vega-Redondo (1993a). An alternative possible interpretation is that those firms with sufficiently below-average performance change their management or are simply taken over by other firms (see (iii) below). This is then taken to imply, in some sense, a new firm with a large flexibility to change its previous technological profile.

(iii) Entry

Different formulations could be adopted with similar implications.[18] Here, I shall discuss one of the simplest possible. It merely postulates that the firms of economy $i = 1,2$ which exit at any t are replaced at $t+1$ by an identical number of new firms. These are chosen to be the first ones (i.e., with lowest index) among those which have not yet entered. This implies that the number of active firms remains constant in each economy throughout the process. We shall assume that this number is the same in both economies and equal to $K \in \mathbb{N}$.

(iv) Technological change

Let $\Theta_{ik}(t)$ denote the set of technologies available to firm k of economy i. If this firm, labelled ik, is not active at t (i.e., $ik \notin A_i(t)$), we simply write

$$\Theta_{ik}(t) = \{\#\} \tag{7.9}$$

where # is interpreted as 'inaction'. For all active firms $ik \in A_i(t)$ we have the following law of motion:

$$\Theta_{ik}(t) = H_\beta(\Theta_{ik}(t-1) \cup N_{ik}(t) \cup M_i(t)); \tag{7.10}$$
$$t = 1,2,..., \quad i = 1,2,$$

where the interpretation is analogous to (7.5) above. On the one hand, the set $N_{ik}(t)$ consists of a random sample among the successors of $\theta_{ik}(t-1)$, the previously adopted technology. (If the firm was previously inactive, it is assumed that this set is empty.) On the other hand, we make:

$$M_i(t) = (\underset{k}{\bigcup} \Theta_{ik}(t-s)) \cup (\underset{k}{\bigcup} \Theta_{jk}(t-s^*)), \ i = 1,2, \ i \neq j, \qquad (7.11)$$

where, possibly, the diffusion lags s and s^* ($s \leq s^*$) are not the same for the technological information flowing within and across borders.

(v) Payoffs

Both economies are assumed to be integrated into a common international market. In a reduced form, this is modelled through payoff functions

$$\pi_{ik}: \Theta^{l_1} \times \Theta^{l_2} \to \mathbb{R} \qquad (7.12)$$

which specify the profit accruing to each firm ik depending on the world technological profile. (This function could be viewed as incorporating suitably formulated output or price decisions which are contingent on prior technological choice; in particular, it could reflect a situation where firms produce different goods, each one of them linked to a different 'technological choice'.)

The functions $\pi_{ik}(\cdot)$ represent *gross* payoffs. Net payoffs are obtained from them by subtracting the switching costs associated with any technological adjustment, as presently described.

If the firm in question is an incumbent firm, i.e., previously active, such switching costs are given by some function $C(\cdot)$, as given by (7.6) and (7.7).

For new entrants, the 'switching cost' is assumed to depend on the technology profile prevailing in the economy where it enters. If the new entrant adopts a technology currently being used in its economy, then the switching cost, indeed an entry cost, is assumed uniform and finite. Otherwise, it is assumed to be infinite. Thus, essentially, this amounts to restricting the initial choice of a new entrant to a technology which is in current use within its own economy. The motivation here is that an entrant has to make use of the currently available know-how of the economy to which it belongs before being able to assimilate new knowledge from abroad. Although admittedly too drastic, this assumption conveniently reflects the constraints which the current technological base of a given economy will impose on its newcomers. It could be easily generalized, simply imposing, for example, a bound on the extent to which a new entrant may be technologically more advanced than the current frontier of its economy.

A further simplification of our framework is provided by the following assumption, which establishes a useful representation for the payoff functions (whose arguments are technological profiles) in terms of corresponding functions of real variables:

(A.4) There is some non-negative function $\rho: \Theta \rightarrow \mathbb{R}_+(\rho(\#) = 0)$ such that, for each firm $ik \in I_i$ and $\underline{\theta} \in \Theta^{I_1} \times \Theta^{I_2}$, $\pi_{ik}(\underline{\theta}) = f_{ik}(\underline{\rho}(\underline{\theta}))$ where $\underline{\rho}(\underline{\theta}) = (\rho(\theta_{ik}))_{i,k}$ and the set of functions $f_{ik}: \mathbb{R}^{(I_1 + I_2)} \rightarrow \mathbb{R}$, $ik \in I_i$, $i = 1,2$, are 'anonymous' (i.e., invariant under index permutation), uniformly continuous and increasing in their respective $\rho_{ik} \equiv \rho(\theta_{ik})$.

Moreover, $\forall \varepsilon > 0 \; \exists \delta > 0$ such that:

$$\forall \rho \in \mathbb{R}^I, \; \forall i,j = 1,2, \; \forall k,k', \frac{\rho_{ik}}{\rho_{jk'}} \leq \delta \Rightarrow \frac{f_{ik}(\rho)}{f_{jk'}(\rho)} \leq \varepsilon.$$

The first part of (A.4) asserts the existence of a real representation of the 'values' of technologies, the vector of which is in turn the argument of the payoff functions of firms. These values may be interpreted, for example, as production costs. Alternatively, one could view them as indicators of product quality. They play an important role in simplifying the analysis.

The second part of (A.4) indicates that, if the ratio between the technological values of two firms becomes sufficiently large, then the corresponding ratio between their (gross) profits will also become arbitrarily large. This simply reflects the role of 'technological value' as an indicator of relative competitiveness.

(vi) Firm behaviour

As with other components of the model, different paradigms of firm behaviour may be postulated without affecting the essence of our results. Let me verbally describe two of them which are possible.

(a) At each t, every firm $ik \in A_i(t)$ chooses a (the) technology in $\Theta_{ik}(t)$ which maximizes its net payoff, given the technological profile prevailing at the preceding period. This formulation may be rationalized by assuming that firms are boundedly rational, in that they are unable to predict (or react to) any change occurring during the current period.

(b) A somewhat polar paradigm is the following. Every t, active firms play a Nash equilibrium of the simultaneous-move game defined by the profile of status quo technologies $(\theta_{ik}(t-1))_{i,k}$, the current technological sets $(\Theta_{ik}(t))_{i,k}$, and the above described payoff functions. As opposed to (a), this implicitly assumes that all active firms have all such information and are able to compute (and play) a corresponding Nash Equilibrium.[19]

As indicated, every one of our upcoming results apply under any of the two former behavioural paradigms. These results are summarized in the next section.

4.2. Results

First, it is confirmed that the essential nature of our previous results remains valid in the new context.

In order to bridge the gap between the two models, some counterparts for the previous clearcut notions of economy-wide productivities and technological distance need to be proposed. As for the productivity notion, a natural candidate to substitute for it in the present context is the aggregate gross profit of each economy.[20] Given a technological profile $\underline{\theta} \equiv (\underline{\theta}_1, \underline{\theta}_2) \in \Theta^{I_1} \times \Theta^{I_2}$, it is defined by:

$$\tilde{\pi}_i(\underline{\theta}) \equiv \sum_{ik \in I_i} \pi_{ik}(\underline{\theta}), \; i = 1,2. \tag{7.13}$$

As for a counterpart of the previous notion of technological distance between economies, a specially simple one is defined as follows. Given the technological profile $\underline{\theta}$, denote by $A_i(\underline{\theta})$ the K active firms of economy $i = 1,2$. The technological distance from economy i to economy j is then defined by:

$$\tilde{\gamma}(\underline{\theta}_i, \underline{\theta}_j) \equiv \min\{\gamma(\theta_{ik}, \theta_{jk}), \; \theta_{ik} \in A_i(\underline{\theta}), \; \theta_{jk} \in A_j(\underline{\theta})\}. \tag{7.14}$$

That is, the technological distance from economy i to economy j is identified with the smallest distance across pairs of respectively used technologies. Based on these concepts, the following analogues of Theorems 1 to 4 can be established for the richer model discussed in this section:[21]

Theorem 1′: Assume $|\underline{\mathcal{L}}| = \infty$. There exists some $\underline{s} \in \mathbf{N}$ such that if $(s^* \geq) \, s \geq \underline{s}$, then every technological path $\{\underline{\theta}_1(t), \underline{\theta}_2(t)\}_{t=1,2,...}$ satisfies, with probability one:

(i) $Lim_{t \to \infty} \tilde{\gamma} \; (\underline{\theta}_i(t), \underline{\theta}_j(t)) = \infty, \; i,j = 1,2;$

(ii) $Sup_{t=1,2,...}\{\max \, [\dfrac{\tilde{\pi}_i(\underline{\theta}_i(t))}{\tilde{\pi}_j(\underline{\theta}_j(t))}, \; i,j = 1,2]\} = \infty.$

Theorem 2′: There exists some $\bar{s} \in \mathbf{N}$ such that if $(s \leq) \, s^* \leq \bar{s}$, then every technological path $\{\underline{\theta}_1(t), \underline{\theta}_2(t)\}_{t=1,2,...}$ satisfies:

(i) $\exists M \in \mathbf{R}$ s.t. $Sup_{t=1,2,...}\{\max \, [\tilde{\gamma}(\underline{\theta}_i(t), \underline{\theta}_j(t)), \; i,j = 1,2]\} \leq M;$

(ii) $\exists M' \in \mathbb{R}$ s.t. $\mathrm{Sup}_{t=1,2,...}\{\max [\dfrac{\tilde{\pi}_i(\Theta(t))}{\tilde{\pi}_j(\underline{\Theta}(t))}, i,j = 1,2]\} \leq M'$;

(iii) $\forall t = 1,2,...$, if $\tilde{\pi}_i(\underline{\Theta}(t)) \geq \tilde{\pi}_i(\underline{\Theta}(t))$ then, with probability one, there exists some $t' > t$ s.t. $\tilde{\pi}_i(\underline{\Theta}(t)) < \tilde{\pi}_j(\underline{\Theta}(t))$.

Theorem 3': Let $\mathfrak{L} = \varnothing$. Then Parts (i), (ii) and (iii) of Theorem 2' apply to every technological path $\{\underline{\Theta}_1(t),\underline{\Theta}_2(t)\}_{t=1,2,...}$

Theorem 4': Assume that $|\mathfrak{L}| = \infty$ and (Θ,μ) is a stationary digraph. Let $\underline{s},\bar{s} \in N$ be as in Theorems 1' and 2' and consider the (stochastic) paths $\{\underline{\tilde{\theta}}_1(t),\underline{\tilde{\theta}}_2(t)\}_{t=1,2..}$, $\{\underline{\hat{\theta}}_1(t),\underline{\hat{\theta}}_2(t)\}_{t=1,2..}$, starting from identical initial conditions but subject to diffusion lags $(\tilde{s}^* \geq) \tilde{s} \geq \underline{s}$, and $(\hat{s} \leq) \hat{s}^* \leq \bar{s}$, respectively. Then, $\exists T \in \mathbb{N}$, $\exists \alpha \in \mathbb{R}$, s.t. $\forall t \geq T$, $\forall i = 1,2$,

$$E [\ln\rho(\underline{\hat{\theta}}_i(t)) - \ln\rho(\underline{\tilde{\theta}}_i(t))] \geq \alpha(t-T)$$

The intuition underlying the former set of results is quite similar to that of their respective counterparts of Section 3. The key point to understand here is that, due to the postulated criterion of firm bankruptcy[22], profit heterogeneity *within* each economy is bounded throughout, even in the case of recurrent technological branching. On the other hand, if such branching exists and technological diffusion is slow, the economies as a whole will tend to diverge technologically from each other for much the same reasons as in our original simple model. Being this the case, their profit gap will eventually grow to an arbitrary extent in full probability (Theorem 1'). As in the original model, the conclusion is reversed if either there is no technological branching (Theorem 3') or, even if in the presence of it, the diffusion lag is sufficiently small (Theorem 2'). Finally, the comparison of each of the two polar scenarios in terms of their expected long-run performance (Theorem 4') is fully analogous to that of Section 3.

Well beyond the above reassuring analogies between the basic model and its subsequent elaboration, the explicit microeconomics of the latter allows a substantial enriching of our analysis. I provide two illustrative examples of this, which will close our formal discussion of the chapter.

Both illustrations refer to a technological context with recurrent branching ($|\mathfrak{L}| = \infty$). The first one (Theorem 5 below) indicates that, even though technological heterogeneity will indeed arise within both economies, both of them can be viewed as developing an idiosyncratic technological specialization in relatively similar technologies. The second result (Theorem 6 below) establishes that the process of technological development unfolding in each economy will be of a 'Schumpeterian nature'; specifically, it will involve a process of creative destruction, with new innovations recurrently inducing the exit of incumbent firms (and thus the 'destruction' of their corresponding 'technological trajectories').

In order to formalize these matters, define the technological span of the profile $\underline{\theta}_i$ for economy $i = 1,2$ by:

$$\omega(\underline{\theta}_i) \equiv \max \{\gamma(\theta_{ik},\theta_{ik'}); \; \theta_{ik},\theta_{ik'} \in A_i(\underline{\theta})\}. \tag{7.15}$$

We then have:

Theorem 5: Assume $|\mathcal{L}| = \infty$. There exists some $\underline{s} \in \mathbb{N}$ such that if $s \geq \underline{s}$, $\forall D > 0$, $\exists T \in \mathbb{N}$ s.t. $\forall t \geq T$, the technological path $\{\underline{\theta}_i(t),\underline{\theta}_j(t)\}_{t=1,\ldots}$ satisfies:
$$E[\gamma(\underline{\theta}_i(t),\underline{\theta}_j(t)) - \omega(\underline{\theta}_i(t))] \geq D; \; i,j = 1,2, \; i \neq j.$$

Theorem 6: Assume $|\mathcal{L}| = \infty$. There exists some $\underline{s} \in \mathbb{N}$ such that if $s \geq \underline{s}$, $\forall \varepsilon > 0$, $\exists \Delta > 0$ s.t. if $t'-t \geq \Delta$, there is probability no smaller than $1-\varepsilon$ that the technological path $\{\underline{\theta}_1(t),\underline{\theta}_2(t)\}_{t=1,\ldots}$ satisfies:
$$A_i(t') \cap A_i(t) = \varnothing, \; i = 1,2.$$

Theorem 5 establishes that, under technological branching and slow diffusion, each economy will develop some degree of technological specialization. More precisely, the technological span covered by its technologies in use will be arbitrarily smaller (in expected terms) than the technological distance which separates it from the other economy.

Theorem 6 asserts that, under the previous conditions, the process of technological change will induce, within each economy, a continuous process of firm turnover. Specifically, with arbitrarily high probability, no firm should be expected to remain active for more than some pre-established length of time.

The intuition underlying these results may be explained along already familiar lines. Under technological branching, all firms (even those firms within a given economy) will eventually end up proceeding along independent technological paths. When this happens, they also become unavoidably vulnerable to quick technological advance by their competitors (in particular, their domestic ones). This, in the end, leads to their forced exit, producing the type of turnover indicated by Theorem 6. Combining such a turnover with the rules postulated for fresh entry (in particular, with the fact that entrants have to imitate one of the current technologies in its own economy) eventually there obtains the degree of domestic specialization established by Theorem 5.

5. SUMMARY AND CONCLUDING COMMENTS

In this chapter, a new approach to modelling technological change has been proposed whose main purpose is to stress its path-dependent nature. To capture such path dependence, the space of technologies has been endowed with the structure of a directed graph. On this digraph, the postulated direction induces the course followed by invention, whereas an appropriate notion of technological gap defined on the digraph determines the magnitude of the switching costs involved in any technological shift.

In such a technological scenario, two subsequent models of increasing complexity have been studied. In the first simple one, two economies, each identified with a single representative agent, are assumed to evolve side by side, with innovation and lagged diffusion between them unfolding as time proceeds. Depending on the particular features of the underlying digraph (essentially, the extent of 'branching' it displays) and the parameters of the model (in particular, the magnitude of the diffusion lag), quite different qualitative behaviour arises. Specifically, it can range from the eventual materialization of arbitrarily large differences in relative development to a scenario where both economies remain relatively close, both technologically and in terms of respective development levels. Issues related to the effect of economic integration on the overall level of development of both economies have also been studied.

In the second model, the objective has been to elaborate on the preceding context by enriching the internal description of each economy. Specifically, the previous representative agent has been replaced by a number of different firms which independently innovate, imitate, and compete in the world market, entering and exiting it as determined by their particular fortunes. In this context, the overall behaviour turns out to be qualitatively analogous to that resulting from the original simple model, adding to it some new considerations pertaining to the 'microeconomics' of the process. In particular, it has been explained that, as time proceeds, one will witness a never-ending Schumpeterian process of 'creative destruction', firms exiting and entering the market as their respective technological trajectories, too mature to be re-directed, become obsolete.

The model proposed in this chapter is admittedly too stylized for many of the interesting questions which one would like to address on the complex problem of technological evolution. Furthermore, it abstracts from important considerations (such as the endogeneity of innovation, which in the chapter is identified with mere 'learning by doing') that are undoubtedly crucial to understand the phenomenon. However, as a first step in the direction of incorporating certain important path-dependence features of the process which have been ignored by previous literature, such shortcomings may be viewed as suggestions and challenges for future research.

NOTES

1. This chapter was written while I was visiting the Institute for Advanced Studies in Vienna. I thank this institution for its hospitality. I also acknowledge financial support by the CICYT (Spanish Ministry of Education), project nos PB 89–0294 and PS 90–0156.
2. Representative instances of it are Romer (1986, 1990), Lucas (1988), or Grossman and Helpman (1991).
3. See, for example, Nelson and Winter (1982) or Dosi, Pavitt and Soete (1990).
4. A directed graph (also called a 'digraph') is simply identified with a certain set of points, some of which are taken to be connected by directional links or 'arrows'.
5. See Vega-Redondo (1993, 1994).
6. This is fully relaxed in the multi-firm model of Section 4, where every one of the firms operating in each economy can be interpreted to be producing a different (divisible) good.
7. That is, a reflexive, anti-symmetric, and transitive binary relation on Θ. Such a relation is called 'partial', if it is not the case that every two elements of the set are ordered.
8. For simplicity, it will be assumed that there is some technology which precedes all others. Thus, the set $Q(\theta, \theta')$ is always non-empty.
9. This could be modified by contemplating some costs linked to the number of draws being obtained. Vega-Redondo (1993) includes this formulation in a context of industrial competition (see the sections below), thus endogenizing the magnitude of the innovation process at each point in time. This complicates matters substantially since it makes the decision problem of the agents unavoidably dynamic. Since such complications are not germane to the main gist of the present paper, I choose to abstract from them.
10. This requirement can be precisely specified in terms of corresponding restrictions on the parameter values of the model. For our present purposes, however, it is unnecessary to make them explicit.
11. An illustrative example discussed by Mokyr is the introduction of the potato in Ireland during the 18th century. As it is well known, this new crop increased very significantly the agricultural yields in this country, allowing it to confront the risk of famines much more effectively. Eventually, however, it became a source of economic stagnation, since potatoes were ill-suited for the application of the subsequent technological developments that produced large productivity gains in other crops.
12. In these illustrations, only the path-related features of technologies are incorporated. In order to match Assumption (A.3) fully, one has to associate with each technology a corresponding productivity level which satisfies the contemplated requirements.
13. As advanced, I shall not provide formal proofs of the results presented in this paper. Those of this subsection can be found in Vega-Redondo (1994); those of Subsection 4.2 below in Vega-Redondo (1993).
14. It is perhaps worthwhile emphasizing that, in this paper, the concept of economic integration bears on the idea of integrated technological environments (specifically, on the speed of technological diffusion), not on the alternative one related to the openness of international markets and trade.
15. Essentially, a stationary digraph is one which displays the same structure from any given point onwards. Or more precisely, one for which all its sub-graphs are μ-isomorphic.
16. Everything else (utility and switching-cost functions, invention probabilities, etc.) is identical in both contexts.
17. Thus, they can be identified with the set of natural numbers $\mathbf{N}$.

18. For example, in Vega-Redondo (1993) the number of firms is endogenously determined, with potential entrants deciding whether to enter or not depending on the current conditions and an entry cost.
19. A further level of sophistication which shall not be pursued here is to postulate that firms are aware of the intertemporal setting in which they are participating and can evaluate their decisions accordingly. This is the scenario studied in Vega-Redondo (1993) as a stochastic game. As it would have been natural to expect, some of the conclusions obtained for paradigm (b) (and (a)) are still obtained in the stochastic-game framework if the firms are sufficiently myopic, i.e., they discount the future quite enough.
20. One could also use net, instead of gross, profit with identical implications. In our simple context, profit and income may be identified.
21. The relevant parts of Assumptions (A.1) to (A.4) are assumed throughout.
22. Recall the formulations of exit and entry described in (ii) and (iii) of Subsection 4.1.

REFERENCES

Arthur, W.B. (1989), 'Competing Technologies, Increasing Returns, and Lock-in by Historical Events', *Economic Journal*, 99, 116–31.

Cardwell, D.S.L. (1972), *The Turning Points in Western Technology*, New York: Neal Watson Academic Publications.

David, P. (1985), 'Clio and the Economics of Qwerty', *American Economic Review*, 75, 332–6.

Dosi, G., K. Pavitt and L. Soete (1990), *The Economics of Technical Change and International Trade*, Brighton: Harvester Wheatsheaf.

Foray, D. and A. Grübler (1991), 'Morphological Analysis, Diffusion, and Patterns of Technological Evolution: Ferrous Casting in France and the FRG', in *Diffusion of Technologies and Social Behaviour*, Berlin: Springer-Verlag.

Freeman, C. (1991), 'Networks of Innovators', *Research Policy*, 20, 499–514.

Grossman, G.M. and E. Helpman (1991), *Innovation and Growth in the Global Economy*, Cambridge, Mass.: The MIT Press.

Lucas, R. (1988), 'On the Mechanics of Economic Development', *Journal of Monetary Economics*, 22, 3–42.

Mokyr, J. (1990), *The Lever of Riches: Technological Creativity and Economic Progress*, Oxford: Oxford University Press.

Nelson, R. and S. Winter (1982), *The Evolutionary Theory of Economic Development*, Cambridge, Mass.: Harvard University Press.

Romer, P. (1986), 'Increasing Returns and Long-Run Growth', *Journal of Political Economy*, 94(5), 1002–37.

Romer, P. (1990), 'Endogenous Technological Change', *Journal of Political Economy*, 98(5), S71–S103.

Swan, P. (1991), 'Rapid Technological Change, 'Visions of the Future', Corporate Structure and Market Structure', paper presented for the Colloquium on Management of Technology, Paris, May.

Vega-Redondo, F. (1993), 'Competition and Culture in the Evolution of Economic Behaviour', *Games and Economic Behaviour*, 5, 618-31.

Vega-Redondo, F. (1993), 'Technological Change and Institutional Inertia: A Game-Theoretic Approach', *Journal of Evolutionary Economics*, 3, 199-224.

Vega-Redondo, F. (1993), 'Technological Change, Path Dependence, and Industrial Dynamics', Working Paper A Discusión, WP–AD 93–4, Universidad de Alicante.

Vega-Redondo, F. (1994), 'Technological Change and Path Dependence: A Co-Evolutionary in a Directed Graph', *Journal of Evolutionary Economics*, 4, 59-80.

8. Catching-Up From Way Behind. A Third World Perspective on First World History

Erik S. Reinert[1]

Schumpeter once said that 'the upper strata of society are like hotels which are ... always full of people, but people who are forever changing' (Schumpeter 1934: 156).[2] It is tempting to use the same metaphor on nations. Taking a long view, many nations have in sequence joined the upper strata hotel: Britain, the United States, Germany, Japan and others. Once there, however, they have tended to stay. The country occupying the best suites have changed, but all who ever moved into the hotel, still – compared to the Third World – 'constitute "the rich", a class ... who are removed from life's battles', to continue quoting Schumpeter on this issue (Schumpeter 1934: 156). These countries, however, are the home of only a minority of world population.

The last 10 years have brought about a changing perspective on how economic growth actually happens. This improved understanding, however, has mainly evolved around the countries which are already living in Schumpeter's upper strata hotel – the Triad of Europe, Japan, and the United States. In this chapter I shall mentally leave this hotel, and see the world from the Third World point of view. Unfortunately, the focusing on the upper strata is somewhat in the spirit of the master himself. Schumpeter's own aristocratic manners, habits, and tastes were not exactly compatible with viewing the world from the point of view of the 'losers' or laggards.

There is a second, and less obvious, reason for studying the problems of the Third World. Understanding underdevelopment in the Third World can contribute effectively to a better understanding of the growth process in the industrialized countries. The economic problems of the industrialized world give weak and unclear symptoms, much in the same way that early stages of an illness produce general and unspecific symptoms: a fever or a headache. As the illness advances – as the patient gets sicker – stronger and more specific symptoms appear, making a diagnosis possible. My contention is that the study of the economically very sick nations can significantly contribute to the understanding of the developed world, for example the European Community running a slight fever.

We traditionally place the catching-up of the Third World in a different profession – that of development economics – from that of industrialized country catching-up. In doing this, we perpetuate a fragmentation of economic science which is instrumental in blocking our path towards a better understanding of the process of economic development.[3]

The long distance to be covered today by the Third World to get to the present theoretical possibility-frontier of living standards and technology, is very similar to the long distances which in the past were faced – at different times in history – by countries like England and Japan. These countries, as did the US and Germany, at some point in history went through remarkably successful catching-up processes starting from very far behind what was then the *avant garde* countries economically. For this reason history becomes a very useful laboratory, where successful strategies for catching-up from way behind can be studied. Economic ideologies of successful national take-off periods in different countries, although separated by centuries, have key common elements. These common elements also distinguish them as a group from the neoclassical economic policy which today is the foundation of the IMF and World Bank policy towards the Third World. My premise is that historically all *long-distance* catching-up processes have shared certain important elements. With marginal exceptions for tiny economic areas, there appears to be only *one* type of national strategy which has led to long-distance catch-up through the centuries. I shall call this the *List-cum-Smith* model. There is reason to believe that this will be the only possible strategy also in the future.

In this chapter I attempt to do the following: Part 1 focuses on the recent insights in the growth process, but looks at them from the point of view of the Third World. Part 2 looks at successful long-distance catch-up strategies in a historical perspective going back 500 years and more. A key insight provided by history is the view that economic development at any point in time is *activity-specific*. Historically, there has been a clear perception that only some activities induce growth – these are 'better' than normal economic activities. In Part 3 I attempt to isolate the factors causing some economic activities to be 'better' than others, and to provide a Quality Index or Quality Meter for ranking economic activities according to their potential for creating development with growth. Part 4 describes the diffusion process of gains from new technologies – why technological progress in some cases is appropriated by the producing nations, and sometimes spreads entirely to the consumers. The Clinton administration's emphasis on 'high quality jobs' is an example of an intuitive approach to the same set of problems. At any point in time, the people and nations who capture the high quality activities inhabit the top floors of Schumpeter's hotel.

I argue that historically the common interventionist strategy of the industrialized world created a 'platform', above which the virtuous circles of development later became self-sustaining under a non-interventionist policy. I call this the *List-cum-Smith* strategy, because it combines the nurturing of 'superior' economic activities with competitive markets. Later 'path dependence' took off from these platforms, created by skilful use of both regulation and market. Below this platform, similar cumulative processes, in the form of vicious circles, work towards a convergence of the poor countries.[4] The Quality Meter and the alternative modes productivity gains spread in the world economy, are mechanisms which create two convergence groups of nations – one rich and one poor – with a remarkable lack of *middle-class* countries.

1. THE VIEW OF THE VANQUISHED – A THIRD WORLD LOOK AT RECENT THEORETICAL INSIGHTS

Understanding the problems of *under*development is in a way a process of turning the many recent insights in the process of economic growth and development upside down. This often implies simply looking at the same evidence, but from the side of the loser, not the winner. Historically, a parallel to this can be found in the similarity of dynamic world view that underlies both Marx and Schumpeter, in spite of their very different conclusions. This similarity is readily admitted by Schumpeter,[5] who suggests that the similarities between Marx and himself are 'obliterated by a very wide difference in general outlook' (Schumpeter 1951: 161). Marx tended to see the destructive side of the capitalist system, while Schumpeter emphasized the creative aspect of that destruction. Schumpeter saw the rise of the cotton textile mills in Manchester, Marx (1867: 389) saw the bones of the cotton weavers who previously supplied India and England 'bleaching the plains of India'. Similarly, Chandler, Porter, Lundvall/Nelson and Perez/Freeman, emphasize the winners – the *star industries* in Porter's first book – without paying much attention to what happens to the losers – Porter's *dog industries* – that are necessarily a part of the same system. Their focus is on understanding the frontiers of technological development, as if all economic activities could be at that frontier. In the following examples I apply the view from the 'dog' industries – a *view of the vanquished* – to what are probably the six most significant new theoretical insights into the economic growth process of the industrialized world to have emerged during the last decade: 1) Chandler's 'scale and scope', 2) Porter's 'competitive advantage', 3) Lundvall and Nelson's 'national innovation systems', 4) Perez and Freeman's 'techno-economic paradigms', 5) Nelson and Winter's 'evolutionary theory', and 6) Chandler and Lazonick's 'organizational capabilities'. All of these, although insightful, have the common feature that they only look at 'frontier' industries, the 'high quality jobs' in Robert Reich's terms.

1. Alfred Chandler has given us a theory of the growth of big business which has greatly improved our understanding of the development of the industrialized world – the First World. In order to understand the Third World we must keep in mind that for every spectacularly successful US Steel Corporation, there was an equally spectacular failure of a US Leather Corporation which tried the same strategy as US Steel.[6] Understanding *development* means being able to pinpoint the potential US Steels out there, understanding *underdevelopment* is understanding *why US Leather Corporation failed* where US Steel succeeded.

2. Michael Porter's first book on industrial strategy (Porter 1980) is in many ways a list of recipes and prescriptions for avoiding being in a business where the assumptions of neoclassical economics are valid – how to avoid working where there are no barriers to entry, no economies of scale, and where information is reasonably perfect. Understanding under-development is understanding what happens to the industries where Porter's strategies don't work – the industries he tells his customers to keep away from, the 'dogs' in his classification (Porter 1980). In the Porter book which economists read – *The Competitive Advantage of Nations* – the author carries the conclusions drawn from the arena of industrial competition to the national level (Porter 1990). The core of the advice he gives to nations is essentially the same that he gives to corporations: grow 'star' industries – 'good' industries – and keep away from the 'dog' industries. However, aggregate world demand consists of products both from 'star' industries and 'dog' industries, thus opening up for a game with very variable payoffs. Limited by demand for 'star' industry products, the winners in Porter's game can only be a small fraction of the world population. What are the solutions for the rest, the vast majority of the world population? 'Competitiveness' in Porter's scheme consists of positioning your own country in the 'star' activities, where imperfect markets will shuffle wealth your way. The core of Porter's theory is like observing, correctly, that doctors make more money than lettuce pickers, and then recommend that the world population should consist exclusively of doctors. Later in the chapter I shall argue that Porter's national strategy recommendations are essentially a more sophisticated version of the

recommendations of the dynamic part of two very old schools of economic thought: the mercantilists and the cameralists.

3. A third important development is the research around the concept of *National Innovation Systems*, generally associated with Bengt-Åke Lundvall (1992) and Richard Nelson (1993). Interactive learning, research and development and the resulting innovation are, correctly in this writer's eyes, seen as crucial factors in explaining economic growth. If the 'national innovation system' approach is extended from being another recipe book for the growing of 'star' industries, into being a more generalized theory of economic development, it is haunted by an implicit assumption very similar to the one which haunts Porter: it does not discuss sufficiently the fact that, at any time in history, economic activities possess widely different opportunities for learning. As long as there is demand also for goods in the non-learning areas, trade is no longer a win/win game. That would only happen if learning potential was the same in all activities – that one 'unit of learning' in every activity changes the output by the same quantity. The cumulative nature of knowledge is frequently, and correctly, pointed out. You are not likely to build a 747 if you have not built other, simpler aircraft previously. But there is more to it than that: at any point in time, world learning focuses – is 'available' – only in a few out of the total spectrum of economic activities. We tend to name historical periods after the economic activities where learning took place at that time: in the stone-working industry in the stone age, in the bronze-working industry in the bronze age, and in manufacturing industry in the machine age.

4. Radical changes in the technology systems, penetrating the majority of economic activities, were named changes in the 'techno-economic paradigm' by Perez (1983). The new technological paradigms, however, not only penetrate different industries to different degrees, new technology often 'hits' some activities in the *value chain*[7] of an industry and not others. In my student days in Cambridge, Massachusetts, this fact was visualized by a very old uniformed man from Western Union. He daily plodded across the Charles River bridge to deliver by hand international cables which at an incredible speed had been carried around the world by satellite – except for the last one mile. Today, thousands of people in Haiti are making a living producing baseballs using a needle-and-thread technology which has changed minimally over the last few hundred years, while golf balls are made with machines. The machine age came to the harvesting of wheat, but not yet to the harvesting of strawberries. The neglected historical *sequence of mechanization,* and the resulting trade patterns, has profound implications for explaining differences in GNP per capita. Understanding growth is understanding how to grab the activities which first create or benefit from the new techno-economic paradigms.

Understanding poverty is understanding the trade patterns caused by the *sequence* in time and space of introduction of these new paradigms.

5. In their *Evolutionary Theory of Economic Change*, Nelson and Winter (1982) describe markets as a selection mechanism among firms. This selection is strongly influenced by the *capabilities of the firm,* in addition to the important effects of random events. Understanding the process of economic development and underdevelopment requires changing the unit of analysis; applying the analysis of the evolutionary selection process to what happens between *nations,* not firms. Markets are a selection mechanism by which different economic activities are distributed among nations, according to the capabilities of these nations. One key mechanism at work is that economic activities requiring few capabilities (needle-and-thread technology) are automatically shed by the rich countries to the poor. For this reason, among others, random events like production with new technologies are far from randomly distributed among nations. Through the logical selection process of the market, low wages – in short: being poor – become the key success factor for Third World manufacturing businesses. A consequence of this strategy is that poor countries specialize in the economic activities where the industrialized countries have not found any scope for learning.

6. The final factor which I would like to discuss from the point of view of the Third World is Chandler's and Lazonick's (1991) view of *organizational capabilities* as the key to the success of a firm. Thomas McCraw of Harvard Business School suggests that the national counterpart of *organizational capabilities* in firms is the Listian concept of *National Productive Power*[8] (see McCraw 1993, addendum). In such a framework the national standard of living of a country – and indeed sometimes the physical survival of its inhabitants – will be determined by the same selection process as the one which determines the profit rate – or survival – of a firm. This is a potentially very useful connection between micro- and macroeconomic theory. To understand underdevelopment, the key question is not how to build *capabilities* and *productive power*, it is: what happens if you stick to your comparative advantage in an activity whose capabilities have become commonplace, with skills which have played out their course, in activities left over from exhausted techno-economic paradigms? What are the economic consequences of being a populous and skilled nation specialized in stone-age technology, if the rest of the world is far into the iron age already?

Faced with the compelling logic of the market, that activities which cannot be further mechanized should be carried out by cheap labour, any attempt at 'technology transfer' to the Third World tends to run against the extremely strong forces of the world market. 'Technology transfer' therefore becomes one of the slogans based more on wishful thinking than on any real understanding of the mechanisms at work, on a par with 'new world economic order'.

2. HISTORICALLY SUCCESSFUL LONG-DISTANCE CATCH-UP STRATEGIES: ECONOMIC DEVELOPMENT AS ACTIVITY-SPECIFIC

The striking contrast between the historically successful long-distance catching-up strategies – Britain, the United States, Germany, Japan – and today's economic theory is that these strategies were *activity-specific*. The solution to problems of economic development was to *get into the right business*, which almost inevitably meant manufacturing. This view is expressed in literally hundreds out of the thousands of mercantilist tracts written, particularly in Britain, Germany, and France, starting in the early sixteenth century.[9] Following Adam Smith, today's studies of mercantilism have concentrated on the monetary aspects of their theories. I suggest that there is an important '*Realökonomisch*-mercantilist' school, whose national economic strategies were responsible for a fairly even development within Europe, in contrast with that of the Third World.

To the early economists, all economic activities were different – much in the same way all professions today are different from an individual's point of view. To an individual, his choice of profession will to a large extent determine his future income and social standing. In pre-Ricardian times, society's future income and standing between nations was determined by its *choice* of economic activity. The neoclassical notion that 'all economic activities are alike' would be as meaningless to a pre-Ricardian economist as it is to a young person today facing the problem of choosing a profession. To a person, choosing a career of washing dishes in a restaurant provides a dramatically different future than deciding to become an engineer. Pre-Ricardian national strategy broadens this argument into one where a nation of engineers will be better off than a nation of dishwashers.

The *activity-specific* outlook on wealth creation can be traced back to the strategic importance the Venetians gave to their salt pans, already before the turn of the Millennium.[10] The strategic decision of being in the right business had to be backed up in the political and military spheres by protecting supplies and markets for the 'superior' and 'wealth-creating' activities. Use of force was needed to protect the static and dynamic rents created by *being in the right business*. Historian Frederic Lane (1979) – in a book venturing into economic theory – explains the rise of empires as a result of '*increasing returns* from the use of force as an economic service'.[11]

Following Venice, England presents the most spectacularly successful use of the *activity-specific* strategy. Daniel Defoe describes the English strategy in his *Plan of English Commerce* in 1728.[12] In the early 15th century, England was a poor country, heavily indebted to her Italian bankers. Her chief export was raw wool. Henry VII, who came to power in 1485, had lived in exile in wealthy Burgundy, where English wool was being spun into cloth. The Tudor strategy which started with him was to bring England into the wealth-creating downstream activities in wool manufacturing that Henry had observed abroad. The English strategy was gradual, starting with import substitution. In 1489 tariffs on cloth were increased, and local cloth manufacturing was encouraged. The Crown paid for foreign workers to be brought in, and businessmen were paid bounties for establishing textile manufacturing firms. When sufficient manufacturing capacity had been achieved, England prohibited all export of raw wool. This development paved the way for what has been called 'the closest approximation to a businessman's government' among the *ancien régimes* of Europe (O'Brien 1993: 125). As the wave of mechanization extended from wool to other areas of manufacturing, these new industries were in turn given the same preferential treatment given initially to the production of woollen cloth. Friedrich List (1844: 12) later put it this way: 'The principle *sell manufactures, buy raw material* was during centuries the English substitute for an (economic) theory'.

Taking up the example set by England, the economic strategies of the great industrial nations in their pre-take-off period share a core theme of the *activity-specific* nature of growth.[13] This theme can be followed in economic writings from the early 1500s in Italy and England and France, a little later in the German cameralists. It is introduced to the United States through Alexander Hamilton[14] and his favourite economist, the English mercantilist Malachy Postlethwayt, and from Friedrich List's involuntary exile in the US it is reinforced again in the Germany of the Zollverein. In Meiji Japan the *doitsugaku* school – favouring the German model – came to be the most influential for the building of society, at least until 1945 (Yagi 1989: 29 and Bernd 1987). The Japanese took over the policies which dominated the German historical school: a basic distrust in free trade and an activity-specific attitude towards economic development, part of which was a belief in the superior 'productive powers' of manufacturing. In Japan, after 1883, 'a stream of German teachers of political economy and related disciplines continually flowed in' (Sugiyama and Mizuta 1988: 32). After World War II, the Japanese strategy was challenged by the American occupants, who suggested that the Japanese should specialize, according to their Ricardian comparative advantage, in cheap labour. Japanese policy-makers in that period strongly rejected what we today could call the World Bank / IMF strategy of a 'Ricardian' specialization in low-cost labour. The 'Asian Tigers' headed by South Korea have in their turn inherited much of their activity-specific philosophy from Japan. Freeman talks about the osmosis[15] in the development process from Japan to Korea, and Vogel (1991: 90) shows how 'the Japanese model was of great importance to Taiwan, South Korea, Hong Kong and Singapore'.

A common thread of successful long-distance catching-up through the centuries, is a shared distrust of free trade until the nation is firmly established in what were seen to be the *right* economic activities – the *specific activities* which gave the nation 'productive powers'. The United States over the last decade have – until the election of Bill Clinton – provided a counter-example to this strategy. Somewhat paradoxically, while postwar United States rode on the crest of perhaps the strongest technological wave history has seen, in that same country the neoclassical paradigm, with no room for technology, was perfected. Doubly confident both in her economic power and in the intellectual underpinnings of the neoclassical paradigm (boldly so even in spite of its unrealistic assumptions), the United States unlearned the activity-specific economic strategy which had dominated the nation's policy over the last 100 years (although not always in the academic theory). The nation self-confidently faced the coming of a post-industrial society with the belief that the market can do no wrong. With the election of Bill Clinton, the United States is painfully rediscovering, now also in practical policy, that manufacturing matters, although there is little theoretical understanding as to why this is so. Interestingly, that manufacturing mattered was thoroughly accepted by the 19th century policy-makers in the United States, this was precisely the essence of what was called The American System (Dorfman 1947, vol. 2: 566–97). Then, as today, there were 'high quality jobs' and 'low quality jobs' both from the point of view of the individual and from the point of view of a nation. These terms are Robert Reich's of today, but the same understanding was the foundation of the 19th Century 'American System', offering protection to manufacturing. In Part 3 of this chapter, I attempt to build a framework for understanding *high quality* and *low quality* jobs.

There was always a considerable lag in the economic understanding of *why* some economic activities created more wealth than others. If a remedy worked, it was not always considered important to understand *why*. The first to identify the qualities that made an activity 'good' for a nation was Antonio Serra in 1613.[16] Serra associated 'good' activities as being the result of *increasing returns,* and associated these primarily with manufacturing. Most early works on national trade strategies, however, merely list the characteristics of 'good' and 'bad' activities for a nation without giving any explanation as to *why*. One hundred years after Serra, Charles King's detailed list of 'good' and 'bad' trade was very influential. Exporting manufactures was 'good', importing them was 'bad', except when manufactured goods were traded for other manufactured goods which was 'to ... mutual advantage' of the trading nations (King 1721: 3). King gives no explanations as to why this is so, but if one associates manufacturing with Schumpeterian 'historical increasing returns', and non-manufacturing with diminishing returns, the strategy makes sense.

Moving on to the next century, it is perfectly clear that increasing returns, to quote Schumpeter, were 'an important feature of nineteenth-century analysis'.[17] Increasing returns are very much present until and including the early editions of Alfred Marshall's *Principles of Economics,* the first being in 1890. Marshall (1890: 452) emphasizes that national income may be increased by taxing commodities produced at diminishing returns and paying bounties to producers of commodities produced at increasing returns. This is probably the best description we shall ever get of Japanese growth strategy, but this key insight is lost in the later editions of *Principles.*

Marshall's dismissal of increasing returns from economic theory over the life of his *Principles,* starting in 1890, represents an important watershed in economic theory. Marshall thereby opened the way for the world of economic theory to be inhabited by clones of 'the representative firm' – a world view which lasts until this very day. The reason why increasing returns disappeared from mainstream economic theory, is the same reason they were not allowed back after Frank Graham's article on the subject in 1923: they are not compatible with equilibrium (see e.g. Viner 1937: 475–82).

The *activity-specific* strategies common to all presently industrialized countries – protecting for centuries manufacturing as 'good' economic activities – created a common platform from which growth became self-sustaining. The remarkable lack of long-distance catch-up processes starting in the (neoclassical) 20th century seems to be associated with a lack of long-term *activity-specific* strategies in the presently underdeveloped world. Third World nations are stuck with what we later shall describe as 'growth-inhibiting' economic activities.

Graham's 1923 article represents an important conceptual bridge between pre-20th century economic thought and today's gradual rediscovery of economies of scale and technical change – Schumpeter's 'historical increasing returns' – as important factors causing uneven economic growth. Crossing that bridge, First World historical growth strategies and today's theories and problems can be woven into a very meaningful whole. History starts to make more sense.

What kind of conclusions can we draw from the historical sequence of catching-up strategies of the presently developed countries? Most presently industrialized countries have through the centuries passed through two distinct stages: 1) A *List-cum-Smith stage* of strong intervention against free trade to establish the nation in the 'right' industries. 2) A pure *Smithian stage* emphasizing free trade. Sequentially – after Venice – England was the first country to reach an industrial plateau where free trade would lead to a higher welfare level than continued protectionism. This stage was reached much later by Germany, the United States and Japan, who in the meantime continued their *List-cum-Smith* strategies. Only long after it was possible to trade manufactures for manufactures, a free trade regime was established between the industrialized countries.[18]

I would suggest that history presents us with two important *stylized facts:*

1. No nation of any size has ever joined what today is the rich convergence group – inhabiting the upper strata hotel – without a prolonged Listian phase of economic policy. In a Listian system 'some economic activities are better than others'. In terms of the circular flow, the focus is on man as the *producer.*

2. Once world leadership has been achieved, the Smithian phase takes over in the successful catch-up country. In a Smithian system, 'all economic activities are alike'. In terms of the circular flow, the focus is on man as the *consumer.*

Growth theory in the 1990s is focusing, no doubt correctly, on technical change, innovation, and learning – in addition to the traditional factor, capital. The enormous diversity of economic activity today obscures our view of what is a 'good' and 'bad' economic activity. Going back to 15th century England it is possible to see things more clearly.

At the time of Henry VII, out of all existing human activities, only *one* experienced rapid technical change: the manufacturing of woollen textiles. All other activities were basically carrying on as before. This one activity absorbed capital, because only here were there large scale investments to be made. This one activity had technical change and innovation. Only in this activity were there economies of scale and scope. Only this one activity offered any possibility for new learning. Only this activity created a *demand* for 'organizational capabilities'. At that moment in time it was clear that economic progress was *activity-specific* – it was basically taking place in one economic activity and not in any of the others. The basis for building a 'National Innovation System' was to protect and support the one economic activity where innovation was taking place.

Studies of patents confirm the idea that economic progress develops through changing 'focal points' of technological change (MacLeod 1988). The concentration of patenting in changing areas of manufacturing – and its almost complete absence in agriculture and services – give us a clue as to why the winning combination of *innovation* and *imperfect competition* is found mostly in manufacturing. The combination *innovation* + *imperfect competition* produces the kind of economic growth which 'sticks' in the producing nation.[19] The mercantilist 'national innovation system' achieved this combination by protecting any economic activity in the process of being mechanized – the 'good' economic activities. In the remainder of this chapter we discuss issues related to this:

- How to determine 'good' and 'bad' economic activities.
- The two modes of diffusion of the benefits of new technologies.

3. THE 'QUALITY' OF ECONOMIC ACTIVITIES AS A DETERMINANT FOR ECONOMIC DEVELOPMENT

The obstacle to our understanding the distribution of wealth and poverty between nations is embedded deeply in an economic theory which sees all economic activities as being alike. 'All Chinese look alike to me' is hardly a scientific approach to a study of China and Chinese culture. In neoclassical economic theory, on the other hand, the core assumptions make all economic activities 'alike'. In a world with perfect information, no scale effects, and full divisibility of all factors, the outcome of increased world trade will be factor-price equalization. In the real world the gap between rich and poor nations is increasing steadily, in spite of huge increases in world trade. Clearly *relative efficiency* in the export sector is not a main determinant of wealth: the world's most efficient golf ball producer (in an industrialized country) receives a monetary wage 30 times higher than the world's most efficient baseball producer (in Haiti) – 30 cents an hour compared to a typical industrial country wage of 9 dollars an hour.

We have seen that the growth of the presently rich countries was based on a theory where economic development is *activity-specific:* it happens only in a small part of the whole spectrum of economic activities at any one point in time. Today, locating these 'superior' activities concentrated in any broad industrial category, as in the past, is difficult. Almost all activities and industries, even the most pedestrian ones, have some segments offering the winning combination of innovation and imperfect competition. The process is not fully understood until one reaches the product and brand level.

Figure 8.1.

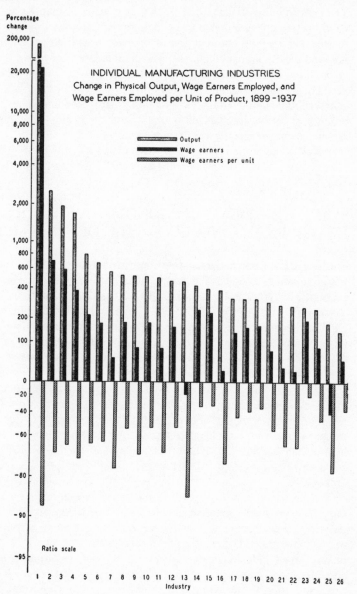

INDUSTRY

1 Automobiles, incl. bodies and parts
2 Chemicals, industrial, incl. compressed gases and rayon
3 Petroleum refining
4 Beet sugar
5 Fruits and vegetables, canned
6 Ice
7 Glass
8 Paper and pulp
9 Silk and rayon goods
10 Knit goods
11 Printing and publishing, total
12 Butter, cheese and canned milk
13 Cigars
14 Rice
15 Paints and varnishes
16 Coke-oven products
17 Zinc
18 Liquors, distilled
19 Steel-mill products
20 Tanning and dye materials
21 Copper
22 Explosives
23 Wood-distillation products
24 Fertilizers
25 Blast-furnace products
26 Jute goods

INDUSTRY

27 Cotton goods
28 Hats, wool-felt
29 Shoes, leather
30 Cane sugar
31 Salt
32 Meat packing
33 Cottonseed products
34 Leather
35 Woolen and worsted goods
36 Liquors, malt
37 Shoes, rubber
38 Carpets and rugs, wool
39 Lead
40 Cordage and twine
41 Gloves, leather
42 Hats, fur-felt
43 Chewing and smoking tobacco
44 Flour
45 Ships and boats
46 Cars, railroad
47 Lumber-mill products
48 Turpentine and rosin
49 Linen goods
50 Locomotives
51 Carriages, wagons and sleighs

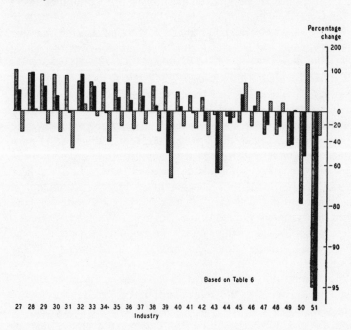

Based on Table 6

Economic development is a process which requires the presence of several *reactants*: capital, education, skills training, institutional factors (property, credit), entrepreneurship, and a technological 'wave' or 'window of opportunity'. The absence of any of these reactants will impede the development process. The understanding of this process is difficult, because not only does the 'formula' – the right mix of reactants – for growth change over time, it also changes from industry to industry at any point in time. Growth-producing innovations have different 'fingerprints' in every industry. In a recent article Moses Abramovitz (1993) enters into these important but neglected problems, but only on an aggregate national level. Further studies into the 'fingerprint' of innovation in different industries would be useful.

An innovation creates *a demand* for education, for skilled labour, for R&D, and for capital. By identifying the economic activities which at any point in time were *in the process of being mechanized* – where new skills were in high demand – the 'primitive' industrial policy of mercantilists and cameralists managed to single out the 'winning' activities, those at the start of a steep learning curve.

Figure 8.1 shows the distribution of technological opportunities in 51 industrial sectors of the US economy from 1899–1937.[20] The growth in productivity rates varies enormously; although we can assume that the same capital, skills and institutional factors were present over the whole spectrum of activities. Clearly, the US would not have taken world leadership if it had been only in industries 27–51. No amount of capital or learning would have achieved the results that in fact were achieved, without the industrial activities on the left side of the chart. Secondary effects spiral from the activities to the left: these activities are the 'wage setters' of the economy, and the upward pressure on wages in turn increase the use of capital in the rest of the economy at the expense of the increasingly more expensive factor labour. Demand grows as the result of higher monetary wages. In the end, the multiplier effect of technological progress in 'wage setting activities' is formidable, and forms a core mechanism in the virtuous circles of development. We tend to forget, however, that technological change comes in focused 'clusters'; in the stone-working industry in the stone age, bronze-working industry in the bronze age, etc.

Uneven distribution of wealth seems to have the same basic causes nationally and internationally. Wage-level differences inside nations are caused by the same mixture of static and dynamic factors, which cause the polarization of the world in a rich and a poor convergence group. Interestingly, in the 1980s sociologists have studied the US economy with a dual-economy approach, an approach used in development economics for a long time (see e.g. Tolbert *et al.* 1980, Hudson and Kaufman 1982).[21] This resulted in a ranking of economic activities similar to that in Figure 8.1 – from 'good' to 'bad' – which is inexplicable, or rather pure nonsense, from a neoclassical viewpoint.[22]

The challenge in economic theory is to find a level of abstraction, where useful generalizations can be made without making all economic activities either *all equal* or *all different*. To a businessman, his firm is unique. The opportunity seen by an entrepreneur is a unique vision, if not in other ways, in the geographical location of his business. At this level of abstraction we are faced with billions of economic agents who are all *unique*. To the other extreme – in neoclassical theory – all economic activities are *equal*.[23] Case studies of firms, industries, and nations are useful building blocks for theories, but a theory on a higher level of abstraction is needed.

What, then, are the characteristics of growth inducing – 'good' – economic activities? Identifying these characteristics must be seen as a task comparable to the measuring of IQ – quantifying the unquantifiable. In economic theory we have defined two extremes of a continuum reasonably well: perfect competition and, at least statically, monopoly. Under perfect competition we would achieve factor-price equalization, we would all be equally rich. Under monopoly, we can predict high rents transferred to the monopoly holder from the rest of the world. A core problem in economic theory is that the profession has, at least until the recent events of new growth and trade theory, *little meaningful to say about varying degrees of imperfect competition,* the conditions under which virtually all economic activities produce and trade. The situation is similar to being able to measure two extremes, black and white, without having any way of measuring the various intermediary shades of grey. This is particularly bothersome in economics, where no activities over any length of time belong to either of the categories we have defined well. In terms of 'degree of perfect/imperfect competition', economic activities are scattered over the spectrum from almost white – where the assumptions of neoclassical theory are reasonably valid – to almost black, where the same assumptions are highly unrealistic. Game theory seems to be in a similar situation, having only the extremes, games with two players and infinite number of players, well defined.

Differences in wage levels, both nationally and between nations, seem to result from varying degrees of imperfect competition – caused by both static and dynamic factors. The factors at work have long been identified both by businessmen and in industrial economics, and they are correlated. In Figure 8.2, I attempt to create an area from light to dark grey where 'the quality' of economic activities at any time can be roughly plotted on a scale from white – 'perfect competition' – to black: 'monopoly'. The latter

Figure 8.2.   The Quality Index of economic activities

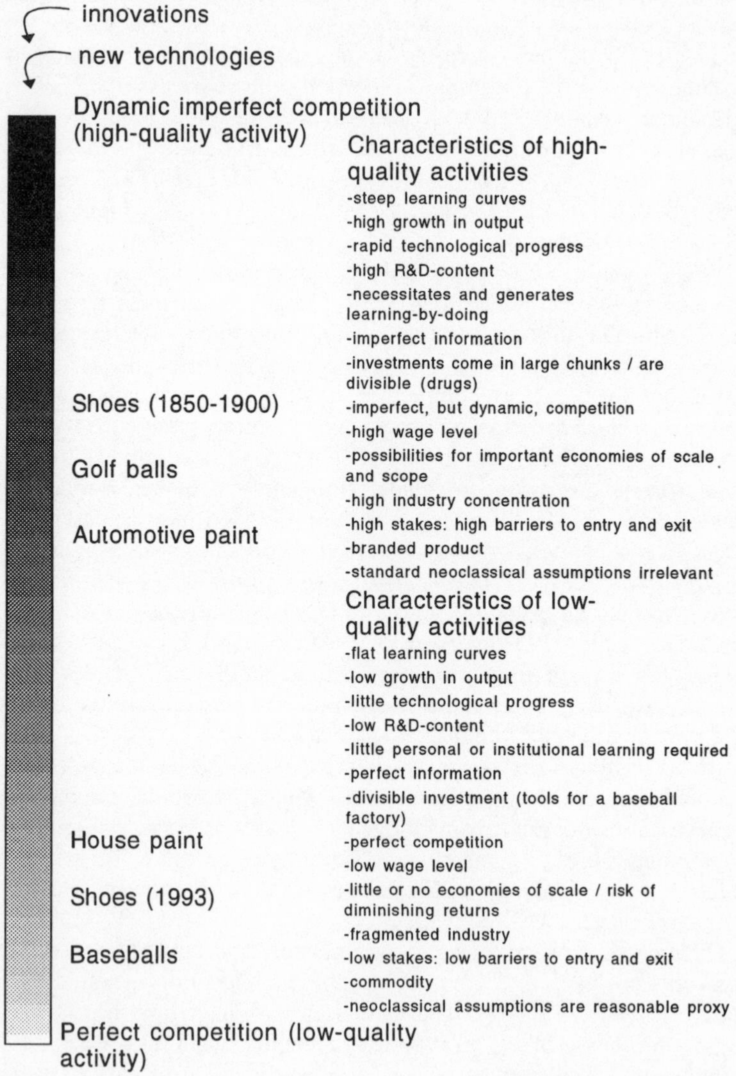

innovations

new technologies

Dynamic imperfect competition (high-quality activity)

Characteristics of high-quality activities
-steep learning curves
-high growth in output
-rapid technological progress
-high R&D-content
-necessitates and generates learning-by-doing
-imperfect information
-investments come in large chunks / are divisible (drugs)

Shoes (1850-1900)
-imperfect, but dynamic, competition
-high wage level

Golf balls
-possibilities for important economies of scale and scope
-high industry concentration

Automotive paint
-high stakes: high barriers to entry and exit
-branded product
-standard neoclassical assumptions irrelevant

Characteristics of low-quality activities
-flat learning curves
-low growth in output
-little technological progress
-low R&D-content
-little personal or institutional learning required
-perfect information
-divisible investment (tools for a baseball factory)

House paint
-perfect competition
-low wage level

Shoes (1993)
-little or no economies of scale / risk of diminishing returns
-fragmented industry

Baseballs
-low stakes: low barriers to entry and exit
-commodity
-neoclassical assumptions are reasonable proxy

Perfect competition (low-quality activity)

is only a temporary state, as new technologies fall towards a lower score as they mature. The upper part of the quality index corresponds to Schumpeter's metaphor of the upper strata of a market economy being like hotels which are indeed full of people, but people who are forever changing. Activities with a high score are *growth inducing,* activities with a low score are *growth inhibiting.* Jaroslav Vanek – in a comment to one of my earlier papers – suggests that the quality axis should be seen as a third dimension in the traditional geometrical presentation of trade theory.

The factors listed are correlated, but clearly not in any way perfectly so. The two lists of factors, those creating high-quality and those creating low-quality activities, exhibit a negative type of correlation: in their extreme form, the characteristics in the two groups are mutually exclusive. Each of the characteristics in one group is, in this form, incompatible with *all* characteristics in the other. The 'quality' of an economic activity for a nation, its ability to pay high wages and potential for high profits, can be read off on this scale. High-quality activities carry with them high risks in innovation and new technologies, and high barriers to entry also carry with them high barriers to exit. Consequently, there is no direct relationship between the quality of and activity and its profit level, only its *potential* profit level. A high-quality activity can be ruined in shake-out periods by huge losses across the industry. These losses are caused by high barriers to exit. However, this normally does not drastically affect wage levels. In spite of the huge losses in the airlines industry in recent years, wages of airline pilots are much higher than those of bus drivers. Airlines are still a high-quality economic activity for a country, due to their potential economies of scale.

As they are presented at the moment, the factors are a blend of causes and effects. I therefore choose to call them 'characteristics'. *Barriers to entry* boils down to being a common denominator of the forces at work. The system is a closed one, except for an opening at the top, in the black end. Here new knowledge – technological change – enters the system as a temporary monopoly, and then falls towards perfect competition over time at greatly differing speeds. Nathan Rosenberg's frequently used example of the innovation with shipping-containers fell reasonably fast on the scale towards perfect competition. Patented drugs fall more slowly. Patents are of course set up for this very reason, to keep profits up in order to encourage investment in research. Even when technological progress no longer takes place in an economic activity, static scale effects may give the activity in question a high value score (= dark grey).

The gravity in the system – the speed with which economic activities fall from temporary monopolies to perfect competition – is also determined by the intensity of competition. More intense competition causes the gravitational power to increase, as we are experiencing in our time with successive generations of computers. A more rapid fall of innovations through the system – more perfect competition and more classical spread of benefits (next section of the chapter) – combined with wage and exchange rigidities, will by itself increase unemployment. This is, in my opinion, a relevant point for the present employment situation in Europe and the US.

This Quality Meter is in my view useful in conceptualizing a number of issues in economics, old and recent: competitiveness, Porter's world view, Bill Clinton's crusade for high-quality jobs, national wage differentials, and, most importantly, the clustering of the world in two groups of nations, the haves and the have-nots. Historically, the Quality Meter opens for an explanation as to why colonialism made sense to the colonial powers. This is not clear in neoclassical analysis, see e.g. Fitzgerald (1988). Colonial economic policy assured the mother-country exclusive access to the activities with the highest score on the Quality Meter. There is also considerable historical evidence that the colonial powers consciously pursued policies based on notions which are compatible with the Quality Index – that access to high-quality activities was prohibited in the colonies. The 'industricides' – the conscious killing off of advanced sectors in colonial economies – testify to this. Perhaps the clearest examples are from British colonial policy: the prohibition of the prosperous woollen industry in Ireland starting in 1699, described by Hely-Hutchinson (1779), and the destruction of the cotton-textile industry in India around 1814 (Chopra 1990). The prohibitions on the export of machinery, in force in Britain until 1843, also indicate an understanding of economic power which is compatible with the Quality Index. The machinery question is described in Berg (1980). All in all, the Quality Index is able to throw new light on why many '*realökonomisch*'-oriented mercantilists were essentially right, although often for the wrong reasons.

If the Marshall Plan worked wonders in a few years in postwar Europe, it was because the nations in question were brought back in the top-floor industries, where they were active before the war. The reason 'technical assistance' to the Third World – originally seen as an extension of the Marshall Plan – has failed so miserably in the Third World in general, is because these countries lacked everything the *List-cum-Smith* stage has given Europe, the United States, and Japan. Most postwar attempts at Third World industrialization under protectionism, like in Mexico and India, did not develop well essentially because the competitive aspect – the *Smithian* element of *List-cum-Smith* – was missing. This led to static rent-seeking and very inefficient industries based on government industrial licences.[24]

4. THE CLASSICAL AND COLLUSIVE MODES OF DIFFUSION OF TECHNOLOGICAL GAINS

To the classical economists, productivity improvements would show up in the economy as lowered prices for the goods which experienced these improvements (see e.g. Smith 1776: 269, and Ricardo 1817: 46–7). At the time of Smith and Ricardo, the gold standard facilitated the result they predicted. In a closed economy, holding velocity of circulation constant, the increase of goods in the economy resulting from technological progress would chase only the same amount of bullion. Prices *would have to fall.* Rapid technological progress would therefore lead to deflation – which it in fact often did until the gold standard was abolished.

When the gold standard was abolished, people in the industrialized countries got rich in a different way than before – instead of seeing the price of industrial goods fall as it used to, they now saw their monetary income rise. Previously deflation had caused awkward social problems: it was difficult to convince people who had to take continuous pay cuts that, in spite of these pay cuts, they were still getting richer, because the price of the goods they purchased fell at an even faster rate than their wages. The monetary policy which followed after the gold standard was abolished became, from the point of view of the industrialized nations, a more sensible one: money supply kept rising with the amount of goods in the economy, or slightly faster, creating a small inflation which seems to have served to oil the machinery of development. Now the producer in an activity not exhibiting productivity improvements – e.g. the barber – got rich by raising his prices at the rate everybody else had their salaries raised, not only by having the price of manufactured goods lowered.

As shown in Figure 8.1, from 1899 through 1937, within the US, labour productivity in the automotive industry increased by about 900%, and many other industries recorded productivity improvements exceeding 100%. However, in many US industries: meat packing, hats, railroad cars, lumber-mill products and others, labour productivity did not change at all in the same period.[25] Yet, the workers in the industries which had no productivity increase at all over this 40-year period had their good share in the unprecedented growth in the US economy over that period. But, as opposed to what was expected in the classical model, this did not come through an improvement in their terms of trade. The increase in real wages came essentially through increased monetary wages as the national stock of money grew, not through improvements in the terms of trade in the 'dog' industries. In this way the huge productivity advances in the 'star' industries spread to a much larger extent *inside the producing nation* than to customers abroad. A similar view on wage determination is held by the

French regulation school (see Boyer 1988).

Terms of trade between developed and developing countries seems to have changed very little, in spite of the widely different changes experienced in productivity between industries within each nation (Figure 8.1). This observation would support the impression that each country keeps its 'average' productivity increase in the form of a higher standard of living. This again suggests that the *choice of economic activity* is strategically crucial to a nation.

The benefits of technology clearly spread in the economy in a different pattern from what the classical and neoclassical economists expect. I call this the *collusive*[26] mode of diffusing the benefits from technological change: the benefits are divided among the capitalists, the workers, and the government *in the producing nation.* (The word collusive does not imply a conspiracy. This collusion comes about by the normal working of the economic, social, and political forces.) Inside a nation, social and democratic forces, labour mobility, and the distributive effects of a huge government sector ensure that the wage level and standard of living in the 'dog' industries do not lag too far behind those of the 'star' industries. Interindustry differences are, of course, much greater in a society like the US than in a 'wage solidarity' culture like the Scandinavian, but the same mechanisms are at work.

Faced with a *collusive spread,* the US during the period covered in Figure 8.1 would grow richer if it could move workers from the hat industry to the automotive industry. Importing hats and exporting cars will – under the collusive diffusion of technological improvements that in fact happened – improve the US welfare position as compared to autarky. This opportunity is created by the fact that not all economic activities are mechanized at the same time and to the same extent. Things would look different, as US economist Henry Vethake said in 1838, 'if improvement in all the arts were to take place *at the same rate.'*[27] This is clearly not the case. A more realistic picture is the one given by Kodama: 'It is more like the principle of surf-riding; the waves of innovation come one after another and you have to invest to ride the waves; if you miss, you are out of the game' (Kodama 1991).

A *classical* spread is the result of the usual assumptions in neoclassical economics. However, in a Schumpeterian world view, a purely classical spread is hardly plausible. The dynamics of the system are generated by the technological change which creates disequilibria – and the higher profits created in the industries experiencing technological change are necessary in order to draw capital to these higher risk and more capital-intensive activities. In addition, a classical spread of the benefits – only in the form of price reductions to customers at home and abroad – would not be seen as fair and democratic in the producing country. That industrialized country workers receive their share in the productivity improvements in terms of higher wages is an integral part of the credo of industrialized societies.

In the late 1930s, the Brookings Institution published a series of books aiming at 'nothing less than a general re-examination, in the light of modern developments, of the operation of the capitalistic system of wealth production and distribution' (Bell 1940). The studies conclude that the benefits of technological progress may be spread in the US economy in two different ways:

1. *Raising money wages (my collusive mode).* 'The most obvious method by which the income of the masses might be expanded... it is the method which has been steadfastly pursued by labor organizations... and it is the method which has been officially experimented with under the auspices of the National Recovery Administration.' (Moulton 1935). It is recognized, however, that this gives a disproportionate wage lead for manufacturing and railway workers.

2. *Price reductions (my classical mode).* The series of studies concluded that 'the *most advantageous* means of broadly distributing the benefits of technological progress was by reducing prices in line with increasing efficiency in production' (Bell 1940). The practical difficulties in achieving this were outlined in a third volume in the series: *Industrial Price Policy and Economic Progress* (Nourse and Drury 1938). The conclusion was that in a market where both the industry in question and the labour unions charge what the market can take for products and labour respectively, a large amount of what from an international trade point of view is a 'collusive spread' is inevitable in a market economy.

Clearly, in most industries, the benefits of technological development spread with elements of both modes. Distribution problems *within* a nation, which was the object of the Brookings Institution study, will be alleviated through competition in the labour market, through labour mobility, through the high government share in GNP, through the relocation of industry to areas in the country with less expensive labour, and, particularly in the case of Europe, through the 'wage solidarity' of labour unions. Internationally, these mechanisms work in a very limited way, as does the huge redistributive machinery of national governments. The inevitability of a 'collusive spread' makes a nation's *choice of economic activity* so crucial. As a result of the collusive spread of technological progress, the world's most efficient baseball producer makes 30 US cents an hour in Haiti, and the world's most efficient golf ball producer makes 30 times as much in an industrialized country, as noted above.

Hans Singer, a former student of Schumpeter, raised the distribution issue of technological progress in his paper to the 1949 meeting of the

American Economic Association. Singer[28] pointed out unquantifiable factors, however, and his important insight drowned in the attention paid to the terms of trade argument presented by Prebisch. Measuring prices – terms of trade – appealed to the traditions and static world view of the economics profession. The remarkable lack of change in terms of trade between industrialized and primary-producing nations over time, showed by Kindleberger and others, really served to reinforce Singer's point: each group of nations is able to keep its own productivity improvements as an increase in national welfare.

Table 8.1 shows the characteristics of the *classical* mode (price reduction) and the *collusive* mode (raising money wages). In a truly classical spread, the innovation immediately falls to the lower level of the Quality Index in Table 8.1. The use of containers could be an example of such an innovation. The two modes are not mutually exclusive – in most cases they are both present to some degree. Under autarky, it makes no immediate difference to GNP whether the benefits spread in a classical or in a collusive way. In an open economy with restricted labour mobility it makes all the difference in the world.

5. REDISCOVERING OLD STRATEGIES FOR DEVELOPMENT IN A NEW ECONOMIC PARADIGM

The neoclassical paradigm in economics is being challenged by new theoretical approaches. A central feature in a Kuhnian change in paradigm is a 'Gestalt-switch', that the object of study – in this case the economy – starts to be perceived as a different *Gestalt*. If economics is to make progress towards understanding the causes of national wealth and poverty, it is necessary to dispense with the view of the world economy as a *Gestalt* consisting of a mass of undifferentiated 'representative firms', all operating under perfect information and competition. The implicit assumption that 'all economic activities are alike' will have to be abandoned. A new and more relevant economic theory will have to consider the differences between economic activities – their use of factors like fixed costs, scale, and knowledge – and the cumulative effects of these factors over time. The description of this new multifaceted world-economy *Gestalt* will require new, but unfortunately less accurate tools than those presently used. The Quality Index of economic activities is one example of such a tool. Simple and absolute 'truths' - like the absolute superiority of free trade under all circumstances - will yield to much more complex, but also more useful, views. The Quality Index of economic activities is one example of such a tool. Simple and absolute 'truths' – like the absolute

Table 8.1. *Characteristics of the two modes of diffusion of productivity improvements*

	The Collusive Mode	The Classical Mode
Characteristics of mode		
Divisibility of investments	Indivisible, comes in 'chunks'	Divisible
Degree of perfect information	Imperfect (e.g., patents, internal R&D)	Perfect (competitive market for technology itself)
Source of technology from user company point of view	Internal, or external in big chunks = high degree of economies of scale	External
Barriers to entry	Increase	No change
Industry structure	Increases concentration	Neutral
Economies of scale	Increase	No change
Market shares	Very important	Unimportant
How benefits spread		
GNP as measured	Highly visible	Tends not to appear (Solow-paradoxes)
Profits level	Increases stakes: possibilities for larger profits or losses	No change
Monetary wages	Increase	No change
Real wages (nationally)	Increase	Increase
Price level	No change	Decreases
Terms of trade	No change	Turns against industries experiencing technological progress
Examples of innovations in the two groups	New pharmaceuticals, mainframe computers, automotive paint production	Electricity, telephones, sewing machines, use of PCs, dispersion paint production, containers
Where found	Mainly in industry, in recent products and processes	In primary and tertiary industry, use of new basic technologies, mature industry

superiority of free trade under all circumstances – will yield to much more complex, but less useful, views. Readers who are worried about this development may find some consolation in Schumpeter's words: 'The general reader will have to make up his mind, whether he wants *simple* answers to his questions or *useful* ones – in this as in other economic matters he cannot have both'.[29]

The evolutionary paradigm will be able to throw new light on mercantilist industrial policy. A new understanding of pre-20th century industrial policy is seeping even into neoclassical economics, without the authors being aware of it. Old practices are being restored, without any historical references, and only used for First World consumption, not for the Third World.[30] The best *realökonomisch*-oriented mercantilists can be seen as having built efficient national innovation systems. Today the goal of enlightened industrial policy is to create the innovation-driven society: positioning the nation in the upper echelons of the Quality Index where growth-inducing activities carried out under imperfect competition create wealth. The economics profession knows, in some place in the right part of the brain – where intuition is seated – that Japan would never have made her way to international economic leadership if she had concentrated on pyjama production instead of car production and electronics. However, the profession as a whole refuses to build this 'knowledge' into the models produced by the left side of their brains. The Quality Index or Quality Meter for economic activities is intended as a device to connect the two parts.

The mercantilists – English, German and French in particular – identified the superior economic activities with the use of machinery.[31] In a world where very few economic activities had been mechanized, the use of new machinery was synonymous at once with innovation, technological change, learning, imperfect competition, high profits, high wages, and national welfare. Today the economists who were associated with the most spectacular catching-up operations in human history, England starting in the late 15th century, United States and Germany starting in the 19th century, are not even mentioned in the textbooks. A basic reason for this, of course, is that the strategic factors used to create and maintain wealth historically, contradict the very foundations of the neoclassical theoretical construction: perfect information and the absence of increasing returns to scale.

If a nation's economic activities historically are concentrated in the lower area of the Quality Index, the workings of the market will reinforce this position by assigning only mature products, produced with common knowledge and technology, to the poor nation. As the pressures of an increasingly perfect competition weigh on a product, cheap and unskilled labour becomes a key success factor for companies. Therefore, the production of a product like baseballs – until now unmechanized – is farmed out to Haiti, while the mechanized production of golf balls and tennis balls is kept in the industrialized countries.[32] As a result, the Third World receives the activities working under perfect competition and a *classical spread* of benefits, while the First World monopolizes the upper part of the Quality Index, the top floor of Schumpeter's capitalist hotel. The Third World mainly receives the destructive part of the Schumpeterian *creative destruction* – the destruction of the existing non-market economies. The invisible hand tends to shuffle the gains from technological progress to the industrialized countries in the form of rents, through the mechanisms described in this chapter. An understanding both of the historical strategies of the First World, and of the differing 'qualities' of economic activities are necessary ingredients in economic strategies of poor nations facing a long-distance catching-up process.

NOTES

1. The author is grateful to Daniele Archibugi, Charles Edquist, Keith Smith and the editors of this volume for helpful comments. The usual disclaimer applies.
2. This part has been added since the first German edition, Leipzig, Duncker & Humblot, 1912.
3. In an earlier work (Reinert 1980), I have argued for studying underdevelopment in a framework including First World historical national strategies, technological change, and industry analysis.
4. Reinert (1980: 39 and 41) shows the characteristics of the two circles.
5. In the foreword to the Japanese edition of his *Theorie der wirtschaftlichen Entwicklung*, Schumpeter describes how he looked for 'a source of energy within the economic system which would of itself disrupt any equilibrium that might be attained .... It was not clear to me at the outset ... that the idea and the aim are exactly the same as the idea and the aim which underlie the economic teachings of Karl Marx' (Schumpeter 1951: 160).
6. The success of the trusts which sought static rents like the Leather Trust, part of the Beef Trust, was limited to the lobbying for tariffs.
7. Porter (1985) elaborates on the concept of 'value chains'.
8. This concept seems to have originated with Adam Müller. His 1809 book is the main work of a German school of economics which is sometimes referred to as the 'Romantic School'.
9. The bibliography of the German cameralist (mercantilist) literature (Humpert 1937) lists over 14,000 entries for Germany alone.
10. Hocquet (1990). In the early days of the Republic, much of the government revenue came from the sale of salt. See also Lane (1973: 58).
11. The parallel with more recent days is striking.
12. Palgrave regards Defoe as 'an important authority for economic history'. See Higgs (1963).
13. This is described in Reinert (1992).
14. It has been shown that Hamilton knew his Adam Smith, but rejected particularly the free trade conclusion. Excerpts from Postlethwayt's *Universal Dictionary of Trade and Commerce* were scattered through Hamilton's Army Pay Book, see Morris (1957). Hamilton's view on the English classical economists was similar to that taken 80 years later by the Japanese, see Morris-Suzuki (1989).
15. Personal communication.

16. Serra's remarkable dynamic 'model' shows how wealth is created without the benefit of natural resources (Venice) on the one hand, and poverty remains in the midst of great natural resources (Naples) on the other. The parallel with modern Japan is interesting.
17. *History of Economic Analysis,* p. 259. The republishing of Serra's work in 1801 may, or may not, have influenced this.
18. This is the strategy recommended by King in 1721, and it also follows as the best strategy from Paul Krugman's 1979 and 1981 papers.
19. Innovations applied under near-perfect competition, like the invention of the container, tend to lower prices and GDP as measured, and therefore create 'Solow-Paradoxes'.
20. This chart is taken from Solomon Fabricant (1942).
21. The concept can be traced back to the first years of this century, see The Royal Tropical Institute (1961).
22. I am grateful to Tom McCraw of Harvard Business School for pointing these articles to me.
23. See, however, Lucas (1988, 1993) for examples of neoclassical models incorporating differences with regard to learning between activities.
24. List was writing on Germany, where he wanted free trade established between more than 30 small states, each with high tariff barriers. That ferocious competition would erupt once these barriers were removed goes without saying.
25. Data from Fabricant, op. cit., pp. 90–91.
26. This matter is discussed more in detail in Reinert (1990).
27. Italics in original.
28. Published as Singer (1950).
29. Schumpeter in his foreword to F. Zeuthen (1930).
30. Paul Krugman of MIT, whose contributions to the rediscovery of increasing returns has already been mentioned, with hindsight now approves of Canada's protectionist policies (Krugman 1992: 42). See also endnote 31.
31. This policy is being rediscovered in the US, see De Long and Summers (1991).
32. This argument can be seen as an extension of the product life-cycle effects associated with Raymond Vernon and Lou Wells, see Vernon (1966) and Wells (1972).

REFERENCES

Abramovitz, M. (1993), 'The Search for the Sources of Growth: Areas of Ignorance, Old and New', *Journal of Economic History*, Vol. 53, No. 2, June, 217–43.

Bell, S. (1940), *Productivity, Wages and National Income*, Washington, DC: The Brookings Institution, 3.

Berg, M. (1980), *The Machinery Question and the Making of Political Economy 1815–1848*, Cambridge: Cambridge University Press.

Bernd, M. (ed.) (1987), *Japans Weg in die Moderne. Ein Sonderweg nach deutschem Vorbild*, Frankfurt: Campus Verlag.

Boyer, R. (1988), 'Technical Change and the Theory of "Régulation"', in G. Dosi *et al.*, *Technical Change and Economic Theory*, London: Pinter, 67–94.

Chopra, P.N. (1990), *The Gazetteer of India*, New Delhi: Ministry of Education and Social Welfare, Vol. 2, 613–15.

Clemence, R.V. (ed.) (1951), *Essays of J.A. Schumpeter*, Cambridge, Mass.: Addison-Wesley Press, 160.

Defoe, D. (1728), *Plan of English Commerce*, London: C. Rivington.

De Long, B. and L. Summers, (1991), 'Equipment Investment and Economic Growth', *Quarterly Journal of Economics*, Vol. 106, May, 445–502.

Dorfman, J. (1947), *The Economic Mind in American Civilization*, Vol. 2, London: George Harrap.

Dosi, G., K. Pavitt, and L. Soete (eds) (1990), *The Economics of Technical Change and International Trade*, Hemel Hempstead: Harvester Wheatsheaf.

Fabricant, S. (1942), *Employment in Manufacturing. An Analysis of its Relation to the Volume of Production*, New York: National Bureau of Economic Research, 90–91.

Fitzgerald, E.P. (1988), 'Did France's Colonial Empire Make Economic Sense? A Perspective from the Postwar Decade', *Journal of Economic History*, Vol. 48 (2), 373–85.

Friedman, M. (1953), 'The Methodology of Positive Economics', in *Essays in Positive Economics*, Chicago: Chicago University Press, 3–43.

Graham, F.D. (1923), 'Some aspects of protection further considered', *Quarterly Journal of Economics*, Vol. 37, February, 199–227.

Hely-Hutchinson, J. (1779), *The Commercial Restraints of Ireland Considered, in a Series of Letters to a Noble Lord, Containing an Historical Account of the Affairs of that Kingdom, so far as they Relate to this Subject*, Dublin: William Hallhead. (All copies of this book were ordered to be burned by the Dublin hangman on publication, few escaped.)

Higgs, H. (ed.) (1963), *Palgrave's Dictionary of Political Economy*, Vol. 1, New York: Kelley, 535.

Hocquet, J.-C. (1990), *Il Sale e la Fortuna di Venezia*, Roma: Jouvence.

Hudson, R. and R. Kaufman, (1982), 'Economic Dualism: a Critical Review', *American Sociological Review*, Vol. 47, 727–39.

Humpert, M. (1937), *Bibliographie der Kameralwissenschaften*, Köln: Schroeder.

King, C. (1721), *The British Merchant; or, Commerce Preserved*, London: John Darby, Vols 1, 3. This part of the book was first published in 1713.

Kodama, F. (1991), 'Changing global perspective: Japan, the USA and the new industrial order', *Science and Public Policy*, Vol. 8, No. 6, December, 388.

Krugman, P. (1979), 'Increasing Returns, Monopolistic Competition and International Trade', *Journal of International Economics*, Vol. 9, No. 4, November, 469–79.

Krugman, P. (1981), 'Trade, Accumulation and Uneven Development', *Journal of Development Economics*, Vol. 8, 149–61.

Krugman, P. (1992), *Geography and Trade*, Cambridge, Mass.: MIT Press, 92.

Krugman, P. and M. Obstfeld (1991), *International Economics, Theory and Policy*, 2nd Edition, New York: Harper Collins, 153.

Lane, F. (1973), *Venice. A maritime Republic*, Baltimore: Johns Hopkins, 58.

Lane, F. (1979), *Profits from Power. Readings in protection rent and violence-controlling enterprises*, Albany: State University of New York Press, 45–8.

Lazonick, W. (1991), *Business organization and the myth of the market economy*, Cambridge: Cambridge University Press.

List, F. (1844), *Das Nationale System der politischen Oekonomie*, Basel: Kyklos, 1959, 12.

Lucas, R.E. (1988), 'On the Mechanics of Economic Development', *Journal of Monetary Economics*, Vol. 22, 3–42.

Lucas, R.E. (1993), 'Making a Miracle', *Econometrica*, Vol. 61 (2), 251–72.

Lundvall, B.-Å. (ed.) (1992), *National Systems of Innovation*, London: Pinter.

MacLeod, C. (1988), *Inventing the Industrial Revolution. The English Patent System*

1660–1800, Cambridge: Cambridge University Press.

Marshall, A. (1890), *Principles of Economics*, London: Macmillan, 452.

Marx, K. (1867), *Das Kapital*, Vol. 1, page numbers quoted refer to the reprinted version published by Ullstein: Frankfurt, Ullstein, 1967, 389.

McCraw, T. (1993), 'Adam Smith and Friedrich List: The invisible hand versus industrial policy', paper presented at the Business History Conference, Harvard Business School, March 19–21.

Moulton, H.G. (1935), *Income and Economic Progress*, Washington, DC: The Brookings Institution, 102.

Morris, R.B. (1957), *Alexander Hamilton and the Founding of the Nation*, New York: Dial Press, 285.

Morris-Suzuki, T. (1989), *The History of Japanese Economic Thought*, London: Routledge.

Müller, A. (1809), *Elemente der Staatskunst*, Vol. 5, Berlin: J.D. Sander.

Nelson, R. (ed.) (1993), *National Innovation Systems*, New York: Oxford University Press.

Nelson, R., and S. Winter (1982), *An Evolutionary Theory of Economic Change*, Cambridge, Mass.: Harvard University Press.

Nourse, E.G. and H.B. Drury (1938), *Industrial Price Policy and Economic Progress*, Washington, DC: The Brookings Institution.

O'Brien, P.K. (1993), 'Political preconditions for the Industrial Revolution', in P.K. O'Brien and R. Quinault, *The Industrial Revolution and British Society*, Cambridge: Cambridge University Press, 125.

Perez, C. (1983), 'Structural change and the assimilation of new technologies in the economic and social system', *Futures*, Vol. 15, 357–75.

Porter, M. (1980), *Competitive Strategy. Techniques for analyzing Industries and Competitors*, New York: Free Press, 362–3.

Porter, M. (1985), *Competitive Advantage*, New York: Macmillan.

Porter, M. (1990), *The Competitive Advantage of Nations*, London: Macmillan, 552–6.

Reinert, E. (1980), *International Trade and the Economic Mechanisms of Underdevelopment*, Ann Arbor, University Microfilm Publications, 237–9.

Reinert, E. (1990), 'How do productivity improvements become visible in economic data – or: is the *Solow Paradox* a paradox at all?', mimeo.

Reinert, E. (1992), 'Thoughts before Takeoff. Hva mente økonomene i de nåværende iland om næringspolitikk og økonomisk vekst før disse landene ble rike?', Parts 1 and 2, Oslo, STEP-Group, mimeo.

Ricardo, D. (1817), *Principles*, London: Dent, reprinted 1973 (page numbers refer to the reprint).

The Royal Tropical Institute, Amsterdam (various authors) (1961), *Indonesian Economics. The Concept of Dualism in Theory and Policy*, The Hague: van Hoeve, 1961.

Schumpeter, J.A. (1934), *The Theory of Economic Development*, Cambridge, Mass.: Harvard University Press, 156.

Schumpeter, J.A. (1951), Foreword to the Japanese edition of *Theorie der wirtschaftlichen Entwicklung*, Reprinted in: Clemence, R.V. (ed.), *Essays of J.A. Schumpeter*, Cambridge, Mass.: Addison-Wesley Press.

Schumpeter, J.A. (1954), *History of Economic Analysis*, New York: Oxford University Press.

Serra, A. (1613), *Breve trattato delle Cause che possono far abbondare li Regni d'Oro e Argento dove non sono miniere. Con applicazione al Regno di Napoli*, Napoli:

Lazzaro Scorriggio.

Singer, H. (1950), 'The Distribution of Gains between Investing and Borrowing Countries', *American Economic Review, Papers and Proceedings,* Vol. II, No. 2, May.

Smith, A. (1776), *Wealth of Nations,* Chicago: University of Chicago Press, reprinted 1976 (page numbers refer to the reprint).

Sugiyama, C. and H. Mizuta (1988), *Enlightenment and Beyond. Political Economy Comes to Japan,* Tokyo: University of Tokyo Press.

Tolbert, C. *et al.* (1980), 'The Structure of Economic Segmentation: a Dual Economy Approach', *American Journal of Sociology,* Vol. 85, March, 1095–116.

Vernon, R. (1966), 'International Investment and International Trade in the Product Cycle', *Quarterly Journal of Economics,* Vol. 80, May, 190–207.

Vethake, H. (1844), *The Principles of Political Economy,* 2nd Edition, Philadelphia: J.W. Moore, 95.

Viner, J. (1937), *Studies in the Theory of International Trade,* New York: Harper, 475–82.

Vogel, E. (1991), *The Four Little Dragons. The Spread of Industrialization in East Asia,* Cambridge Mass.: Harvard University Press.

Wells, L. (ed.) (1972), *The Product Life Cycle and International Trade,* Boston: Harvard Business School.

Yagi, K. (1989), 'German Model in the Modernization of Japan', in *The Kyoto University Economic Review,* Vol. 29, No. 1–2, April–October, 29.

Zeuthen, F. (1930), *Problems of Monopoly and Economic Welfare,* London: Routledge.

9. Technological Revolutions and Catching-Up: ICT and the NICs[1]

Christopher Freeman

1. INTRODUCTION

The literature on 'catching-up' and 'convergence' from the mid-1980s placed heavy emphasis on technological 'spillovers' as a main reason for expecting such convergence to come about (Baumol 1986, the chapter by Beelen and Verspagen and other contributions to this book). At the same time, it was pointed out that convergence did not extend to all countries. Baumol (*op. cit.*) suggested that there were 'clubs' of countries for which convergence had been partially achieved, but other clubs which showed little evidence of convergence and some of falling further behind. Abramovitz (1986) argued that 'social capabilities' were the main factors differentiating those catching up from those falling behind.

This chapter examines the role of technology in catching-up, by investigating the potential contribution of Information and Communication Technology (ICT) in the modern world. It aims to show that these advances produce their full impact only when adopted as a system, in which case they can give rise to a technological 'revolution'. The systemic nature of the technologies implies that piecemeal technological spillovers, even of 'radical' technological advances are likely to have only limited ability to bring about economic convergence. The effects are demonstrated by examining in greater detail one of the suggested convergence 'clubs' – the Newly Industrializing Countries (NICs) of East Asia. This analysis helps to clarify the 'capabilities' required for catching-up. While the technologies are in principle available to all other countries, the more successful are differentiated by the major indigenous efforts to develop through such a technological revolution. Catching-up based on new technologies is far from the passive process that language like 'spillovers' and 'imitation' might seem to suggest. To pursue the argument, it is first necessary to define a taxonomy of innovations (see Table 9.1).

Some historians would deny the very existence of 'technological revolutions' or of 'radical innovations'. These are categories which are not self-evident from the infinite myriad of 'facts' about individual specific inventions and innovations. The category of 'radical innovations' is clearly selective as these amount to only a small proportion of the total universe of innovations, whilst the use of the expression 'technological revolution' implies a judgement about the inter-relationship between large numbers of innovations and society as a whole. This chapter will attempt to justify the use of both these categories and to show that they help us to understand both the past and the present trends in the global economy and in global technology.

Table 9.1 sets out the working definitions which are used in this chapter. The first two refer to individual innovations, the third and fourth to their combinations and inter-relationships.

Many researchers on innovation have made a distinction between 'radical' or 'major' innovations and 'incremental' or 'minor' innovations. This has sometimes appeared as academic hair-splitting and it is true that like most boundary definitions the distinction is not always easy to make. Nevertheless, it is actually extremely important.

The advocates of gradualism and incrementalism, like those who reject

Table 9.1.   Taxonomy of innovations

---

1. Incremental Innovations

Gradual improvement of existing array of products, processes, organizations and systems of production, distribution and communication.

2. Radical Or Basic Innovations

A discontinuity in products, processes, organizations and systems of production, distribution and communication, i.e. a departure from incremental improvement, involving a new factory, new market or new organization.

3. New Technology Systems ('Constellations' Of Innovations)

Economically and technically inter-related clusters of innovations (radical and incremental).

4. Technological Revolution ('Change Of Techno-Economic Paradigm')

A pervasive combination of system innovations affecting the entire economy and the typical 'common-sense' for designers and managers in most or all industries.

---

the notion of a British 'industrial revolution' in the late 18th and early 19th centuries, do have a point. If one wishes to confine the use of the term 'revolution' to events which occur within a few days or hours, then it is obviously out of place in relation to technology. This is a matter of choice of terminology in relation to time scales. A world without electricity is sufficiently different from one in which electric power is used in almost every enterprise and household, as to justify for many authors some such description, even if the rate of growth of electric power production and consumption may have been less than ten per cent per annum for long periods, or less than five per cent in some countries. By the same token a world where electronic computers are used in almost every factory and every office, as well as many homes, is so different from a world without electronic computers that it is quite justifiable to describe this as a revolutionary transformation in technology, even though it is already over half a century since the first electronic computer was developed by Zuse in Berlin. The use of the expression 'information revolution' or 'information and communication revolution' seems quite legitimate to describe a change of this magnitude.

Mensch (1975) defined radical innovations (or *'Basis-Innovationen'*) as those which require a new factory and/or a new market, whereas incremental innovations take place within existing work-places and existing markets i.e. they are simply improvements to existing processes and the existing product range. Mensch regarded many incremental innovations as *'Schein-Innovationen'* i.e. a form of product differentiation rather than genuine novelty. However, much as engineers tried to improve cotton or woollen factories they would never have got to nylon or acrylics, or, as Schumpeter used to say, no matter how many stage-coaches you put together, you would not get a railway. A radical innovation is a *discontinuity* in the production system or in a market (but not necessarily in science or technology). It requires new skills, new equipment and new forms of organization, i.e. it involves structural change in the economy.

Although some radical innovations, such as the float glass process, may appear as relatively isolated events, typically they emerge in clusters of related innovations. Such clusters result both from technological inter-relationships and inter-dependencies and from economic inter-relationships and were well described by Keirstead (1948) as 'constellations' of innovations. Obvious examples are 'families' of drug innovations, such as antibiotics and the related innovations in fermentation technology, in process equipment and in testing techniques. The systemic aspects of most innovations have been stressed by many historians of technology, especially Gille (1978) and Hughes (1982). Gaps and weaknesses in technology systems (for example, unsatisfactory materials or components) frequently act as 'focusing devices' which stimulate further innovations, thus reinforcing the clustering effects (Rosenberg 1976, Hughes 1982).

Finally, some new technology systems or combinations of systems are so pervasive that they influence the entire economy and penetrate almost every branch. It is these pervasive systemic changes that merit some such description as 'technological revolution'. Since they involve clusters of radical innovations as well as numerous incremental innovations, they lead to far-reaching changes in work organization and management systems, affecting both production and distribution. Organizational innovations, such as the assembly line or containerization or self-service, may sometimes precede and sometimes follow more narrowly technical innovations, but whichever is the case the social changes are very extensive and lead to the emergence of a new 'common-sense' about 'best practice' in management. Carlota Perez (1983) has described this type of pervasive change as a 'change of techno-economic paradigm'.

2. INFORMATION AND COMMUNICATION TECHNOLOGY AS A TECHNOLOGICAL SYSTEM

In Section 1 it has been argued that developments in Information and Communication Technology have led to a technological transformation, variously described as the 'Information Revolution', the 'Micro-electronic Revolution' or the 'Computer Revolution'. This chapter uses the expression 'information and communication technology' both to indicate a new range of products and services *and* a technology, which is capable of revolutionizing the processes of production and delivery of all *other* industries and services. The *scope* for such a new technology itself is new, having emerged in the last couple of decades as a result of the convergence of a number of inter-related advances in the field of micro-electronics, fibre optics, software engineering, communications, laser and computer technology. An approach to information activities which ignores the specific features of the new technologies is in danger of overlooking many of the economic and social consequences of these technologies including their employment and skill effects. This approach puts the emphasis on the new *technology* and not just on the *information*.

The pervasiveness of ICT is now more or less universally accepted and despite the classification problems many features of this pervasiveness can be measured. Measures of R&D show that in most leading industrial countries electronic and telecommunication R&D account for between 20 per cent and 30 per cent of total manufacturing and services R&D (Table 9.2). The classification problems hinder international comparability and for this reason, the OECD has chosen to combine 'electrical' and 'electronic'.

Table 9.2. *Percentage of business enterprise R&D performed in the electronic, electrical and office machinery industries, 1990*

	Electronic and Electric	Office Machinery
Canada	22.5	6.7
France	25.2	3.6
Ireland	31.8	12.6
Italy	20.3	5.8
Japan	34.0	–
Norway[*]	13.6	6.2
Turkey	46.9	–
Sweden[*]	19.8	–
Finland[*]	20.6	0.6
Germany	26.6	3.3[*]
UK	23.3	7.4
EC	24.5	4.5
South Korea	41.0[**]	

[*] 1989. Source: OECD (1992).
[**] Electronics only. Source: Dong Jin Koh (1992).

Nevertheless, this group is predominantly electronic and so too is 'office machinery' which some countries still classify separately. But these measures exclude most software applications development. Canada was the first country to attempt systematic measurement of this software R&D performed outside R&D Labs. It amounted to 23 per cent of total industrial R&D in Canada in 1988. This means that in the leading industrial countries electronics plus software development probably accounts for about half of all new R&D in industry. In Korea and Japan it probably accounts for over half. This is an extraordinarily high concentration of R&D activities and fully justifies the description of ICT as a technological revolution. Figures of investment tell a similar story.

The statistics for international trade (Table 9.3) show that ICT goods, classified by GATT as 'office machinery' and 'telecommunication equipment' are by far the fastest growing category in international trade.

They account already for more than a quarter of all exports of manufactures from Japan and several other East Asian countries.

Table 9.3.   Rates of growth of exports in 1980–1989

All Primary Commodities	2
of which	
Fuels	–5
Food	3
Raw materials	4
Ores, minerals	4
All Manufactures	8
of which	
Iron and steel	4
Textiles	6
Chemicals	7
Clothing	10
Machinery and transport	8
of which	
ICT Goods	13

Source: GATT (1990).

ICT not only affects every industry and service but also every *function* within each industry i.e. R&D, Design, Production, Marketing, Transport and general administration. It is *systemation* rather than automation, integrating the various previously separate departments and functions. Examples can be chosen at all levels of the production process.

In *design and development* every industry now depends on computers. This is not just a question of a product such as Computer Aided Design (CAD), although this is of great and growing importance. It is also a question of the accuracy, speed and volume of all kinds of calculations and access to data banks at all stages of the research and development process. Moreover, the use of CAD systems means that component and assembly firms are increasingly linked together and both are linked to data banks on the properties of new and old materials. Roy Rothwell (1991) has described this process as the 'electronification of design', as in the network of inter-linked computers used to design the Boeing 777. The new developments in telecommunications also mean that research laboratories, design offices, and manufacturing plants in different locations can exchange data, designs and calculations, divide and coordinate tasks in a matter of seconds. Speeding up design and development and the corresponding shortening of lead times is certainly not an entirely new feature of R&D management (see Freeman 1962, for an example in mining machinery), but it has received far greater attention with the diffusion of ICT.

Flexible *production* systems are of course directly related to widespread computerisation: numerical control, Flexible Manufacturing Systems (FMS) and Computer Integrated Manufacturing (CIM). The *Economist* magazine (30 May, 1987) in a special supplement on the 'factory of the future' described these as a change in production *system*, even though the investment may take place incrementally and involve much trial and error:

> For the first time in three-quarters of a century the factory is being reinvented from scratch. Long narrow production lines with men crawling all over them – a feature of manufacturing everywhere since the early days of the car-making dynasties – are being ripped apart and replaced with clusters of all-purpose machines huddled in cells run by computers and served by nimble-fingered robots. The whole shape of the industrial landscape is changing in the process. The name of the game in manufacturing has become not simply quality or low cost but 'flexibility' – the quest to give the customer his or her own personalised design, but with the cheapness and availability of mass-produced items. Savile Row at High Street prices. In short, nothing less than a whole new style of manufacturing is in the process of being defined.

It is because of this 'new style of manufacturing' that diffusion research can no longer concentrate, as in the 1960s, exclusively on discrete products but must take account of system changes as well. For this reason, there is now a proliferation of studies on the diffusion of 'computer-integrated manufacturing', 'flexible manufacturing systems', 'computer-aided manufacturing', 'computer-aided design' and so forth (see for example, Arcangeli *et al.* 1991, Ayres 1991).

These studies of diffusion, whether they are of individual products or of systems point unanimously to the conclusion that there are few 'standard' solutions in the machine-building and other metal-working industries. Configurations of robots, machine-tools, guided vehicles and other equipment vary enormously and so too does the programming and organization of the production process. All are path dependent and related to the locally available skills, training systems, managers, industrial relations systems and so forth. Fleck's (1988, 1993) work on robotics in particular has shown that the adaptation of robot design to local situations and needs has been one of the strong points of the relatively successful diffusion in Japan. He coined the expressions 'innofusion' and 'diffusation' to characterize the dependence of diffusion on site-specific incremental innovations.

The integration of functions within the firm is no less relevant to *marketing* than to production and design. Speed of response to market changes and reduction of stocks at various points in the distribution chain are typical of the competitive advantages achieved by firms like IKEA and Benetton, which have computerized warehousing and distribution systems, linked to retail outlets downstream and suppliers upstream. The involvement of future *users* of new products and services is nowhere more important than in the introduction of computerized systems and new software.

All of these conclusions apply *a fortiori* to service industries as well as to service functions within manufacturing industries. A particularly important feature of the ICT revolution is the scale of technical and organizational change in service activities, especially those like financial services which are mainly concerned with the storage, analysis, processing and transmission of vast quantities of information. The scale of investment in these industries is now greater than that in most manufacturing industries and (usually for the first time) R&D activities are beginning to be significant, mainly in the development of new software and associated services. Service industry R&D in the United States has increased from less than 2 per cent in the 1960s to nearly 10 per cent of total business R&D in 1989. These figures almost certainly underestimate service R&D because of the problem of software R&D, already referred to. These changes within service industries have led Barras (1986, 1990) to re-define the relationship between hardware suppliers and service industries as the latter increasingly make their own innovations and cease to be so dependent on hardware suppliers, as they were with earlier waves of technical change.

There can therefore be little doubt that the institutional changes associated with the diffusion of ICT are vast in extent, difficult to accomplish, and so far incomplete in their systemic linkages. They are not simply 'off the peg' for copying.

3. TECHNO-ECONOMIC SYSTEMS AND THE DIFFUSION OF ICT

Section 2 showed that ICT fulfilled the requirements of a 'new technology system' according to the definition supplied in Table 9.1. The systemic interpretation of the technology meant going beyond conceptions of IT simply as 'information' or as 'automation'. In this section, the object is to explain in further detail the less narrowly technological aspects of the ICT-based economy and to justify the claim that ICT represents a new 'techno-economic paradigm'.

Carlota Perez (1983, 1990) argued that slow-down in productivity would result from 'mis-match' between the old institutional framework and a new technology system. This can be observed in many cases – for example, the complexity of the transition from the Fordist techno-economic paradigm to the ICT paradigm may well explain part of the slow-

Table 9.4.   Change of techno-economic paradigm

'Fordist' Old	ICT New
Energy intensive	Information intensive
Design and engineering in 'drawing' offices	Computer-aided designs
Sequential design and production	Concurrent engineering
Standardized	Customized
Rather stable product mix	Rapid changes in product mix
Dedicated plant and equipment	Flexible production systems
Automation	Systemation
Single firm	Networks
Hierarchical structures	Flat horizontal structures
Departmental	Integrated
Product with service	Service with products
Centralization	Distributed intelligence
Specialized skills	Multi-skilling
Government control and sometimes ownership	Government information, coordination and regulation
'Planning'	'Vision'

Source: Adapted from Perez (1990).

down in productivity growth rates (especially capital productivity) in almost all leading industrial countries in the 1970s and 1980s. However, as both she and Johnson (1992) have stressed, institutions are not only sources of inertia ('institutional drag') but also facilitators of change. Whilst some industries and countries may be 'locked in' to old ways of doing things, others may initiate reforms which enable them to produce and to use ICT products and services very widely and efficiently. Table 9.4 gives a schematic and over-simplified summary of some of the major changes in company organization and work structure associated with the 'techno-economic paradigm' based on ICT.

Rothwell (1991), in discussing the 'electronification of design', is careful to point out that the organizational and managerial capability to use such systems efficiently varies a great deal by firm, by industry and by country. Even more important as a managerial function is the ability to integrate capabilities relating to a range of functions. Many observers have commented on Japanese techniques of integrating R&D, production and marketing. Baba (1985) spoke of using 'the factory as laboratory'. Takeuchi and Nonaka (1986) spoke of 'playing rugby' instead of 'running relay races'. The MIT world vehicle project showed in some detail how design and production engineering were integrated to generate shorter lead times in the automobiles industry (Graves 1992). It must be emphazised that not all of these management techniques depended on computerization or other technical innovations. 'Lean production systems' preceded computerization as did other management innovations associated with the 'Toyota-Ohno' system. Speed to market and the shortening of lead times as described above involve not just adoption of particular techniques such as CAD, but managerially driven improvements such as fast prototyping and total quality control. Customization of ICTs may also be crucial to performance, as noted for the case of robots.

The capability to initiate such institutional changes is very uneven in different parts of the world economy and so too is their efficient implementation. In part this is a matter of the scale and nature of the institutional heritage from the past (path dependence). An obvious example is the educational and training system. As Diebold insisted already in 1952, computerization of production systems is possible only when accompanied by a vast transformation of the skill profile of the work force. As against those who stressed unemployment and de-skilling as the probable consequence of computerization, he stressed on the contrary the need for creative skills in the re-design of the entire capital stock and in the maintenance of this new capital and argued that this would require the breaking down of departmental and disciplinary barriers within organizations and completely new forms of organization which facilitated horizontal communication and original initiatives at all levels of the work force.

On the whole, experience has vindicated his standpoint. Computerization does indeed demand a huge number of new skilled people as well as the re-training and re-skilling of most others. Every computer requires software so that there has been a persistent shortage of software engineers and programmers in almost every industrialized country for decades. Whilst it is true that some analysts now argue that the software shortages are over, it is more probable that new developments in parallel processing multi-media inter-active services and virtual reality will generate a vast new demand for software skills (Freeman and Soete 1993). Despite numerous innovations in software design and engineering there has been a permanent software crisis and innumerable examples of system failures because of software problems (Brady 1986, Brady and Quintas 1991, Quintas 1993). Spectacular failures have occurred not only with computer integrated manufacturing systems (CIM) but also in banks, in weapon systems, in government departments and in distribution.

This means that those countries which had an educational and training system capable of a rapid and effective response to these huge demands for new skills had a big comparative advantage in the efficient implementation of ICT. Countries which had considerable inertia and rigidity in these systems, on the other hand were placed at a disadvantage and experienced relative stagnation in their production systems and competitive strength. Much depended too on management style, on industrial relations and structure of the software industry.

One solution to the software problem is of course to use standard packaged software for standard functions in areas such as accountancy, pay-roll, stock control and so forth. The US software industry has excelled in the development and marketing of these standard packages world-wide, aided by the early US lead, the English language predominance in the computer industry and, until recently, some proprietary standards.

However, as we have seen, many software applications involve unique features so that an organization which relied entirely on standard packages would be relatively limited in its capacity to initiate changes in its design, production and marketing systems. It would also be limited in its response to external changes in hardware and software systems. Another solution is to use consultancy services with software capability or the services of the hardware suppliers themselves. It is notable that the big hardware suppliers have been making intensive efforts to extend their service consultancy business and their software activities generally in response to the extraordinarily rapid growth of these activities, which has been far more rapid than that of the hardware industry. The market capitalization of Microsoft early in 1993 was equal to that of Intel or IBM.

There can be no doubt that consultancy services are an extremely important feature of the new techno-economic paradigm and it is significant that recent studies of diffusion have drawn attention to their enhanced role. Whereas previously the pattern of diffusion was attributed primarily to the characteristics and proximity (cultural or geographic) of the adopter population (epidemic models) or to the sales push of suppliers, now the role of third parties, whether public agencies or private consultancies, is increasingly stressed (see e.g. Midgley *et al.* 1992). Often they are capable of advising their clients on both technical and managerial problems and it is notable that consultants who were previously almost entirely concerned with technical and engineering problems have moved increasingly into management consultancy and vice versa. This reflects the intense interdependence of technical and organizational problems in this paradigm change. The availability and efficiency of consultancy services varies very much in different countries, despite their globalization.

Finally, however, the efficiency and innovative capability of any firm will depend not only on its ability to use standard packages and the services of consultants but also on its own in-house capacity for R&D, design and software development. Comparisons of the Japanese and US software industries suggest that the main *structural* difference lies in the relatively greater size (and perhaps better quality) of the in-house software teams in Japanese firms, whereas the independent software houses and consultants are the great strength of the US industry, both in packaged and customized software (Baba *et al.* 1993). This probably accounts for the efforts of some cable firms in the US to acquire software capability by acquisitions or alliances.

Maintenance is a key issue in software activities. Some studies have suggested that a high proportion of software designers and programmers are now occupied with maintenance. However, *physical* deterioration and dis-repair is not a problem with software as it is with buildings or machinery. It has even been suggested that the software industry could decline drastically once most users have installed reasonably efficient systems, since the software itself is relatively indestructible. This brings out the point that the industry depends on *permanent innovation*. Software 'maintenance' is not in fact maintenance in the old sense at all but is a new type of maintenance involving continuous adaptation both to changes in the user organization and to changes in the external environment, including new hardware and software systems, as well as networking relationships. It is an extremely creative function and probably should be described as 'innovative maintenance' or some such expression. It is true of course that electro-mechanical maintenance can also be creative and used for continuous incremental innovation and those firms and countries where this has already been recognized, will probably have a comparative advantage. Once again, Diebold (1952) anticipated this key role of the skilled creative maintenance function.

These two examples of education and training and of software services have served to bring out the fundamental point that national (and regional) systems vary a great deal. Economists and sociologists concerned with technical change have been increasingly preoccupied with these differences, using the expression 'national systems of innovation' (Lundvall 1992, Nelson 1988, 1993, Mjøset 1992) to describe all those institutions which affect the innovative performance of a national economy. Whereas, at one time, there was a tendency to think primarily of the R&D system in this connection, it became increasingly evident during the 1970s and 1980s that technical change depended on a wide variety of other influences as well as formal R&D. In particular, *incremental* innovations came from production engineers, from consultants, from technicians and from the shop floor and were strongly related to different forms of work organization.

Furthermore, many improvements to *products* and to services came from interaction with the market and with related firms, such as subcontractors, suppliers of materials and services (see especially Lundvall 1985, 1988, 1992, Sako 1992). Formal R&D was usually decisive in its contribution to *radical* innovations but it was no longer possible to ignore the many other contributions to, and influences upon the process of technical change at the level of firms and industries. Networking has always been a feature of manufacturing under capitalism but its role has been greatly enhanced with ICT with computerized networks playing a rapidly growing part. National and regional aspects of networking were shown to be of great and continuing importance despite the availability of global telecommunication networks (*Research Policy*, Special Issue 1991).

Not only were inter-firm and market-production relationships shown to be of critical importance, but the external *linkages* within the narrower professional science-technology system were also shown to be decisive for innovative success with radical innovations. Finally, research on diffusion revealed more and more that the *systemic* aspects of innovation were increasingly influential in determining both the rate of diffusion and the productivity gains associated with any specific diffusion process (see especially Carlsson and Jacobsson 1993). As information and communication technology diffused through the world economy in the 1970s and 1980s, all these systemic aspects of innovation assumed greater and greater importance.

4. CATCHING-UP IN ICT

At the *international* level two contrasting experiences made a very powerful impression in the 1980s both on policy-makers and on researchers: on the one hand the extraordinary success of first Japan and then South Korea in technological and economic catch-up; and on the other hand the collapse of the Socialist economies of Eastern Europe. At first in the 1950s and 1960s the Japanese success was often simply attributed to copying, imitating and importing foreign technology and the statistics of the so-called 'technological balance of payments' were often cited to support this view. They showed a huge deficit in Japanese transactions for licensing and know-how imports and exports and a correspondingly large surplus for the United States. It soon became evident, however, as Japanese products and processes began to out-perform American and European products and processes in various industries, that this simplistic explanation was no longer sufficient. Japanese industrial R&D expenditures as a proportion of civil industrial net output surpassed those of the United States in the 1970s and total civil R&D as a fraction of GNP surpassed USA in the 1980s. The Japanese performance was now often explained more in terms of R&D-intensity, especially as Japanese R&D was highly concentrated in the fastest growing civil industries, such as electronics. Patent statistics showed that the leading Japanese electronic

Table 9.5. Top 20 firms in US patenting (patents granted) 1984–1988

	US	EC	J
Electronic consumer goods and photography	5	2	13
Motor vehicles	5	5	10
Mechanical engineering	9	3	8
Electronic capital goods	10	3	7
Electrical machinery	11	4	5
New materials	12	3	5
Chemicals	11	8	1
Raw materials and processing	16	4	0
Defence	15	5	0

Source: SPRU Databank.

firms outstripped American and European firms not just in domestic patenting but in patents taken out in the United States (Patel and Pavitt 1991, Freeman 1987). Japanese electronic firms came to occupy the leading positions in patenting in the USA displacing the erstwhile leaders, such as IBM and GE. Only in materials, chemicals, defence and electrical machines did United States firms continue to dominate patenting activity (Table 9.5).

However, although these rough measures of research and inventive activity certainly did indicate the huge increase in Japanese scientific and technical activities, they did not in themselves explain how these activities led to higher quality of new products and processes (Grupp and Hofmeyer 1986, Womack *et al.* 1990), to shorter lead times (Graves 1992, Fujimoto and Clark 1990, Mansfield 1988) and to more rapid and efficient diffusion of some ICT technologies such as robotics (Fleck 1983, 1988, 1993) and CNC. Moreover, the contrasting example of the (then) Soviet Union and other East European countries showed that simply to commit greater resources to R&D did not in itself guarantee successful innovation,

Table 9.6.   Social innovations in the Japanese national system of innovation (1970s–1990s)

---

(1) Horizontal information flows and communication networks within firms and groups yielding shorter lead times and better processes ('The factory as laboratory').

(2) The firm as a continuous learning and innovating organization by universal training and re-training.

(3) Capital market providing funds for long-term 'patient' investment in R&D, training and equipment.

(4) Collaborative research networks facilitated by 'Keiretsu' structure and stimulated/coordinated by central government with long-term strategic perspective ('vision').

(5) 'Fusion' research facilitated and stimulated by same approach ('Mechatronics', 'Chematronics'), engineering research associations.

(6) Links between basic research organizations through increasing performance of basic research in industry.

---

diffusion and productivity gains. It was obvious that *qualitative* factors affecting the national systems had to be taken into account as well as the purely *quantitative* indicators.

Some major features of the Japanese national systems are summarized in Table 9.6. Comparison with the United States, as for example, in the MIT Study 'Made in America' (Dertouzos *et al.* 1989) and with most EC countries suggests that Japanese organizational and managerial innovations were relatively well adapted to the use and improvement of ICT.

A similar sharp contrast can be made between the national systems of innovation typically present in Latin American countries in the 1980s and those in the '4 Dragons' of East Asia, and especially between two 'newly industrializing countries' (NICs) in the 1980s: Brazil and South Korea (Table 9.7). In the 1960s and 1970s, the Latin American and East Asian ('Four Dragons') countries were often grouped together as very fast-growing NICs, but in the 1980s a sharp contrast began to emerge. Whereas the East Asian countries' GNP grew in the 1980s at an average annual rate of about 8 per cent, in most Latin American countries, including Brazil, this fell to less than 2 per cent, which meant in many cases a falling per capita income. There are of course many explanations for this contrast.

The World Bank (1993) Report on the 'East Asian Miracle' denies any role for active industrial and technology policies and has little to say about new technology, except to stress the importance of public and private investment in education. Moreover, it often treats the countries of South East Asia (Indonesia, Thailand, Malaysia) as though they were at the same level of development and could be analysed in the same way as the earlier successful industrialization in South Korea and Taiwan. It thus ignores the importance of regional interdependence and the role of Korean, Taiwanese, Hong Kong and Singapore investment and technology transfer (as well as Japanese) to these later industrializing countries. It is astonishing that such a report should ignore the role of industrial R&D, technology up-grading and technological accumulation in firms and the active stimulus of government policies in South Korea, Taiwan and Singapore. For example, the Samsung Trading Company only entered the electronics industry (as late as 1969!) because of the inducements offered by the Korean government. A policy of *laissez-faire* for industries implies an approach which has been described as 'free competition and let the chips fall as they may'. That the most important chips (VLSI Circuits) fell in Samsung was hardly accidental. Its enormous success and that of many other Korean firms cannot be attributed simply to the free play of market forces.

The Asian countries started from a *lower* level of industrialization in the 1950s, so that their catching-up and overtaking performance is all the

Table 9.7.   National systems of innovation: 1980s. Some quantitative indicators

Various Indicators of Technical Capability and National Institutions	Brazil	South Korea
% Age group in 3rd level (higher) education (1985)	11	32
Engineering students as per cent of population (1985)	0.13	0.54
R&D as per cent GNP (1987)	0.7	2.1
Industry R&D as .% total (1988)	30	65
Robots per million employed (1987)	52	1060
Telephone lines per 100 (1989)	6	25

Source: Freeman (1993).

more remarkable. In the early stages ICT was not an important factor in their rapid growth but it became increasingly important in the 1970s and 1980s. Clearly a process of structural and technical change of this magnitude in this time would have been impossible without a well-functioning national system of innovation. In the case of Brazil and South Korea it is possible to give some more detailed quantitative indicators of some contrasting features which became especially obvious in the 1980s. As Table 9.7 shows, the contrast in educational systems was very marked as well as enterprise-level R&D, telecommunication infrastructure and the diffusion of new technologies (see Nelson 1993 for more detailed comparisons and Villaschi 1993, for a detailed study of the Brazilian NS). The East Asian countries were characterized by many features similar to those of Japan (Table 9.8).

Like Japan, South Korea was and is a very heavy importer of foreign technology, but also like Japan, is making intense efforts to upgrade its own technology by indigenous R&D. As Tables 9.9 and 9.10 show, the Korean ICT industries are moving from simple licensing increasingly to Joint Development. They also show that Japan is now the main source of foreign technology for Samsung as for many other Korean companies, despite the political and economic conflicts. However, Korea is now itself

Table 9.8.   Characteristics of East Asian national systems of innovation

---

1. Continuous learning and re-training in firms.
2. Rapid changes in design and product mix.
3. High level of general education and high proportion of engineers.
4. High priority for strategic industries and technologies
     Subsidies
     Protection
     Coordination
     Interest Rates
5. High investment in new (telecommunication) infrastructure.
6. Major structural change in patterns of production and trade (ICT).
7. Strong export networks with government and private promotion.
8. Combining technology import and inward investment with in-house
     technology capacity.

---

becoming a source of overseas investment and technology. Hobday (1993) has shown in considerable detail how the Korean companies have managed this upgrading of their technology. As could be expected, education and training activities play a key part. A recent study of Samsung (Dong Jin Koh 1992) describes recent developments in the *in-house* training activities:

> In 1989, Samsung Group established SATTI (Samsung Advanced Technology Training Institute) at Kihung near by SAIT mainly for vocational training dealing for electronics-related core technologies such as applied Software, CAD/CAM (Computer-Aided Design/Computer-Aided Manufacturing), micro-processors, semiconductors and so on. Over 340 researchers and engineers are accommodated for intensive programmes at any one time. Courses are designed for experienced employees to strengthen their professional knowledge. Lectures and experiments are directed by professors in universities, current senior researchers and engineers. Semesters consist of short term (i.e. one week) and long term (i.e. three months) programmes. As well as the Group educational institution, SEC opened ETTC (Electronics Technology Training Centre) in July 1990. SEC invested $200 million in the construction of the training centre. ETTC can accommodate 750 people in four separate classrooms and ten laboratories, complete with an array of scientific equipment. SEC plans to use the ETTC for its own researchers and engineers as well as those of affiliated firms such as Samsung Electro-Mechanics, Samsung Electron Devices and Samsung Corning. According to the Centre's plans, the employees of some 2,000 SMEs in Korea who supply components and parts to SEC will make up about 20 per cent of the total.

Table 9.9.   Samsung electonic company (South Korea) Technology acquisition in office machinery and telecommunications*

Year	Firm	Country	Technology / Product	Type of agreement
1982	BTM	Belgium	Digital Public Switches Production	Licensing
1984	Alcatel	France	Optical Fiber & related tech.	Licensing
1985	Toshiba	Japan	Fax & Mobile Phone Production	Licensing
1988	Italtel	Italy	Transmitter Production	Licensing
	DHT/MPI	USA	Office Equipment	Joint Development
1989	SEIKO	Japan	Fax Component	Joint Development
	Meitec	Japan	Fax Component	Joint Development
1990	EMI	USA	Office Equipment	Joint Development

Source: SEC Report (SCR), 1991.
* This includes only major products.

Many studies of East Asian 'Tigers' suggest that these developments are by no means atypical of these countries.

These features enabled them as well as Japan to gain a very strong competitive advantage in exports. While the export performance of the Asian countries has often (and rightly) been stressed, the commodity composition of these exports has received less attention. Table 9.3 has already shown that ICT products were by far the fastest growing category of commodities in world trade in the last 15 years. The extraordinary specialization of Japan and other Asian countries in these commodities is brought out in Table 9.11. One does not have to look much further to realize why the trade surplus of Japan has been so stubbornly increasing despite massive revaluation of the Yen in the 1980s and 1990s.

Table 9.10.   Samsung electronics company (South Korea) Technology acquisition in consumer electronics

Year	Company of Origin	Country of Origin	Technology	Type of Agreement
1981	FROG	Germany	C-TV & VCR	Joint Development
1981	Toshiba	Japan	MWO Production	Licensing
1982	Philips	Netherlands	CTV Patent	Licensing
1983	Toshiba	Japan	Air-Conditioner Production	Licensing
1983	JVC	Japan	VCR Patent	Licensing
1983	Sony	Japan	VCR Patent	Licensing
1983	GE	USA	MWO	OEM
1984	Toshiba	Japan	Washing Machine Production	Licensing
1985	Toshiba	Japan	Air-Conditioner Production	Licensing
1985	Matsushita	Japan	Magnetron Production	Licensing
1987	UNITEK	Japan	VCR Production	Licensing
1987	AMPEX	USA	VCR Patent	Licensing
1988	D.V.A.	Germany	CDP Patent	Licensing
1988	Toshiba	Japan	VCR Production	Licensing
1989	Tenking	Japan	VCR Drum	Joint Development
1989	Thomson	USA	CDP Patent	Licensing
1990	TRD	Japan	Camcorder	Joint Development
1990	ITECS	Japan	CDP	Joint Development
1990	JVC	Japan	S-VHS Patent	Licensing

Source: SEC Report (SCR), 1991, Dong Jin Koh (1992).
CTV = Colour Television   VCR = Video Cassette Recorder
MWO = Micro Wave Oven   CDP = Compact Disc Player

Table 9.11. Share of office machinery and telecom equipment in total merchandise exports (ranked by value of 1989 exports)

	1980	1989
Japan	14	28
USA	8	13
FRG	5	5
UK	5	9
Singapore	14	34
South Korea	10	22
Taiwan	14	25
Hong Kong	12	16
France	4	7
Netherlands	5	7
Canada	3	4
Sweden	6	8
Brazil (estimate)	2	3

Source: GATT (1990), Table IV.40, Vol. II.

5. CONCLUSION

The chapter has shown that ICT has the capability to act as the basis of a technological revolution in countries aiming to catch up the world's industrial leaders. However, ICT is not just a 'new technology system' in the sense of Table 9.1, as outlined in Section 2 above. In practice, it is argued here that its effective implementation requires a new 'techno-economic paradigm', combining the organizational, managerial and training aspects with the technological (see Section 3). Countries such as the East Asian NICs which have been more successful in catching-up have implemented strategies which have focused on and pushed ahead with these broader implications (Section 4). Singapore, for example, now has a telecommunication infrastructure superior to most European countries and has pressed through a whole series of measures which oblige even small firms to use computerized data networks and to record information such as that required for customs formalities through these networks.

The policy implications are fairly obvious. It is not sufficient to rely on technological 'spillovers' for catching-up – the key is in the indigenous efforts to develop and act upon suitable techno-economic systems. Although this places the responsibility rather firmly in the lap of the country aiming to catch up, it is evident from the growing inequalities of the global economic system that countries cannot be left simply to fend for themselves. Countries do not begin in this prospective technological revolution from the same starting line. Examples include the collapse of the East European economies and the catastrophic situation in Africa. The innovative development and strengthening of the *international* institutional economic framework is now essential for harmonious global economic development to overcome the enormous social tensions generated by the uneven and disruptive effects of the ICT revolution. Vast international flows of investment and technology and the strengthening of local capacities for technical change everywhere in the Third World offer the most hopeful and constructive solution.

NOTE

1. This chapter is partly based on a talk to the Annual PICT Conference in Kenilworth, May 1993.

REFERENCES

Abramovitz, M. (1986), 'Catching up, forging ahead and falling behind', *Journal of Economic History*, 66, 385–406.

Arcangeli, F., G. Dosi and M. Moggi (1991), 'Patterns of diffusion of electronics technologies: an international comparison', *Research Policy*, 20(6), 515–31.

Ayres, R.U. (1991), *Computer Integrated Manufacturing*, London: IIASA and Chapman Hall.

Baba, Y. (1985), 'Japanese colour TV firms. Decision-making from the 1950s to the 1980s', DPhil dissertation, Brighton: University of Sussex.

Baba, Y., S. Takai and Y. Mizuta (1993), *The Evolution of the Software Industry in Japan: a comprehensive analysis*, Tokyo: RACE, University of Tokyo.

Barras, R. (1986), 'Towards a theory of innovation in services', *Research Policy*, 15(4), 161–73.

Barras, R. (1990), 'Interactive innovation in financial and business services: the vanguard of the service revolution', *Research Policy*, 19(3), 215–37.

Baumol, W.J. (1986), 'Productivity, growth, convergence and welfare. What the long run data show', *American Economic Review*, 76, 1072-1085.

Brady, T.M. (1986), *New Technology and Skills in British Industry*, Skills Series 5,

London: Manpower Services Commission.

Brady, T. and P. Quintas (1991), 'Computer software: the IT constraint', in C. Freeman, M. Sharp and W. Walker (eds), *Technology and the Future of Europe*, London: Frances Pinter.

Carlsson, B. and S. Jacobsson (1993), 'Technological systems and economic performance: the diffusion of factory automation in Sweden', in D. Foray and C. Freeman (eds), *Technology and the Wealth of Nations*, London: Frances Pinter.

Dertouzos, M.L., R.K. Lester and R.N. Solow (eds), (1989), *Made in America*, Cambridge, Mass.: MIT Press.

Diebold, J. (1952), *The Advent of the Automatic Factory*, New York, Van Norstrand.

Dong Jin Koh (1992), 'Beyond Technological Dependency, Towards an Agile Giant', M.Sc. Dissertation, SPRU, University of Sussex.

Fleck, J. (1983), 'Robots in manufacturing organisations', in G. Winch (ed), *Information Technology in Manufacturing Processes*, London: Rossendale.

Fleck, J. (1988), 'Innofusion or diffusation? The nature of technological development in robotics', ESRC Programme on Information and Communication Technologies (PICT), Working Paper series, University of Edinburgh.

Fleck, J. (1993), 'Configurations crystallising contingency', *The International Journal of Human Factors in Manufacturing,* 3(1), 15–36.

Freeman, C. (1962), 'Research and development: a comparison between British and American industry', *National Institute Economic Review*, 20, 21–39.

Freeman, C. (1987), *Technology Policy and Economic Performance: Lessons from Japan*, London: Frances Pinter.

Freeman, C. (1993), 'Interdependence of technological change with growth of trade and GNP', in M. Nissanke and A. Hewitt (eds), *Economic Crisis in Developing Countries*, London: Frances Pinter, 157–77.

Freeman, C. and L. Soete (1993), *Information Technology and Employment*, Paris: IBM.

Fujimoto, T. and K.B. Clark (1990), 'Lead time in automobile product development: explaining the Japanese advantage', *Journal of Engineering and Technology Management*, 6, 25–58.

GATT (1990), *International Trade 1989–90*, Vol. II, Geneva: GATT.

Gille, B. (1978), *Histoire des Techniques*, Paris: Gallimar.

Graves, A. (1992), 'International competitiveness and technological development in the world automobile industry', DPhil thesis, Brighton: University of Sussex.

Grupp, H. and O. Hofmeyer (1986), 'A technometric model for the assessment of technological standards and their application to selected technology comparisons', *Technological Forecasting and Social Change*, 30, 123–37.

Hobday, M. (1993), 'Science and Technology institutions in the Four Dragons of East Asia', SPRU, Brighton: University of Sussex.

Hughes, T.P. (1982), *Networks of Power: Electrification in Western Society 1800-1930*, Baltimore, MD: Johns Hopkins University Press.

Johnson, B. (1992), 'Institutional learning', in B.-Å. Lundvall (ed.), *National Systems of Innovation*, London: Frances Pinter.

Keirstead, B.S. (1948), *The Theory of Economic Change*, Toronto: Macmillan.

Lundvall, B.-Å. (1985), 'Product innovation and user-producer interaction', *Industrial Development Research Series*, 31, Aalborg: Aalborg University Press.

Lundvall, B.-Å. (1988), 'Innovation as an interactive process: from user-producer interaction to the national system of innovation', in G. Dosi *et al.* (eds), *Technical Change and Economic Theory*, London: Frances Pinter.

Lundvall, B.-Å. (ed.) (1992), *National Systems of Innovation: Towards a Theory of Innovation and Interactive Learning*, London: Frances Pinter.

Mansfield, E. (1988), 'Industrial Innovation in Japan and the United States', *Science*, 241, 1760–64.

Mensch, G. (1975), *Das technologische Patt*, Frankfurt: Umschau.

Midgley, D.F., P.D. Morrison and J.H. Roberts (1992), 'The effect of network structure in industrial diffusion processes', *Research Policy*, 21(6), 533–52.

Mjøset, L. (1992), *The Irish Economy in a Comparative Institutional Perspective*, Dublin: National Economic and Social Council.

Nelson, R.R. (1988), 'Institutions supporting technical change in the United States', in G. Dosi *et al.* (eds), *Technical Change and Economic Theory*, London: Frances Pinter.

Nelson, R.R. (1992), 'National innovation systems: a retrospective on a study', *Industrial and Corporate Change*, 1(2), 347–74.

Nelson, R.R. (ed.) (1993), *National Innovation Systems*, New York: Oxford University Press.

OECD (1992), *Technology and the Economy: The Key Relationships*, Paris: OECD.

Patel, P. and K. Pavitt (1991), 'Large firms in the production of the world's technology: an important case of "non-globalisation"', *Journal of International Business Studies*, 22(1), 1–21.

Perez, C. (1983), 'Structural change and the assimilation of new technologies in the economic and social system', *Futures*, 15(5), 357-375.

Perez, C. (1990), 'Technical change, competitive restructuring and institutional reform in developing countries, *World Bank Strategic Planning and Review*, Discussion Paper No. 4, Washington: World Bank.

Quintas, P. (ed.) (1993), *Social Dimensions of Systems Engineering*, Chichester: Ellis Harwood.

Rosenberg, N. (1976), *Perspectives on Technology*, Cambridge: Cambridge University Press.

Rothwell, R. (1991), 'External networking and innovation in small and medium-sized manufacturing firms in Europe', *Technovation*, 11(2), 93–112.

Sako, M. (1992), *Contracts, Prices and Trust: How the Japanese and British Manage Their Subcontracting Relationships*, Oxford: Oxford University Press.

SEC Report (1991), Annual Report, Samsung Electronics Company, Seoul.

Takeuchi, H. and I. Nonaka (1986), 'The new product development game', *Harvard Business Review*, January/February, 285–305.

Villaschi, A.F. (1993), 'The Brazilian National System of Innovation: opportunities and constraints for transforming technological dependency', DPhil Thesis, University of London.

Womack, J., D. Jones and D. Roos (1990), *The Machine that Changed the World*, New York: Rawson Associates (Macmillan).

World Bank (1993), Policy Research Report: *The East Asian Miracle; Economic Growth and Public Policy*, Washington, DC: World Bank.

Authors Index

Subject Index

226